# Sardar Vallabh Bhai Patel

# Sardar Vallabh Bhai Patel

Dr. C.P. Raj
Dr. Ved Prakash

AMIGA PRESS. INC
Delhi -110051

**AMIGA PRESS. INC**

H.O :- 28-A, Indra Park, Chander Nagar

Delhi :- 110051 (India)

Tel :- 011-22504028, +91-98736-57000

Email :- amigapress@gmail.com

amigaeditorial@gmail.com

Website :- www.amigapress@co.in

This edition is published by Amiga Press.Inc

ISBN : 978-93-84533-26-7



First Published 2018



---

PRINTED : REPLIKA PRESS PVT. LTD.

# Preface

Sardar Vallabhbhai Patel (31 October 1875—15 December 1950) was a political and social leader of India who played a major role in the country's struggle for independence and guided its integration into a united, independent nation. In India and across the world, he was often addressed as Sardar which means Chief in many languages of India.

Vallabhbhai Patel, the 'Iron Man of India', was born in Nandiad, Gujarat, to Ladbai and Jhaverbhai Patel. He was one of their six children, five boys and a girl. There is no record of his date of birth. The generally accepted date, 31 October 1875, is taken from his matriculation certificate. It was an agriculturist family in which Vallabh was born and not a well-to-do one. His childhood was spent working on the family's ten acre farm at Karamsad, just like any other farmer's son, away from books. His education was thus erratic, though he was sent to the middle school at Karamsad from where he passed in his late teens. To continue his education, he joined the High School at Nandiad and passed the matriculation examination in 1897 at the age of twenty-two. In the meanwhile, he was married at the age of sixteen to Javerbai, a girl from a nearby village. Javerbai died in 1909 when Vallabhbhai was thirty three but he did not remarry. The couple had two children, a son, Dhayabhai and daughter, Manibehn.

Vallabhbhai took to spinning the charkha, boycotted foreign goods and clothes and burned his foreign possessions on public bonfires. He even discarded the western dresses he once so coveted. There was no stopping Vallabhbhai. He participated in the Nagpur flag satyagraha from May to August in 1923 in protest against the stopping of a procession which carried the national flag.

He started his practice in Ahmedabad and soon he became aware of the local life, activities and people's problems. He became an extremely popular person and he got elected in the Municipal Corportaion in 1917. Around 1915, he came across Mahatma Gandhi. The Swadeshi Movement was at its peak. Gandhiji gave a lecture at a place in Ahmedabad where Patel heard him and was very impressed and started actively participating in the freedom movement. The British government's atrocities were increasing. The government declared to confiscate all the lands of farmers. He forced the British government to amend the rules. He brought together the farmers and encouraged them and hence got the title of 'Sardar' and thus became famous.

Vallabhbhai successfully led peasants revolt in Kheda and the revolt ended in 1919 when the British government agreed to suspend collection of revenue and roll back the rates. Kheda Satyagraha turned Vallabhbhai Patel into a national hero. Vallabhbhai supported Gandhi's Non-Cooperation Movement, and as president of the Gujarat Congress, helped in organizing bonfires of British goods in Ahmedabad. He gave up his English clothes and started wearing Khadi. Sardar Vallabh Bhai Patel was elected Ahmedabad's municipal president in 1922, 1924 and 1927. During his terms, Ahmedabad was extended a major supply of electricity and underwent major education reforms. Drainage and sanitation systems were extended over all the city.

Vallabhbhai Patel, after his embrace of Gandhi's philosophy and a completely Indian way of life Supported by Congress volunteers Narhari Parikh, Mohanlal Pandya and Abbas Tyabji, Vallabhbhai Patel began a village-to-village tour in the Kheda district, documenting grievances and asking villagers for their support for a statewide revolt by refusing the payment of taxes. Patel emphasised potential hardships with the need for complete unity and nonviolence despite any provocation.

The book has been written with intention to primarily focus on the life, work and political philosophy of Vallabhbhai Patel commonly known as Sardar Patel.

—*Editor*

# Contents

# 1

# Life Sketch of Patel

Vallabhbhai Patel was born on October 31, 1875, in a farmer's family in Nadiad, Gujarat. His father, Zaverbhai, had served in the army of Jhansi ki Rani, and his mother, Ladbai, was a deeply religious woman. Vallabhbhai's initial schooling was in Gujarati. His brother Vithalbhai, after completing middle school, had enrolled himself in English tutorial classes in a nearby town. Vallabhbhai followed suit. Vallabhbhai's superior organizational skills became evident while he was in high school at Petlad when he coordinated the entire campaign for a poor teacher who he thought deserved a seat on the local municipal committee. Vallabhbhai persuaded his fellow students to work for the campaign. So impressively was the campaign handled that the teacher was elected over the rich local businessman. Vallabhbhai matriculated from Nadiad High School in 1897.

Vallabhbhai was married to Zaverbai in 1891. The couple had two children-a daughter Manibehn, born in April of 1904, and a son Dayabhai, born in November of 1905. Zaverbai died in January of 1909. Vallabhbhai sailed for England in August of 1910 to study law. He qualified as a barrister in 1913 and returned to India to a lucrative practice in Ahmedabad. He joined the Gujarat Club and took to western dressing and a comfortable lifestyle.

Gandhiji started coming to the Gujarat Club to give lectures. He came again and again, propagating the idea of his newly wielded weapon of "satyagraha" or truth force. Vallabhbhai was impressed with Gandhiji and slowly began to adopt his view. The relationship between Gandhiji and Vallabhbhai was concretely defined when Gandhiji was elected the President of the Gujarat Sabha and Vallabhbhai the Secretary, in 1917. It was a relationship of a guru (teacher) and disciple.

Vallabhbhai got his first opportunity to utilize Gandhiji's philosophy of satyagraha in 1918 for the farmers of Kaira who had lost their crops to heavy rains and floods that year. The government disregarded the farmers' misery and insisted on collecting land revenue. Vallabhbhai organized the No Tax campaign on peaceful, Gandhian lines. The government held out and began confiscating land and what little crops and cattle the farmers still had. Vallabhbhai, now decked in a dhoti, kurta and cap urged the farmers not to buckle. The government eventually relented and returned the confiscated property. This was the first victory of satyagraha for Vallabhbhai. He was jubilant.

Vallabhbhai took to spinning the charkha, boycotted foreign goods and clothes and burned his foreign possessions on public bonfires. He even discarded the western dresses he once so coveted. There was no stopping Vallabhbhai. He participated in the Nagpur flag satyagraha from May to August in 1923 in protest against the stopping of a procession which carried the national flag.

On March 12, 1930, Sardar Patel left for Dandi to prepare for Gandhiji's Salt satyagraha. He went to villages to organize for the food and lodging of the marchers. In every village he went, he made stirring speeches, rousing the people to join the march to Dandi. The Government swooped down and arrested him while he was in the village of Ras. This was Sardar Patel's first prison sentence. He was released after the Gandhi-Irwin pact of March 1931. That year he presided over the Congress session in Karachi.

Gandhiji sailed for London to attend the Round Table Conference in 1931. Sardar Patel regularly updated him on the situation in India. Ironically, the British Government in India stepped up repression just when the Conference was going on in London. Gandhiji was arrested on his return from the Conference. Sardar Patel and Jawaharlal Nehru were also imprisoned. Sardar Patel was imprisoned with Gandhiji in Yeravada Jail, Pune, where they spent 16 months together. While Sardar Patel was in jail, his mother and brother died. He refused to be released to attend to their last rites.

In 1937, elections for the provincial governments were held under the Government of India Act of 1935. Sardar Patel was elected Chairman to the Parliamentary Sub-Committee which was to select Congress candidates and organize the elections. Sardar Patel's hard work resulted in the Congress forming majority governments in most Provinces. All the Congress ministries resigned when the British arbitrarily included India in the war effort against Germany and Japan. Gandhiji planned an individual satyagraha to protest India's inclusion in the war without being consulted. Sardar Patel was among the first batch of leaders to offer satyagraha. Arrests of the participants followed.

On August 8, 1942, the Congress and Gandhiji passed the "Quit India" resolution, calling upon the British to withdraw from India. The Government responded with arrests of Sardar Patel, Jawaharlal Nehru, Gandhiji and other eminent Congress leaders. Sardar Patel was imprisoned in Ahmednagar Fort while Gandhiji was kept in Aga Khan Palace.

On March 23, 1946, the Labour Prime Minister of Britain arrived in India to assure independence for India. An Interim Government was proposed and Sardar Patel once again was asked to handle the campaign for the Congress. Again the Sardar delivered. The Congress won thumping majorities in almost all provinces. Jawaharlal Nehru became Prime Minister in September 1946 and Sardar Patel held the portfolios of Home and Information and Broadcasting. On August 15, 1947, India became free, but only after Pakistan was created.

When Pakistani infiltrators attacked Kashmir, Sardar Patel proposed withholding Pakistan's share of cash balances left by the British. Gandhiji felt such an act would be morally wrong and went on a fast unto death. Sardar Patel tried to prevail over Gandhiji, but he finally relented in order to save the life of the "Father of the Nation."

Sardar Patel handled the portfolio of Home Minister, Minister of States and Minister of Information and Broadcasting. As Home Minister he had to deal with communal disturbances that continued to rock the nation after partition. He transferred army units from Pune and Madras to deal with the disturbances in Delhi. He had the army move ten thousand Muslims to Red Fort to protect them from the riots.

Sardar Patel handled the integration of all the princely states into the Indian Union with great expertise. Under the Cabinet Mission, all the princely states had the right to join Pakistan, India or remain independent. The Sardar declared that "we are all knit together by bonds of blood and feelings... Therefore, it is better for us to make laws sitting together as friends." Sardar Patel dealt with Hyderabad and Junaghad firmly when these states tried to join Pakistan or remain independent. Gandhiji was full of praise.

As time passed, differences in opinion formed between Sardar Patel and Jawaharlal Nehru. Gandhiji wanted both to work together for the betterment of India. On January 30, 1948, Sardar Patel met Gandhiji who expressed his wish that Sardar Patel work side by side with Nehru. The same day Gandhiji was assassinated. Sardar Patel was crushed. He was further hurt when he was criticized for not protecting Gandhiji. Sardar Patel wanted to post plain-cloth policemen at the Gandhiji's prayer meetings, but Gandhiji had forbidden it. After Gandhiji's death, Sardar Patel acted as Gandhiji had wished and worked closely with Nehru.

Sardar Patel formed the Indian Administrative Service, Indian Police Service and other Central Services to assist in the process of nation building.

The "Iron Man of India" died in Bombay in December 1950. He left behind a united India.

## EARLY LIFE

### Young Vallabhbhai, When a Student

Vallabhbhai Jhaverbhai Patel was born at his maternal uncle's house in Nadiad, Gujarat. His actual date of birth was never officially recorded—Patel entered 31 October as his date of birth on his matriculation examination papers. He was the fourth son of Jhaverbhai a Hindu by religion and his wife Ladba Patel. They lived in the village of Karamsad, in the Kheda district where Jhaverbhai owned a homestead. Somabhai, Narsibhai and Vithalbhai Patel (also a future political leader) were his elder brothers. He had a younger brother, Kashibhai and a sister, Dahiba. As a young boy, Patel helped his father in the fields and bimonthly kept a day-long fast, abstaining from food and water—a Hindu cultural observance that enabled him to develop physical toughness. When he was eighteen years old, Patel's marriage was arranged with Jhaverba, a young girl of twelve or thirteen years from a nearby village. As per custom, the young bride would continue to reside with her parents until her husband started earning and could establish their household.

Patel travelled to attend schools in Nadiad, Petlad and Borsad, living self-sufficiently with other boys. He reputedly cultivated a stoic character—a popular anecdote recounts how he lanced his own painful boil without hesitation, even as the barber supposed to do it trembled. Patel passed his matriculation at the late age of 22; at this point, he was generally regarded by his elders as an unambitious man destined for a commonplace job. But Patel himself harboured a plan—he would study to become a lawyer, work and save funds, travel to England and study to become a barrister. Patel spent years away from his family, studying on his own with books borrowed from other lawyers and passed examinations within two years. Fetching Jhaverba from her parents' home, Patel set up his household in Godhra and enrolled at the bar. During the many years it took him to save money, Vallabhbhai—now a pleader—earned a reputation as a fierce and skilled lawyer. His wife bore him a daughter, Manibehn, in 1904 and later a son, Dahyabhai, in 1906. Patel also cared for a friend suffering from Bubonic plague when it swept across Gujarat. When Patel himself came down with the disease, he immediately sent his family to safety, left his home and moved into an isolated house in Nadiad (by other accounts, Patel spent this time in a dilapidated temple); there, he recovered slowly.

## Vallabhbhai Patel, When a Young Lawyer

Patel practised law in Godhra, Borsad and Anand while taking on the financial burdens of his homestead in Karamsad. When he had saved enough for England and applied for a pass and a ticket, they arrived in the name of "V. J. Patel," at Vithalbhai's home, who bore the same initials. Having harboured his own plans to study in England, Vithalbhai remonstrated to his younger brother that it would be disreputable for an older brother to follow his younger brother. In keeping with concerns for his family's honour, Patel allowed Vithalbhai to go in his place. He also financed his brother's stay and began saving again for his own goals.

In 1909, Patel's wife Jhaverba was hospitalised in Mumbai (then Bombay) to undergo a major surgical operation for cancer. Her health suddenly worsened and despite successful emergency surgery, she died in the hospital. Patel was given a note informing him of his wife's demise as he was cross-examining a witness in court. As per others who witnessed, Patel read the note, pocketed it and continued to intensely cross-examine the witness and won the case. He broke the news to others only after the proceedings had ended. Patel himself decided against marrying again. He raised his children with the help of his family and sent them to English-medium schools in Mumbai. At the age of 36, he journeyed to England and enrolled at the Middle Temple Inn in London. Finishing a 36-month course in 30 months, Patel topped his class despite having no previous college background. Returning to India, Patel settled in the city of Ahmedabad and became one of the city's most successful barristers. Wearing European-style clothes and urbane mannerisms, he also became a skilled bridge player. Patel nurtured ambitions to expand his practise and accumulate great wealth and to provide his children with modern education. He had also made a pact with his brother Vithalbhai to support his entry into politics in the Bombay Presidency, while Patel himself would remain in Ahmedabad and provide for the family.

## Fighting for Independence

At the urging of his friends, Patel won an election to become the sanitation commissioner of Ahmedabad in 1917. While often clashing with British officials on civic issues, he did not show any interest in politics. Upon hearing of Mohandas Gandhi, he joked to Mavlankar that Gandhi would "ask you if you know how to sift pebbles from wheat. And that is supposed to bring independence." But Patel was deeply impressed when Gandhi defied the British in Champaran for the sake of the area's oppressed farmers. Against the grain of Indian politicians of the time, Gandhi wore Indian-style clothes and emphasised the use of one's mother tongue or any Indian language as opposed to English—the lingua franca of India's intellectuals. Patel was particularly attracted to Gandhi's inclination to action—apart from a resolution condemning the arrest of political leader Annie Besant, Gandhi proposed that volunteers march peacefully demanding to meet her.

Patel gave a speech in Borsad in September 1917, encouraging Indians nationwide to sign Gandhi's petition demanding *Swaraj* — independence — from the British. Meeting Gandhi a month later at the Gujarat Political Conference in Godhra, Patel became the secretary of the Gujarat Sabha—a public body which would become the Gujarati arm of the Indian National Congress—at Gandhi's encouragement. Patel now energetically fought against *veth*—the forced servitude of Indians to Europeans—and organised relief efforts in wake of plague and famine in Kheda. The Kheda peasants' plea for exemption from taxation had been turned down by British authorities. Gandhi endorsed waging a struggle there, but could not lead it himself due to his activities in Champaran. When Gandhi asked for a Gujarati activist to devote himself completely to the assignment and Patel volunteered, much to Gandhi's personal delight. Though his decision was made on the spot, Patel later said that his desire and commitment came after intensive personal contemplation, as he realised he would have to abandon his career and material ambitions.

## QUIT INDIA

When World War II broke out, Patel supported Nehru's decision to withdraw the Congress from central and provincial legislatures, contrary to Gandhi's advice, as well as an initiative by senior leader Chakravarthi Rajagopalacharya to offer Congress's full support to Britain if it promised Indian independence at the end of the war and install a democratic government right away. Gandhi had refused to support Britain on the grounds of his moral opposition to war, while Subhash Chandra Bose was in militant opposition to the British. The British rejected Rajagopalacharya's initiative, and Patel embraced Gandhi's leadership again. He participated in Gandhi's call for individual disobedience, and was arrested in 1940 and imprisoned for nine months. He also opposed the proposals of the Cripps' mission in 1942. Patel lost more than twenty pounds during his period in jail.

While Nehru, Rajagopalacharya and Maulana Azad initially criticized Gandhi's proposal for an all-out campaign of civil disobedience to force the British to *Quit India*, Patel was its most fervent supporter. Arguing that the British would retreat from India as they had from Singapore and Burma, Patel stressed that the campaign start without any delay. Though feeling that the

British would not quit immediately, Patel favoured an all-out rebellion which would galvanize Indian people, who had been divided in their response to the war, In Patel's view, an all-out rebellion would force the British to concede that continuation of colonial rule had no support in India, and thus speed power transfer to Indians. Believing strongly in the need for revolt, Patel stated his intention to resign from the Congress if the revolt was not approved. Gandhi strongly pressured the All India Congress Committee to approve of an all-out campaign of civil disobedience, and the AICC approved the campaign on 7 August 1942. Though Patel's health had suffered during his stint in jail, Patel gave emotional speeches to large crowds across India, asking people to refuse paying taxes and participate in civil disobedience, mass protests and a shutdown of all civil services. He raised funds and prepared a second-tier of command as a precaution against the arrest of national leaders. Patel made a climactic speech to more than 100,000 people gathered at Gowalia Tank in Bombay (Mumbai) on August 7:

> *"The Governor of Burma boasts in London that they left Burma only after reducing everything to dust. So you promise the same thing to India?... You refer in your radio broadcasts and newspapers to the government established in Burma by Japan as a puppet government? What sort of government do you have in Delhi now?...When France fell before the Nazi onslaught, in the midst of total war, Mr. Churchill offered union with England to the French. That was indeed a stroke of inspired statesmanship. But when it comes to India? Oh no! Constitutional changes in the midst of a war? Absolutely unthinkable...The object this time is to free India before the Japanese can come and be ready to fight them if they come. They will round up the leaders, round up all. Then it will be the duty of every Indian to put forth his utmost effort — within nonviolence. No source is to be left untapped; no weapon untried. This is going to be the opportunity of a lifetime."*

Historians believe that Patel's speech was instrumental in electrifying nationalists, who had been skeptical of the proposed rebellion. Patel's organising work in this period is credited by historians for ensuring the success of the rebellion across India. Patel was arrested on 9 August and was imprisoned with the entire Congress Working Committee from 1942 to 1945 at the fort in Ahmednagar. Here he spun cloth, played bridge, read a large number of books, took long walks, practised gardening. He also provided emotional support to his colleagues while awaiting news and developments of the outside. Patel was deeply pained at the news of the deaths of Mahadev Desai and Kasturba Gandhi later in the year. But Patel wrote in a letter to his daughter that he and his colleagues were experiencing "fullest peace" for having done "their duty." Even though other political parties had opposed the struggle and the British had employed ruthless means of suppression, the Quit India movement was "by far the most serious rebellion since that of 1857," as the viceroy cabled to Winston Churchill. More than one hundred thousand people were arrested and thousands killed in police firings. Strikes, protests and other revolutionary activities had broken out across India. When Patel was released on 15 June 1945 he realised that the British were preparing proposals to transfer power to Indian hands.

## Independence, Integration and Role of Gandhi

In the 1946 election for the Congress presidency, Patel stepped down in favour of Nehru at the request of Gandhi. The election's importance stemmed from the fact that the elected President would lead free India's first Government. Gandhi asked all 16 states representatives and Congress to elect the right person and Sardar Patel's name was proposed by 13 states representatives out of 16, but Patel respected Gandhi's request to not be the first prime minister. As a Home Minister, Patel merged all parts of India under federal control but Jammu and Kashmir was left out because of Nehru.

After the election of Nehru as the party's president, Patel began directing the Congress campaign for the general elections of the Constituent Assembly of India.

In the elections, the Congress won a large majority of the elected seats, dominating the Hindu electorate. But the Muslim League led by Muhammad Ali Jinnah won a large majority of Muslim electorate seats. The League had resolved in 1940 to demand Pakistan—an independent state for Muslims—and was a fierce critic of the Congress. The Congress formed governments in all provinces save Sindh, Punjab and Bengal, where it entered into coalitions with other parties.

## CABINET MISSION AND PARTITION

When the British mission proposed two plans for transfer of power, there was considerable opposition within the Congress to both. The plan of 16 May 1946 proposed a loose federation with extensive provincial autonomy, and the "grouping" of provinces based on religious-majority. The plan of 16 June 1946 proposed the partition of India on religious lines, with over 600 princely states free to choose between independence or accession to either dominion. The League approved both plans, while the Congress flatly rejected the June 16 proposal. Gandhi criticised the May 16 proposal as being inherently divisive, but Patel, realizing that rejecting the proposal would mean that only the League would be invited to form a government, lobbied the Congress Working

Committee hard to give its assent to the 16 May proposal. Patel engaged the British envoys Sir Stafford Cripps and Lord Pethick-Lawrence and obtained an assurance that the "grouping" clause would not be given practical force, Patel converted Nehru, Rajendra Prasad and Rajagopalacharya to accept the plan. When the League retracted its approval of the 16 May plan, the viceroy Lord Wavell invited the Congress to form the government. Under Nehru, who was styled the "Vice President of the Viceroy's Executive Council," Patel took charge of the departments of home affairs and information and broadcasting. He moved into a government house on 1, Aurangzeb Road in Delhi—this would be his residence till his death in 1950.

Vallabhbhai Patel was one of the first Congress leaders to accept the partition of India as a solution to the rising Muslim separatist movement led by Muhammad Ali Jinnah. He had been outraged by Jinnah's Direct Action campaign, which had provoked communal violence across India and by the viceroy's vetoes of his home department's plans to stop the violence on the grounds of constitutionality. Patel severely criticised the viceroy's induction of League ministers into the government, and the revalidation of the grouping scheme by the British without Congress approval. Although further outraged at the League's boycott of the assembly and non-acceptance of the plan of 16 May despite entering government, he was also aware that Jinnah did enjoy popular support amongst Muslims, and that an open conflict between him and the nationalists could degenerate into a Hindu-Muslim civil war of disastrous consequences.

The continuation of a divided and weak central government would in Patel's mind, result in the wider fragmentation of India by encouraging more than 600 princely states towards independence. Between the months of December 1946 and January 1947, Patel worked with civil servant V. P. Menon on the latter's suggestion for a separate dominion of Pakistan created out of Muslim-majority provinces. Communal violence in Bengal and Punjab in January and March of 1947 further convinced Patel of the soundness of partition. Patel, a fierce critic of Jinnah's demand that the Hindu-majority areas of Punjab and Bengal be included in a Muslim state, obtained the partition of those provinces, thus blocking any possibility of their inclusion in Pakistan. Patel's decisiveness on the partition of Punjab and Bengal had won him many supporters and admirers amongst the Indian public, which had tired of the League's tactics, but he was criticised by Gandhi, Nehru, secular Muslims and socialists for a perceived eagerness to do so. When Lord Louis Mountbatten formally proposed the plan on 3 June 1947, Patel gave his approval and lobbied Nehru and other Congress leaders to accept the proposal. Knowing Gandhi's deep anguish regarding proposals of partition, Patel engaged him in frank discussion in private meetings over the perceived practical unworkability of any Congress-League coalition, the rising violence and the threat of civil war. At the All India Congress Committee meeting called to vote on the proposal, Patel said:

> *I fully appreciate the fears of our brothers from [the Muslim-majority areas]. Nobody likes the division of India and my heart is heavy. But the choice is between one division and many divisions. We must face facts. We cannot give way to emotionalism and sentimentality. The Working Committee has not acted out of fear. But I am afraid of one thing, that all our toil and hard work of these many years might go waste or prove unfruitful. My nine months in office has completely disillusioned me regarding the supposed merits of the Cabinet Mission Plan. Except for a few honourable exceptions, Muslim officials from the top down to the chaprasis (peons or servants) are working for the League. The communal veto given to the League in the Mission Plan would have blocked India's progress at every stage. Whether we like it or not, de facto Pakistan already exists in the Punjab and Bengal. Under the circumstances I would prefer a de jure Pakistan, which may make the League more responsible. Freedom is coming. We have 75 to 80 percent of India, which we can make strong with our own genius. The League can develop the rest of the country.*

Following Gandhi's and Congress' approval of the plan, Patel represented India on the Partition Council, where he oversaw the division of public assets, and selected the Indian council of ministers with Nehru. However, neither he nor any other Indian leader had foreseen the intense violence and population transfer that would take place with partition. Patel would take the lead in organising relief and emergency supplies, establishing refugee camps and visiting the border areas with Pakistani leaders to encourage peace. Despite these efforts, estimates on the death toll vary from around two hundred thousand, to over a million people. The estimated number of refugees in both countries exceeds 15 million. Understanding that Delhi and Punjab policemen, accused of organising attacks on Muslims, were personally affected by the tragedies of partition, Patel called out the Indian Army with South Indian regiments to restore order, imposing strict curfews and shoot-at-sight orders. Visiting the Nizamuddin Auliya Dargah area in Delhi, where thousands of Delhi Muslims feared attacks, he prayed at the shrine, visited the people and reinforced the presence of police. He suppressed from the press reports of atrocities in Pakistan against Hindus and Sikhs to prevent retaliatory violence. Establishing the Delhi Emergency Committee to restore order and organising relief efforts for refugees in the capital, Patel publicly warned officials against partiality and neglect. When reports reached Patel that large groups of Sikhs were preparing to attack Muslim convoys heading for Pakistan, Patel hurried to Amritsar and met Sikh and Hindu leaders. Arguing that attacking helpless people was cowardly and dishonourable, Patel emphasised that Sikh actions would result in further attacks against Hindus and Sikhs in Pakistan. He assured the community leaders that if they worked to establish peace and order and guarantee the safety of Muslims, the Indian government would react forcefully to any failures of Pakistan to do the same. Additionally, Patel addressed a massive crowd of an estimated 200,000 refugees who had surrounded his car after the meetings:

> *Here, in this same city, the blood of Hindus, Sikhs and Muslims mingled in the bloodbath of Jallianwala Bagh. I am grieved to think that things have come to such a pass that no Muslim can go about in Amritsar and no Hindu or Sikh can even think of living in Lahore. The butchery of innocent and defenceless men, women and children does not behove brave men... I am quite certain that India's interest lies in getting all her men and women across the border and sending out all Muslims from East Punjab. I have come to you with a specific appeal. Pledge the safety of Muslim refugees crossing the city. Any obstacles or hindrances will only worsen the plight of our refugees who are already performing prodigious feats of endurance. If we have to fight, we must fight clean. Such a fight must await an appropriate time and conditions and you must be watchful in choosing your ground. To fight against the refugees is no fight at all. No laws of humanity or war among honourable men permit the murder of people who have sought shelter and protection. Let there be truce for three months in which both sides can exchange their refugees. This sort of truce is permitted even by laws of war. Let us take the initiative in breaking this vicious circle of attacks and counter-attacks. Hold your hands for a week and see what happens. Make way for the refugees with your own force of volunteers and let them deliver the refugees safely at our frontier.*

Following his dialogue with community leaders and his speech, no further attacks occurred against Muslim refugees, and a wider peace and order was re-established soon over the entire area. However, Patel was criticised by Nehru, secular Muslims and taxed by Gandhi over his alleged wish to see Muslims from other parts of India depart. While Patel vehemently denied such allegations, the acrimony with Maulana Azad and other secular Muslim leaders increased when Patel refused to dismiss Delhi's Sikh police commissioner, who was accused of discrimination. Hindu and Sikh leaders also accused Patel and other leaders of not taking Pakistan sufficiently to task over the attacks on their communities there, and Muslim leaders further criticised him for allegedly neglecting the needs of Muslims leaving for Pakistan, and concentrating resources for incoming Hindu and Sikh refugees. Patel clashed with Nehru and Azad over the allocation of houses in Delhi vacated by Muslims leaving for Pakistan — Nehru and Azad desired to allocate them for displaced Muslims, while Patel argued that no government professing secularism must make such exclusions. However, Patel was publicly defended by Gandhi and received widespread admiration and support for speaking frankly on communal issues and acting decisively and resourcefully to quell disorder and violence.

## POLITICAL INTEGRATION OF INDIA

Under the June 3 plan, more than 600 princely states were given the option of joining either India or Pakistan, or choosing independence. Indian nationalists and large segments of the public feared that if these states did not accede, a vast majority of the people and territory would be fragmented. The Congress as well as senior British officials considered Patel the best man for the task of achieving unification of the princely states with the Indian dominion.

Gandhi had said to Patel *"the problem of the States is so difficult that you alone can solve it"*. He was considered a statesman of integrity with the practical acumen and resolve to accomplish a monumental task.

Patel asked V. P. Menon, a senior civil servant with whom he had worked over the partition of India, to become his right-hand as chief secretary of the States Ministry. On 6 May 1947, Patel began lobbying the princes, attempting to make them receptive towards dialogue with the future Government and trying to forestall potential conflicts. Patel used social meetings and unofficial surroundings to engage most monarchs, inviting them to lunch and tea at his home in Delhi.

At these meetings, Patel stated that there was no inherent conflict between the Congress and the princely order. Nonetheless, he stressed that the princes would need to accede to India in good faith by 15 August 1947. Patel invoked the patriotism of India's monarchs, asking them to join in the freedom of their nation and act as responsible rulers who cared about the future of their people. He persuaded the princes of 565 states of the impossibility of independence from the Indian republic, especially in the presence of growing opposition from their subjects. He proposed favourable terms for the merger, including creation of *privy purses* for the descendants of the rulers. While encouraging the rulers to act with patriotism, Patel did not rule out force, setting a deadline of 15 August 1947 for them to sign the instrument of accession document. All but three of the states willingly merged into the

Indian union—only Jammu and Kashmir, Junagadh, and Hyderabad did not fall into his basket.

Junagadh was especially important to Patel, since it was in his home state of Gujarat. The Nawab had under pressure from Sir Shah Nawaz Bhutto acceded to Pakistan. It was however, quite far from Pakistan and 80% of its population was Hindu. Patel combined diplomacy with force, demanding that Pakistan annul the accession, and that the Nawab accede to India. He sent the Army to occupy three principalities of Junagadh to show his resolve. Following widespread protests and the formation of a civil government, or *Aarzi Hukumat*, both Bhutto and the Nawab fled to Karachi, and under Patel's orders, Indian Army and police units marched into the state. A plebiscite later organised produced a 99.5% vote for merger with India. In a speech at the Bahauddin College in Junagadh following the latter's take-over, Patel emphasised his feeling of urgency on Hyderabad, which he felt was more vital to India than Kashmir:

> *If Hyderabad does not see the writing on the wall, it goes the way Junagadh has gone. Pakistan attempted to set off Kashmir against Junagadh. When we raised the question of settlement in a democratic way, they (Pakistan) at once told us that they would consider it if we applied that policy to Kashmir. Our reply was that we would agree to Kashmir if they agreed to Hyderabad.*

Hyderabad was the largest of the princely states, and included parts of present-day Andhra Pradesh, Karnataka, and Maharashtra states. Its ruler, the Nizam Osman Ali Khan was a Muslim, although over 80% of its people were Hindu. The Nizam sought independence or accession with Pakistan. Muslim forces loyal to Nizam, called the Razakars, under Qasim Razvi pressed the Nizam to hold out against India, while organising attacks with militant Communists on people on Indian soil.

Even though a Standstill Agreement was signed due to the desperate efforts of Lord Mountbatten to avoid a war, the Nizam rejected deals and changed his positions. In September 1948, Patel emphasised in Cabinet meetings that India should take no more, and reconciled Nehru and the Governor-General, Chakravarti Rajgopalachari to military action.

Following preparations, Patel ordered the Indian Army to integrate Hyderabad (in his capacity as Acting Prime Minister) when Nehru was touring Europe. The action was termed Operation Polo, in which thousands of Razakar forces had been killed, but Hyderabad was comfortably secured into the Indian Union. The main aim of Mountbatten and Nehru in avoiding a forced annexation was to prevent an outbreak of Hindu-Muslim violence. Patel insisted that if Hyderabad was allowed to continue with its antics, the prestige of the Government would fall and then neither Hindus nor Muslims would feel secure in its realm. After defeating Nizam, Patel retained him as the ceremonial chief of state, and held talks with him.

## Leading India

Governor General Chakravarti Rajagopalacharya, Nehru and Patel formed the *triumvirate* which ruled India from 1948 to 1950. Prime Minister Nehru was intensely popular with the masses, but Patel enjoyed the loyalty and faith of rank and file Congressmen, state leaders and India's civil services. Patel was a senior leader in the Constituent Assembly of India and was responsible in a large measure for shaping India's constitution. Patel was a key force behind the appointment of Dr. Bhimrao Ramji Ambedkar as the chairman of the drafting committee, and the inclusion of leaders from a diverse political spectrum in the process of writing the constitution.

Patel was the chairman of the committees responsible for minorities, tribal and excluded areas, fundamental rights and provincial constitutions. Patel piloted a model constitution for the provinces in the Assembly, which contained limited powers for the state governor, who would defer to the President — he clarified it was not the intention to let the governor exercise power which could impede an elected government.

He worked closely with Muslim leaders to end separate electorates and the more potent demand for reservation of seats for minorities. Patel would hold personal dialogues with leaders of other minorities on the question, and was responsible for the measure that allows the President to appoint Anglo-Indians to Parliament. His intervention was key to the passage of two articles that protected civil servants from political involvement and guaranteed their terms and privileges. He was also instrumental in the founding the Indian Administrative Service and the Indian Police Service, and for his defence of Indian civil servants from political attack, he is known as the "patron saint" of India's services.

When a delegation of Gujarati farmers came to him citing their inability to send their milk production to the markets without being fleeced by middlemen, Patel exhorted them to organise the processing and sale of milk by themselves, and guided them to create the Kaira District Cooperative Milk Producers' Union Limited, which preceded the Amul milk products brand. Patel also pledged the reconstruction of the ancient but dilapidated Somnath Temple in Saurashtra — he oversaw the creation of a public trust and restoration work, and pledged to dedicate the temple upon the completion of work (the work was completed after Patel's death, and the temple was inaugurated by the first President of India, Dr. Rajendra Prasad).

When the Pakistani invasion of Kashmir began in September 1947, Patel immediately wanted to send troops into Kashmir. But agreeing with Nehru and Mountbatten, he waited till Kashmir's monarch had acceded to India. Patel then oversaw India's military operations to secure Srinagar, the Baramulla Pass and the forces retrieved a lot of territory from the invaders. Patel, along with Defence Minister Baldev Singh administered the entire military effort, arranging for troops from different parts of India to be rushed to Kashmir and for a major military road connecting Srinagar to Pathankot be built in 6 months. Patel strongly advised Nehru against going for arbitration to the United Nations, insisting that Pakistan had been wrong to support the invasion and the accession to India was valid. He did not want foreign interference in a bilateral affair. Patel opposed the release of Rs. 55 crores to the Government of Pakistan, convinced that the money would go to finance the war against India in Kashmir. The Cabinet had approved his point but it was reversed when Gandhi, who feared an intensifying rivalry and further communal violence, went on a fast-unto-death to obtain the release. Patel, though not estranged from Gandhi, was deeply hurt at the rejection of his counsel and a Cabinet decision.

In 1949, a crisis arose when the number of Hindu refugees entering West Bengal, Assam and Tripura from East Pakistan climbed over 800,000. The refugees in many cases were being forcibly evicted by Pakistani authorities, and were victims of intimidation and violence. Nehru invited Liaquat Ali Khan, Prime Minister of Pakistan to find a peaceful solution. Despite his aversion, Patel reluctantly met Khan and discussed the matters. Patel strongly criticised, however, Nehru's intention to sign a pact that would create minority commissions in both countries and pledge both India and Pakistan to a commitment to protect each other's minorities. Syama Prasad Mukherjee and K.C. Neogy, two Bengali ministers resigned and Nehru was intensely criticised in West Bengal for allegedly appeasing Pakistan. The pact was immediately in jeopardy. Patel however, publicly came out to Nehru's aid. He gave emotional speeches to members of Parliament, and the people of West Bengal, and spoke with scores of delegations of Congressmen, Hindus, Muslims and other public interest groups, persuading them to give peace a final effort. The pact was approved and within a year, most of the Hindu refugees had returned to East Pakistan.

## PATEL AND PARTITION OF BENGAL

1. Bengal would be a Free State. The Free State of Bengal would decide its relations with the rest of India.

2. The Constitution of the Free State of Bengal would provide for election to the Bengal Legislature on the basis of a joint electorate and adult franchise, with reservation of seats proportionate to the population among Hindus and Muslims. The seats set aside for Hindus and Scheduled Caste Hindus would be distributed amongst them in proportion to their respective population, or in such manner as may be agreed among them. The constituencies would be multiple constituencies and the votes would be distributive and not cumulative. A candidate who got the majority of the votes of his own community cast during the elections and 25 percent of the votes of the other communities so cast, would be declared elected. If no candidate satisfied these conditions, that candidate who got the largest number of votes of his own community would be elected.
3. On the announcement by His Majesty's Government that the proposal of the Free State of Bengal had been accepted and that Bengal would not be partitioned, the present Bengal Ministry would be dissolved. A new interim Ministry would be brought into being, consisting of an equal number of Muslims and Hindus (including Scheduled Caste Hindus) but excluding the Chief Minister. In this Ministry, Chief Minister would be a Muslim and the Home Minister a Hindu.
4. Pending the final emergence of a Legislature and a Ministry under the new constitutions, Hindus (including Scheduled Caste Hindus) and Muslims would have an equal share in the Services, including military and police. The Services would be manned by Bengalis.
5. A Constituent Assembly composed of 30 persons, 16 Muslims and 14 non-Muslims, would be elected by Muslim and non-Muslim members of the Legislature respectively, excluding Europeans.

After arriving at an agreement among themselves, Suhrawardy, Kiran Shankar Roy and Sarat Chandra Bose tried to secure the approval of the Congress and the League High Commands for the terms of the tentative agreement. But the prevailing misunderstanding between the Congress and the League leaders and the changing political situation completely unnerved the authors of the agreement. The majority of the Congress and League leaders of Bengal denounced the terms of the agreement outright. Influential Hindu dailies of Calcutta and the press belonging to the Khwaja group of the Bengal League started campaigning against the terms of the agreement. While the Khwaja group thought that the agreement would amount to a complete surrender to the Hindus, Congress and Hindu Mahasabha leaders felt that it was designed entirely to extend the frontiers of Pakistan. On 28 May 1947, the Working Committee of the Bengal Provincial Muslim League at its meeting under the Presidentship of Akram Khan denounced the terms of the tentative agreement and reiterated its adherence to the League demand for Pakistan and expressed full confidence in the leadership of Jinnah. The Bengal unity formula received a further setback when, following the statement of the Congress Working Committee, Kalipada Mukherjee, the General Secretary of the Bengal Congress discarded it through a statement issued on 1 June 1947.

In all-India politics, the main opposition to the proposal for a sovereign independent Bengal came from the Indian National Congress. The Congress High Command was frightened of the possibility of permanent domination of Hindus by Muslims in a united Bengal. Both Jawaharlal Nehru and Sardar Vallabhbhai Patel were totally opposed to the concept of a sovereign Bengal. Nehru thought that through this scheme the Muslim League in Bengal would force practically the whole of Bengal to join Pakistan. He further held the view that if Bengal were to remain united it should continue to be a part of the Union of India. He made it clear that Congress would regard a separate state of Bengal as an extension of Pakistan. Sardar Patel too offered determined resistance to the move for Bengal unity. His correspondence with influential Hindu leaders of Bengal during April-June 1947 indicates his role in directing Hindus to the partition of the province as well as his fanatical opposition to the idea of a sovereign Bengal. He condemned those Hindu leaders of Bengal who had got themselves involved in negotiations with the Muslim League leaders of the province.

The approach of the Muslim League High Command to the terms of the tentative agreements was also not favourable. True, Jinnah, was not totally opposed to the proposition. It is evident that he had once offered some encouragement to the scheme. Considering the arguments of Mountbatten that in case of a division of India there should be a partition of the Punjab and Bengal, Jinnah initially was ready to agree to the proposal of a united independent Bengal. His primary consideration was to avert the partition of Bengal; the possibility of a potential alliance between an independent Bengal and Pakistan in the future was of secondary importance to him. But he could not finally settle his mind in favour of the issue. Although apparently he had given his blessings to the move, several factors seemed to have been responsible for making Jinnah reconsider his stand. He rejected the idea in the end, perhaps he felt that it was after all a deviation from the creed of Pakistan. He was not interested in offering any concessions such as joint electorate etc, as incorporated within the terms of the tentative agreement.

The Premier of Bengal had sincerely felt that the formation of a coalition Ministry in the province would be an important step towards bringing the Hindus and Muslims of Bengal closer together as well as preventing the province from being partitioned. But Jinnah never considered these issues to be matters of great urgency. His veto to a coalition cabinet in Bengal proved to be fatal to the Suhrawardy-Bose Formula.

The British were never totally allergic to the idea of a sovereign independent Bengal. Burrows, the Governor of the province, was not at all in favour of the partition of the province. In fact, he was inclined to the Suhrawardy-Bose Formula and had tried his best for its implementation to the last. The Viceroy was also not unwilling to offer united Bengal the status of a Dominion along with India and Pakistan. He had assured Suhrawardy that the British would accept any settlement about Bengal approved by the League and the Congress High Commands. But the British had to look at the question from an all India point of view. They were not eager to compromise the safety of the whole of India for the interest of one province. Hence in the long run the failure of the scheme was inevitable. The final blow to the concept was given when the Congress and the League High Commands accepted Mountbatten Plan (the 3rd June Plan of 1947) for partition of India and for transfer of power to the two Dominions of India and Pakistan.

## CIVIL SERVICE IN TRANSITION AND PATEL

It is not possible to run any kind of government whether a dictatorship or a monarchy or a democracy without a large number servants of the State to ensure that the orders of the Ruler are carried out. Prior to the emergence of democracy, which in itself is a relatively new form of governance, the Ruler appointed his servants from among his courtiers, relatives, and favourites. They were responsible to him and held their office at his pleasure.

A modern Civil Service, with its well-defined regulations, defining what qualifications its members should have, how they should be chosen, the duties they have to perform and their own rights regarding their salaries, their security in service and the like, is linked with democracy and the Rule of Law which is one of its prime functional features.

The first step towards the establishment of a Civil Service seems, however, to have been taken by the Bourbons. This idea was further improved by Napoleon who formalised the system of Prefects (corresponding to our Deputy Commissioner or Collector) and created the three "grands corps" which further extended the functions of the civil services and gave them a high position in society. It is perhaps this ancestry that has made the Civil Service in France, the best organised, the best trained and the most respected of such organizations. It is not by accidents that two of the five Presidents of the Fifth French Republic have been career civil servants.

The history of the Indian Civil Service starts with the East India Company. It was as early as 1800 AD that Lord Wellesley realising that the administrators of the Empire required high education, expertise, and character established the College of Fort William where every employee of the company was to be sent for a three-year course of education of the standards of the universities of Oxford and Cambridge. Among other subjects taught were ethics and international law, and in addition, Indian history and oriental languages. The Directors, however, while accepting the proposal decided that the college should be in England. This is how that, for a whole half-century and more, all members of the Civil Service were educated and given special training at the East India College at Haileybury. The method of recruitment was by competitive examination but the method of entry was by nomination of the Directors. In 1853, the competition became an open one—a full seventeen years before the Home Civil Service could do the same.

The examination for the ICS took place in London and the curriculum, according to which the merit of the candidates was determined was such that Indians had little chance of competing successfully unless they were rich and had studied at a school in England. The constant demand of the Indian National Congress since its birth in 1885 was to increase the numbe of Indians in the ICS. Consequently first the curriculum was widened and then in 1922, a parallel examination began to be held in India. The end-result was that at the time of the transfer of power, half the members of the ICS were Indians.

In the long period in which the ICS had developed, the methods of recruitment and training, the duties, the division of responsibilities, and the salaries had all been very well worked out and standardised. What the methods of recruitment and training were half a century ago would best be illustrated by my own story. Having graduated from Allahabad University, I was sent to England to study Economics, Political Science and the Law with the objective of joining the ICS. Three quarters of the Indian students in England had the same objective; less than a quarter achieved it.

The competitive examination was a joint one for the Diplomatic, the Home, the Indian, and the Colonial Services. The age limit was between 21 and 24 thus giving everyone three chances. The total of the marks for the examination were 1,900. Of this 500 were compulsory for testing out your knowledge of, and ability to write, English and your general knowledge, which included sciences of various kinds. 300 marks were reserved for the *Viva Voce* and for the remaining 1100, you could choose any subject on earth from Astronomy to Zoology. This meant, in effect, the equivalent of two university degrees.

The *Viva Voce* was designed to test personality, moral values, and awareness of what was happening in the world, reactions to problems and situations and the like. The obvious question for me to be asked was that, considering that half of my family was in jail, how was it that I wanted to serve the British Government. My answer was that I wanted to see for myself whether my being in the ICS would help my people. If I found that it would not, I would resign. This earned me 277 marks because what was expected of an ICS officer was truth, courage, honesty and integrity and not cringing sycophancy.

After having been chosen, you had to undergo one or two years' probation in England according to whether you had taken the London or the Indian examination. This period was spent at Oxford, Cambridge, or the School of Oriental Studies in London. It consisted principally of studying Indian Law and procedures, mostly criminal and the Law of Evidence, getting an idea of the revenue system, reading Indian history and learning the language of the province to which you had been assigned. Thereafter, there was one final examination which included, among other things, your ability to ride a horse!

The real training started on one's arrival in India. The new recruit was put in the charge of a Deputy Commissioner or Collector. These trainers were specially selected for their interest in, and capacity for teaching the newcomer not only what his duties were, but to instill into him the proud traditions of the service he had joined. He was also taught what his behaviour should be, how he should acquaint himself with the culture, customs, desires and difficulties of the people in the villages, how to make and keep the revenue records, and how to try both criminal and revenue cases. It was the custom that the trainer invited his new Assistant Commissioner to stay with him. (This was not free of charge, the standard rate for the paying guest, when I arrived in 1934, was Rs. 150 per month, all inclusive.)

The constant company of the teacher with the pupil made it a *guru-chela* relationship. It is a thousand pities that the custom disappeared soon after Independence; no two Indians ate the same food! My guru took me with him on his tours, his inspections, his courts, his *shikar* (which was seldom), to play tennis at the club, and to whichever function he was invited. Apart from this, it was instilled into me, that as a member of the ICS, my integrity, financial, moral and ethical, was to be beyond suspicion.

Every action of mine should therefore be fair, just, helpful and kind. There was to be no fear or favour in my actions or decisions and no listening to *sifarishes* of which I would get plenty. I had to be firm but always polite and courteous. I had to remember that I was not a ruler of the people, but their servant, working for their benefit. I also had to realise that no matter how insignificant I might regard myself to be, in this small rural district, I was a very important person. Whatever I did was expected to be the right and correct thing to do. I had, therefore, to be specially careful.

Thereafter followed the routine training—treasury training for three months in the hills for the summer, six months of "settlement training" when I started as a labourer pulling the "jarib" or iron chain with which the fields were measured and was gradually promoted to the rank of *tehsildar.* During this period, I was prohibited from returning to headquarters and was to go from village to village to know the people by living among them. I was given training for six months as a class-I Magistrate followed by six months of "judicial training" as a subordinate judge, second class. Thereafter I was ready to be given independent charge as Sub-divisional Officer.

The IAS probationer of today gets a far wider and variegated training than I, like my pre-Independence colleagues, ever did. They are far better equipped to handle the far more complicated issues of today. But I have some doubt whether there is today the kind of character-building that I got in the first few months of my service, when I was taught what justified my very existence—that I was there to serve the people. This had to do with humanity and devotion, give them justice within the law, do everything I could to help them improve their condition and to all this without committing even a single act of doubtful integrity.

Times have changed and with them has changed totally, the position of the all-India services. How completely and drastically this has happened can best be illustrated by my describing four incidents. One was during British times; the second, during the regime of Jawaharlal Nehru, when the Rule of Law was still strictly enforced; and the other two are relatively recent.

Sometime in the 1930s, the Finance Member—as cabinet ministers were then called—ordered a new carpet for his office. The price of the carpet was more than the regulations permitted. The excess was detected by audit and the Accountant General, Ganga Ram Kaula, ordered that it should be recovered from the member's salary. The Finance Member was up in arms and wrote an angry letter to the Auditor General saying, "Ganga Ram Kaula is unfit to be an Accountant General". But that was all. Not only was Ganga Ram Kaula eventually promoted to be the first Indian Auditor General but also honoured with a knighthood.

The second case, to which I was a witness was that the Finance Minister T.T.Krishnamachari asked the Chairman of the Central Board of Revenue, Arun Roy, to show him the income tax returns of a particular individual. Arun Roy said that he was sorry he could not do so because they were secret documents. T.T.K was one of the most powerful ministers India has had, with a highly explosive temper and a vengeful nature. He asked, "Haven't you seen them yourself?" Arun's answer was he had. The next question was, "You are my subordinate, aren't you?" The answer: "Yes, sir, I am." Question: "How is it then that I can't see what you have seen?" The answer was that the Chairman of the Board of Revenue was a member of the Income Tax Department, but the minister was not. The minister was furious, but could do absolutely nothing. Arun Roy was promoted to be Economic Secretary in the Finance Ministry and later to be the Auditor General of India.

Now take two relatively recent cases. A young IAS officer went to the minister concerned with the request that the orders for his transfer should be delayed by a few months. The minister asked him what his category was. The officer did not understand what "category" meant. The minister explained that service officers were divided into three categories—A, B, and C. Category A obeyed orders without ifs and buts. Category B raised objections when they thought the orders were against the law, but eventually agreed to carry them out. Category C consisted of those who stuck to their objections and refused to do what the minister wanted. Category A officers alone were of any use. Now and again, category B was also acceptable, but he had no use for category C at all. "Now, tell me to which category do you belong?" The poor officer, who apparently belonged to category C, said goodbye and walked out.

The second case is that of a cabinet minister bringing with him luxury items worth several lakhs from a visit abroad. The Assistant Commissioner at the airport asked for the duty to be paid. The minister's clerk said that these goods belong to the minister. They should be let in duty free. The officer could not accept that interpretation of the law. The duty was paid but within a week was transferred from Delhi to Chennai.

I shall try to describe how, when, and why this revolutionary change took place. There are many reasons for this change. Historically, the first is that the Indian National Congress was highly prejudiced against the ICS and the Indian Police Service. Given the history of the struggle for freedom, this was not surprising. Most freedom fighters did not understand that the service at whose hands they suffered was performing its duty to implement the law. The law was not made by the members of the services. It was made by the Viceroy and the Secretary of State for India in London. Nobody could have stated the difference between making the law and enforcing it better than the judge, C.V. Broomfield of the ICS who sentenced Mahatma Gandhi to six years' imprisonment in 1923. The last sentence of his judgement was, "If the course of events in India makes it possible for the Government to reduce the period and release you, no one will be better pleased than I."

Occasionally they did understand the difference but the masses did not. When my mother was arrested in 1942, the police officer who came to arrest her begged "Mataji," as she was universally called, to pardon him for what he was doing. Mataji told him that he was doing nothing to be pardoned for. His duty was to arrest her because she had broken the law; her duty was to break the law. Both of them were doing nothing more than carrying out their "dharma."

Most of the leaders who became who became ministers after Independence, had very little experience of administration and sometimes none at all. The only such experience that Prime Minister Nehru had had was one year's tenure as chairman of the Allahabad Municipality. They did not understand that the good laws that were about to pass would not automatically enforce themselves. Good governance required a competent, efficient, and disciplined machine, known as the Civil Service, to do so.

The only leader who understood the importance and the essentiality of the All India Services was Sardar Vallabhbhai Patel. In a letter to the Prime Minister on April 27, 1948, he said, "I need hardly emphasize that an efficient, disciplined, and contented service, assured of its prospects as a result of diligent and honest work is a *sine qua non* of sound administration under a democratic regime even more than under an authoritarian rule. The service must be above party and we should ensure that political considerations, either in its recruitment or in its discipline and control, are reduced to the minimum, if not eliminated altogether." He also saw the importance of organizing the Civil Service on an All-India basis with the Central Government having a considerable say in the recruitment, training, and career of its members, as a counter-balance to the emergence of the centrifugal forces that have repeatedly torn apart the political unity of our country. These proposals were strongly opposed by the Chief Ministers of the states who wanted no interference with their authority and wished then, as they do now, to have pliable officials who could be manipulated more easily than members of the All India Services. In his speech to the Constituent Assembly in October 1949, the Sardar said, "The Indian Union will go. You will not have a united India if you do not have a good All India Service which has independence to speak out its advice—if you do not adopt this course, then do not follow the present system, substitute something else." Sardar Patel did ultimately succeed in forcing his proposals down the throat of an unwilling Constituent Assembly. All the articles designed to ensure the independence and the security of the services and to prevent any political interference with them, find themselves in the Constitution because of Sardar Patel.

The Prime Minister, as he gained experience of how in actual fact the ICS worked, was fairly soon converted fully to the Sardar's point of view. During his long tenure of office, no politician dared to interfere with the functioning of the services or bully them into breaking the law. For the first quarter-of-century of our independence, the All India Civil Services continued to function as before.

There had, however, been one change. One of the complaints against the ICS was that it drew "fat salaries," and we were pledged to reduce them. The salaries of the ICS were fixed at very high levels in order to prevent the ICS becoming corrupt in an environment of corruption, both among the Indian rulers and the servants of the Company. These salaries started at Rs. 450 per month for the new entrant and went up to Rs. 4,000 for a Secretary to > the Government of India and a judge of the High Court. They had never been revised during the previous ninety years of rise in prices, so that instead of remaining fat, they became lean. Nevertheless, to fulfil the pledge, they were reduced to Rs. 350 for the entrant and Rs. 3500 for the seniormost posts. Coupled with this, there was steady inflation while rates of income tax were gradually raised to absurdly high levels. Simultaneously with this, we adopted the policy of nationalising, not only "the commanding heights of the economy," as Jawaharlal Nehru wanted, but also of anything that any minister, Central or State, desired. The industry that was left in private hands was so strictly controlled that virtually nothing could be done without government sanction. The license-quota-permit-raj started and when a senior minister of the Union Government started selling these across the table, corruption started to become a way of life. Be it said to the ninety years old tradition of the ICS, that it did not, for a very long time, in spite of their salaries having become meager, become parties to this dishonesty. Corruption descended to the Civil Services from the top and did not do so till it had thoroughly soaked the political world.

Why has the politician been opposed to the independence of the Civil Services from the very beginning and why has he become as corrupt as he is now? The answer to both questions lies in the Indian Constitution. That Constitution is based on ideas which are still not acceptable to the vast majority of the Indian people although they might be acceptable to the tiny minority which has received a westernised education. Those ideas are democracy, equality, secularism, human rights and, above all, the Rule of Law. All these ideas are of foreign origin and they are contrary to our traditions.

Our tradition of government has, for thousands of years, been that of "Raja and Praja." They were in full practice in 1947 in the Princely states and accepted by the people. The powers of the king are absolute, the wishes and desires of the king are the law which the "praja" cannot question and has to obey. One of his prerogatives, never questioned, is to levy whatever taxes he likes and to take whatever proportion of the revenues of the state for his personal use. Nor was it unusual for the king and his courtiers to accept, and indeed demand, presents or gifts for getting favours in return. There is nothing strange about this because the whole world which, till not so long ago, was ruled by Kings and Emperors had the same traditions as ours. The control over the absoluteness of the King started in England with the Magna Carta in 1215 AD, when the King was forced to hand-over a few of his powers to a handful of his nobles. The movement for the transfer of power from the King to the people took, in England, well over seven-hundred years. These years included civil wars, revolutions, and regicide. We in India, on the other hand, suddenly jumped from the absolute power of the Viceroy to all power being transferred to all the people. If King John had given all his powers to the people in 1215 AD, it is doubtful that England would have ever emerged from chaos.

While we go on priding ourselves at being the largest democracy in the world, the fact is that the only part of democracy that we have really understood and adopted is that every citizen of India has the right to vote. But that in a democracy, the laws passed by the representatives of the people have to be obeyed by every citizen, has not yet been accepted. The concept of the common man is that by casting his vote, he is electing a Ruler, and as the Ruler is all powerful, he can do whatever he wishes, including transferring a part of the public revenue to his own pocket. It is his orders that have to be obeyed and not those of the bureaucrat. The laws that are passed in Parliament in the State Assemblies are not meant to be enforced on the elected representative of the people, his family and his supporters. It is for this reason that most laws are passed without a quorum being present in the House.

In this context, where does the civil servant fit in? His function is to implement the law. This is regarded by the politician as a check on his power and that check is unacceptable to him. There is, consequently, a continuous war between civil servants who try and live up to the democratic concept of the Rule of Law. For the minister, it is only category "A" officers who are worthwhile. But ideal civil servants are expected to belong to category "C".

The weapon used to bend civil servants to the minister's will is frequent transfers which ruin a man's life and that threat has changed much of the transferees from category C to A. Once having said goodbye to one's conscience, it would be foolish not to also become a partner in the loot that is so easily available. There is unfortunately no denying the fact that an increasing number of civil servants are now corrupt.

Sardar Patel wanted a civil service without political interference, but he forgot to place any limit on the Chief Minister's power to transfer officers. In developed democracies, there are such limitations. In Britain, senior officers cannot be transferred without the orders of the Prime Minister, who will not, by convention, act except on the advice of the Secretary of the Civil Services Department. In India, it is the custom, both in the states and has now crept into the centre, to transfer dozens of civil servants whenever a government is changed.

The other factor which has changed the position of the civil service is the spread of corruption at all levels throughout the country. Not too long after Independence the whole country seems to have changed its religion.

The worship of God was replaced by the worship of Mammon. The economic policies we adopted, the strict control over private industry and the totally absurd rates of direct taxation placed enormous powers in governmental hands and gave both, the politicians and the bureaucrat, an opportunity to make money.

As the cost of elections goes on increasing and the size of monetary pool goes on getting smaller as a result of liberalisation, the source of money becomes increasingly objectionable.

The very large size of our constituencies make it imperative to raise money for fighting elections. According to recent calculation, the money required by a candidate for the election to the Lok Sabha is Rs. 1.3 crore. That money has to be procured somehow, and those who make it available, now consist largely of members of the underworld, shady characters and criminals of all kinds. Inevitably, the nexus between the politician, the criminal, the corrupt businessman, and the corrupt civil servant gets stronger year after year. Our democracy remains "of the people" but it is neither "by the people" nor "for the people."

Till about twenty years ago, one could say with confidence that there was hardly any member of the IAS who was dishonest or corrupt. These days, I gather that over half of the IAS have joined the politicians in corrupt practices. (They may, if they wish, seek satisfaction in the fact that among the politicians, the percentage on a conservative basis, is well over 80 percent.) It is a matter of credit to the strength of the IAS tradition that they resisted the temptation for so long. This break in the tradition has been helped by the fact that it is only about 50 percent of the IAS who are appointed on the basis of merit through competitive examinations. The other half come through reservation of all kinds and promotions from the State Services. Furthermore, the competitive examination can now be taken by members of some classes till they are well over 30 by which time there is little likelihood that they will be affected by the tradition of the service they join.

The result of all this is two-fold. One is that our system of governance is no longer democratic. The people still elect their MPs and MLAs, but the elected Rulers, who are now getting increasingly accepted as being above the law, are more interested in themselves than the welfare of the people. We abolished 500 or so Maharajas in India but have instead created almost ten times that number of Kings!

Things have come to such a pass that only the other day in the state of Haryana, an MLA along with his supporters, which included muscle men and his security guards, entered the office of a Deputy Commissioner and demanded that he should do something or the other. The DC said that he could not oblige because the Election Commission had temporarily forbidden it. Thereupon, after some abuses, the poor DC was manhandled. In any democratic country, the whole lot of people who were involved would have been immediately arrested on the orders of the Deputy Commissioner, tried for contempt of court, and sentenced to a term of imprisonment. The only thing the poor DC could do was to run to the Chief Minister who did order a case to be registered against the MLA. This was the last that was heard of the matter. How, in circumstances such as these, can the Deputy Commissioner enforce the law? The position of the Indian Police Service is even worse because they are not regarded as the implementors and enforcers of the law, but members of the private army of the Chief Minister. It is not only he alone whose orders have to be obeyed without question, but the desires and wishes of his wife, children, and grandchildren, have also to be attended to. The crimes committed by the members of the "Royal family" are numerous. Apart from taking bribes or fees for favours done, a practice very common indeed, they range from kidnapping for ransom, to rape and murder. If the crime is so open that some action has to be taken under public pressure, the evidence is so tampered with, that not even a *prima facie* case can be made out and taken to court.

Furthermore, the prime duty of the police now seems to be not to protect the common man from crime but to protect the VIP and see to it that he is not discomfited in any way. The definition of VIP has also become very liberal, most MPs and MLAs seem to be included ex officio in that category. It is often said that of the 60,000 policemen in the Delhi Police, no less than 40,000 are employed on VIP duties. Given all these circumstances, is there any wonder if a larger proportion of the Indian Police Service than of the IAS have joined the criminals? The discontent that leads to rebellion, anarchy, and chaos, has many reasons. But the chief reason is our failure to provide to our people that liberty, justice and equality which our Constitution was designed to give them. There is no shortage of good laws we have passed, but we have destroyed the means by which these laws can be implemented.

In order to restart the machine to implement the laws, many fundamental changes have to be made, and can be made without any difficulty if there is the political will to change the existing situation. But that will does not exist. There have been three important reports by commissions appointed by previous governments which have made recommendations that would help in restoring the Rule of Law. The first was the Administrative Reforms Commission, presided over by no less a person than Mr. Morarji Desai. Yet another commission, presided over by Mr. Justice Sarkaria, suggested many valuable reforms which could help greatly in improving our system of governance. The third was the Dharma Vira Commission which would have enabled the police to perform their real functions. These reports have been gathering dust over the years without any action being taken.

Then there have been lying, with the Government of India, for years, proposals for the Supreme Court to amend the basic legislation enacted in the 1860s which, antiquated and out of date as it now is, prevents the administration of justice. There are proposals from the Election Commission to prevent criminals from becoming our representatives. There are proposals from the Law Commission, to change all kinds of laws. Several governments have, over the years, introduced a Lok Pal Bill, but have had to withdraw it.

Our last government, presided over by none other than the present Prime Minister, announced bravely that they would appoint a commission to suggest amendments in the Constitution. A former President of India, the highly respected R. Venkataraman, was appointed Chairman. And then nothing happened. Why did nothing happen? Because MPs of their own coalition told those who started the move that they would not stand by such ideas. After all, they had the democratic system of governance with all powers vested in the elected representatives of the people. Why did their government want to destroy democracy? The explanation for their apathy is simple. The corrupt and criminal caucus in our legislatures is so strong that it can block any change which reduces even slightly the unlimited power that they today enjoy.

I have two great fears about the future. One is that it might happen one day when a criminal with some popular support might turn around to say these black-gowned salaried lackeys have no authority to pass judgement over the elected representatives of the people. In a democracy, the people are sovereign. If they have said, by electing him, that he is not guilty, these paid employees have no right to question their decision. If this ever happens, the chaos will be complete.

The other fear I have is that this theory of absolute power which has succeeded in destroying the Civil Service is now beginning to interfere with the autonomy of the Armed Forces. The last time this political interference was started by Mr. Krishna Menon, the country had to pay a very heavy price. Not only did our Army which had never lost a war, have to bear a shameful defeat, but the consequences were even greater. We had to retreat from the policy of non-alignment which we had preached to the world for so long. Not only did we have to beg for foreign help but had, at least temporarily, to do what they desired.

For the next 35 years, no minister dared to interfere with the appointments postings and promotions of the personnel of the defence forces. Some ministers did try but were warned off by the Generals. For the last two years, there have been disturbing rumours of interference and the much more disquieting news is that the Chiefs of Staff have been weak enough to allow this to happen. If the rumours are true, the elected representatives of the people might get a few more votes, but the defence forces will lose the capacity to defend us and the sovereignty of our country.

## THE CONSTITUENT ASSEMBLY

The Constitution was drafted by the Constituent Assembly, which was elected by the elected members of the provincial assemblies. Jawaharlal Nehru, C. Rajagopalacharya, Rajendra Prasad, Sardar Vallabhbhai Patel, Maulana Abul Kalam Azad and Shyama Prasad Mukherjee were some important figures in the Assembly. There were more than 30 members of the scheduled classes. Frank Anthony represented the Anglo-Indian community, and the Parsis were represented by H. P. Modi and R. K. Sidhwa. The Chairman of the Minorities Committee was Harendra Coomar Mukherjee, a distinguished Christian who represented all Christians other than Anglo-Indians. Prominent jurists like Alladi Krishnaswamy Iyer, B. R. Ambedkar, Bengal Narasingh Rao and K. M. Munshi Ganesh Mavlankar were also members of the Assembly. Sarojini Naidu, Hansa Mehta, Durgabai Deshmukh and Rajkumari Amrit Kaur were important women members. The first president of the Constituent Assembly was Sachidanand Sinha later, Rajendra Prasad was elected president of the Constituent Assembly. The members of the Constituent Assembly met for the first time in the year 1946 on December 9.

## Grand Finale

Thus the task of uniting the country was complete. In the history of India stretched over ages, India became one and united for the first time and that too without shedding a drop of blood. That was the marvel of the personality of Sardar. The sterling qualities of leadership he had shown as leader of Satyagraha, flowered in greater way in the administration of the country, maintenance of law and order and ensuring stability of the country and making it invulnerable. It is because of these strong steps that earned him the title of "The man of steel". Sardar Vallabhbhai passed away in Mumbai on the morning of the 15th December 1950.

## AS CONGRESS PRESIDENT AND THE ELECTION OF 1950

In spite of being ideologically at odds with both the right-wing Vallabhbhai Patel and the left-wing Jawaharlal Nehru-he was elected Congress President for the crucial years around Indian independence in 1947.

After Gandhi's assassination in January 1948, Nehru rejected his demand that the party's views should be sought in all decisions. Nehru, with the support of Patel, told Kripalani that while the party was entitled to lay down the broad principles and guidelines, it could not be granted a say in the government's day-to-day affairs. This precedent became central to the relationship between government and ruling party in subsequent decades.

Nehru, however, supported Kripalani in the election of the Congress President in 1950. The election was considered a vital battle for the party between the left, led by Nehru, and the right, led by Patel. Kripalani went up against Patel's candidate, the Hindu nationalist Purushottam Das Tandon. In an atmosphere soured by communal tension, the controversial reconstruction of the Somnath Temple, the founding of the Jan Sangh, and the Nehru-Liaquat Pact, as well as differences on economic policy, Tandon narrowly defeated Kripalani. Bruised by his defeat, and disillusioned by what he viewed as the abandonment of the Gandhian ideal of a countless village republics, Kripalani left the Congress and became one of the founders of the Kisan Mazdoor Praja Party. This party subsequently merged with the Socialist Party of India to form the Praja Socialist Party.

For a while it was even believed that Nehru, stung by the defeat, was considering abandoning the Congress as well; his several offers of resignation at the time were all, however, shouted down. A great many of the more progressive elements of the party left in the months following the election, however. Congress's subsequent bias to the right was only balanced when

Nehru obtained the resignation of Tandon in the run up to the general elections of 1951.

## Patel and P.Das Tandon

He and Nehru had good relations in the beginning; Nehru who commended the "No Tax" campaign started by Tandon in 1930. In the 1940s the differences between them increased. While Tandon was not perceived to be power-hungry, his relation with Nehru was not on good terms and he was believed to be a protege of Sardar Vallabhbhai Patel. In 1950, his successful election to the post of Congress President against Acharya Kriplani, who was widely believed to be backed by Nehru, put the latter in a tight spot. The relations between the party and the government suffered during that period. Subsequently, it became a sort of unwritten norm for the leader of the government to also be the party president or at the least, have a pliable candidate in the post.

## A Divided Freedom

As the Second World War was moving to its final stage, the British Government released Gandhi in May 1944. On his release, Gandhi proposed to meet Jinnah and discuss the communal situation with him. As a result they held a series of parleys from 9 September till 27 September. In these parleys, the question of Partition was discussed. The discussions were centred on the Rajagopalchari or the CR formula as it was called. The principal provisions of the formula were:

- The Muslim League was to endorse the demand for independence of the country and cooperate with the Indian National Congress in forming an Interim government.
- Contiguous districts in the Northwest and East of India would be demarcated and plebiscite would be held to decide whether or not they should be separated from India.

Gandhi accepted the right of self-determination and even of secession of the two predominantly Muslim territories in India while Jinnah was demanding for Pakistan. In essence Gandhi insisted on independence first and secession later while Jinnah wanted Pakistan first and independence later. Jinnah continued to insist that the Muslims of India constituted a separate nation. This was Jinnah's trump card. In the words of Sri Aurobindo: "*The idea of two nationalities in India is only a newly-fangled notion invented by Jinnah for his purposes and contrary to the facts. More than 90% of the Indian Mussalmans are descendants of converted Hindus and belong as much to the Indian nation as the*

*Hindus themselves. This process of conversion has continued all along; Jinnah is himself a descendant of a Hindu, converted in fairly recent times, named Jinahbhai and many of the most famous Mohammedan leaders have a similar origin"*.

The talks broke down as Jinnah refused to negotiate any further. Durga Das had written earlier regarding the talks: 'Mr Jinnah will never come to an agreement during the war. While he is intransigent he is on top; the moment he settles with the Congress, the League will get merged in the nationalist movement and will never be able to dictate terms to the Congress'. Sri Aurobindo too had remarked: "Instead of doing what is necessary, the Congress is trying to flirt with Jinnah, and Jinnah simply thinks that he has to obstinately stick to his terms to get them. The more they try, the more Jinnah becomes intransigent".

In early 1945, Lord Wavell the Viceroy of India announced a plan 'designed to ease the present political situation and to advance India towards her goal of full self-government'. He proposed that a Conference be held in Simla, the summer capital of India, to which leaders of all the parties in India would be invited. This list included the Congress, the Muslim League, the Scheduled Castes, the Sikhs, and some other groups. The main topic of discussion would be the formation of a new Executive Council. It was suggested that all the members of this body would be Indians, except the Viceroy and the Commander in Chief.

Gandhi raised an objection to the classification 'Caste Hindus' whom the Congress was supposed to represent. Jinnah objected on two counts: first, that the list of members suggested by the Muslim League would be final and second that all Muslim members were to be from the Muslim League alone. Despite these objections, the Conference met and discussions were held. The Viceroy was unable to accept the demands of Jinnah; failing to convince him he announced that the Conference had failed. This act of the Viceroy gave Jinnah the veto power, which he used, to full effect in the following days.

In August 1945, the War came to an end with the dropping of two atom bombs on Japan. No doubt, Britain with the help of the Allies had crushed both Germany and Japan; but in the life and death battle it had exhausted its manpower and economic resources to such an extent that it could never again hope to recover its old power and prestige.

The world situation had completely changed and it was evident that India would get her freedom as a result of new world circumstances. In the words of Leonard Mosley: "From the moment, in 1945, when war was over and the post-war world began to reshape itself, no one of clear mind had any doubt that the Indian people would achieve the independence from British rule.... After Singapore, Burma and the sinking of her finest ships by the Japanese, Britain would never again be able to demonstrate in Asia the background of strength and influence which had for so long enabled her to rule a million people with one man on the spot".

It is clear therefore that it was the world circumstances and not the Quit India movement that was responsible for India's freedom. The question then predominant was no longer the attainment of freedom, which was inevitable, but the communal problem.

Some time towards the end of 1945 elections were held in the Provinces. The Congress won seven provinces, while the Muslim League won in Bengal and Sind. In Punjab it was forestalled by a coalition of the Congress and the Akalis. But one thing became clear in these elections; the Muslims were solidly behind the League while the rest of the country was with the Congress. At the same time two other factors hastened the ushering in of freedom. The first one was the trial of the INA soldiers and the second one was the revolt of the sailors serving in the Indian Royal Navy.

The soldiers of the INA were charged with committing war against the King. A Military Tribunal was set up and three officers were put on public trial; the Indian public did not know much about the INA till then, but as a result of the public trial they came to be regarded as a band of patriotic heroes who fought for the liberation of the motherland. The trial aroused great interest all over the country and popular demonstrations were held leading sometimes to violent demonstrations. The Government quailed before the storm and although the officers were convicted to sentence of transportation for life, it was soon changed to being simply cashiered.

On 18 February 1946, some ratings of the Signal School in Bombay went on a hunger strike in protest against the treatment being meted out to them by Royal Navy. Soon others in different parts of the country joined them and the situation began to get completely out of hand. They took possession of some of the ships and strikes and hartals were organised all over the country. The police had to open fire and the military had to be called in to restore order. Finally, due largely to the efforts of Sardar Vallabhbhai Patel, the ratings surrendered on 23 February.

On 19 February, one day after the Mutiny broke out, the Government announced the decision to send out a special mission consisting of three cabinet Ministers. This group known as the Cabinet Mission was made up of the following members: Lord Pethick Lawrence, Secretary of State for India, Sri Stafford Cripps, President of the Board of Trade and A.V.Alexander, First Lord of the Admiralty. They were, in association with the Viceroy, sent to find an agreement with the leaders of the different political parties on the principles and procedures relating to the constitutional issue. They arrived in India on 24 March 1946. They spent five weeks meeting the leaders of all the parties and representative groups. On 5 May, a conference of leaders of the Congress and Muslim League was held in Simla to consider the grouping of provinces, the character of the federal union and the setting up of the constitutional machinery. But it was unable to arrive at a consensus and therefore the mission issued a statement containing its own proposal on 16 May 1946. The main points of the Cabinet Mission Plan were:

- The formation of an undivided Union of India embracing both British India and the States, which should deal with three subjects: Foreign Affairs, Defence and Communications.
- The provinces would have complete autonomy with all other powers vested in them. The demands of the Muslim League would be thus met.
- A proposal for the creation of an intermediate level between the centre and the provinces. It was proposed that there could be three regional groupings – one in the northwest, one in the northeast and one consisting the rest of the country. The provinces in each group would be allowed to associate themselves in units, each having its own executive and legislature.

Both the Congress and the League seemed to be in two minds with regard to the proposals of the Cabinet Mission; they were reluctant to reject them outright and yet unwilling to accept them as they stood. The Muslim League at first accepted the Plan with the hope that it would ultimately result in the establishment of Pakistan. The Congress, despite its reservations, agreed to join the Constituent Assembly. Then followed an unfortunate incident, which changed the whole course of events. Nehru who was elected President of the Congress gave a Press conference on 10 July. In the words of Leonard Mosley: "And on 10 July after he had been elected President, he called the Press together for a conference to discuss the policy as the new head of Congress. It was a moment in history when circumspection should have been the order of the day. There was much to be gained by silence.

The fortunes of India were in the balance, and one false move could upset them. Nehru chose this moment to launch into what his biographer, Michael Brecher, has described as one of the most fiery and provocative statements in his forty years of public life". He goes on to say: "Did he realise what he was saying? He was telling the world that once in power, the Congress would use its strength at the Centre to alter the Cabinet Mission Plan as it thought fit". That was the flashpoint and soon "the Hindus and Muslims were back in two fuming camps". This was the just the thing that Jinnah was waiting for, arguing that this statement of Nehru represented the real mind of the Congress. Quite inevitably, the Muslim League decided to back out and demanded the immediate establishment of Pakistan. In order to bring this about, Jinnah called upon the Muslims to resort to Direct Action. He explained that the participation of the Muslims in the proposed constitution making machinery was fraught with danger. He said that while the British had machine guns to enforce their will and the Hindus the weapon of civil resistance, the Muslims alone remained defenceless. It followed that they must bid good-bye to constitutional methods and prepare for self-defence and self-preservation by resorting to direct action. 16 August was fixed as the day for Direct Action. While the tension was building the Viceroy decided on 12 August to invite the Congress to form the Interim Government; that proved to be the last straw for Jinnah. Nehru invited Jinnah to participate in the Interim Government but he declined the invitation. At that time, the president of the All-India-Jamaitul Ulma-I-Islam, Shabbir Ahmad Usmani declared that no power on earth can crush the Muslims. 'Living he is a Gazi and killed in action he is a martyr'.

In Calcutta, on 16 August the day began with public demonstrations, hartals and hoisting of the Muslim League flag. Soon clashes began and spread to the whole city. Utter confusion prevailed in the city and the hooligans had a field day indulging in stabbing, killing, arson and criminal assaults on women.

The mob fury continued for four days with the Government standing by and proving to be utterly ineffective to meet the situation. It is estimated that thousands were killed, tens of thousands injured, lakhs left homeless and property worth crores of rupees destroyed. Bengal was then under the Muslim League and the Chief Minister was Suhrawardy. The Statesman wrote: 'this is not a riot. For three days the city concentrated on unrestrained civil war. Upon whom the main guilt for it rests is manifest. Where the primary blame lies is where we have squarely put it – upon the Provincial Muslim League Cabinet and particularly the Chief Minister'. The rioting soon spread to other parts like Noahkali and Tipperah where the Muslims were in a majority. The Hindus were butchered mercilessly and in retaliation the Hindus in Bihar took revenge. All in all it was a sordid story of horror and cruelty. This was the way Jinnah had chosen to prove his point: *Hindus and Muslims could not live together.*

The Interim Government led by Nehru was sworn in on 2 September. The Muslim League refused to participate in it. However on 13 October, Jinnah agreed to participate and sent a list of five ministers who would be accommodated. One of the ministers was Liaquat Ali Khan who was given the important Finance portfolio. 'In the government but against it', Liaquat used his pivotal position to bring the government to a standstill. Elections to the Constituent Assembly were held in the second half of the year and were completed by December. It was decided to convene the Assembly on 9 December. Jinnah called upon the members of the Muslim League to boycott the Assembly. Naturally the Congress demanded that the League should either attend the Assembly or quit the Interim Government. This led to a complete deadlock. Jinnah knew that all that he had to do was to boycott the Assembly in order to render nugatory any decision regarding the Constitution of an Indian Union. Jinnah warned in his speeches that the only alternative to Pakistan was civil war. Under this threat, the British government decided that the decisions of the Constituent Assembly could not be implemented in so far as they affected the areas under Muslim majority. A month later, the League demanded the dissolution of the Assembly.

The country was facing a grave crisis. It was at this time that Prime Minister Atlee took a bold decision. He was of the view that it was necessary to take a clear-cut decision and he decided that the British government should fix a date for the withdrawal of British power in India. As a result, Attlee announced: "The present state of uncertainty is fraught with danger and cannot be indefinitely prolonged. His Majesty's Government wish to make it clear that it is their definite intention to take necessary steps to effect the transference of power to responsible Indian hands by a date not later than June 1948". In order to perform this task he announced that Lord Mountbatten would replace Lord Wavell as Viceroy. Immediately the political tempo was whipped up.

The Muslim League made a desperate attempt to secure control over the Provinces, which it planned to be attached to Pakistan. Direct Action was started in Assam but with little success. But in Sind and the North-West Frontier Provinces a systematic genocide was carried on against the Sikhs and the Hindus who were in a minority. On January 27, 1947 Mian Iftikharuddin said at a Lahore public meeting of Muslims: "We have come here to tell you that if you can carry on the fight with the same determination and discipline as had been displayed during the past three days, not only will you have achieved victory in the Punjab, but you will also have reached nearer to your goal of Pakistan."

Lord Mountbatten arrived in India on 22 March. He was sent with all the powers to effect the transfer of power. Immediately he held meetings and consultations with all parties. He was soon convinced that partition was inevitable. Jinnah was determined to have even a truncated Pakistan. He said: "I do not care how little you give me, so long as you give it to me completely". Sardar Vallabhbhai Patel and Jawaharlal Nehru accepted the plan with a heavy heart. Gandhi however remained adamantly opposed to partition. He even went so far as to suggest that Jinnah could be made the first Prime Minister of a United India. The Congress rejected the proposal outright. Gandhi then not only withdrew his proposal but also withdrew himself from all politics leaving all negotiations to the Working Committee.

Mountbatten then, along with the Hindu, Muslim and Sikh leaders worked out a scheme, which was approved later by the British Cabinet. On 3 June, Prime Minister Attlee announced in the House of Commons the scheme known as the June 3rd or Mountbatten Plan. The Plan dealt with the method by which power would be transferred to Indian hands and particularly the methods by which Muslim majority provinces would choose whether to remain in India or join the new State Pakistan. The next day, Mountbatten announced that the final transfer of power would not be later than June 1948, but a few days later it was decided that the date would be 15 August 1947. On 12 June the Congress Working Committee met and passed a resolution accepting partition. An extract from the resolution: "The Congress had worked hard and sacrificed everything for the sake of unity. But there was a limit beyond which it could not go. The choice today was between accepting the statement of June 3 or committing suicide". Gandhi, who a few days back, opposed the formation of Pakistan now supported the resolution. However there were still some Congress leaders who opposed this resolution. One such person was Purushottam Das Tandon. He said: " Acceptance of the resolution will be an abject surrender to the British and the Muslim League. The admission of the Working Committee was an admission of weakness and the result of a sense of despair. The Partition would not benefit either community – the Hindus in Pakistan and the Muslims in India would both live in fear". Despite all this the plan was accepted and so in less than ten weeks, India was to be free and partitioned. The provinces of Baluchistan, Sind and the North-Western Provinces went to Pakistan. Punjab and Bengal were to be divided. East Punjab and West Bengal were to be part of India while West Punjab and East Bengal were to form part of Pakistan. Boundary commissions were set up to delineate the boundaries between these two provinces.

While all this was happening, the Princely States, which were also ruled by Britain, were left free to decide their own fate. They could become sovereign States or voluntarily join India or Pakistan. If they chose to be free, as at one time it seemed that they would, it would have meant a balkanisation of India with very grave consequences. Sardar Vallabhbhai Patel with the help of VP Menon convinced the princes that it was in their interest to join the Indian Union. By August, most of them had signed the Instrument of Accession by which they became formally part of India. Three States however held out; these were the States of Junagadh, Kashmir and Hyderabad. Soon after India attained independence, Junagadh's eccentric ruler escaped to Pakistan, while the Maharaja of Kashmir acceded to India in the month of October. The Nizam of Hyderabad held out for over a year.

As the boundary lines were being drawn, the communal hatred and cruelty that was seething for the last one year reached its crescendo. There is perhaps no parallel in the history of India to the barbarity and massacre that took place in the following days. The story may be summed up thus: six hundred thousand dead, 14 million driven from their homes, one hundred thousand young girls kidnapped, forcibly converted or sold on the auction block. The Dominion of Pakistan was inaugurated in Karachi on 14 August. On 15 August India became an Independent State. It was a moment of sorrow and destruction but at the same time millions of Indians were celebrating with great joy and enthusiasm.

Gandhi's dreams of nonviolence and Hindu-Muslim unity lay inevitably shattered in pieces, for they were built on castles of sand. On the other hand Sri Aurobindo said: "Pakistan was created by falsehood, fraud and force".

On the midnight of 15 August, Jawaharlal Nehru addressed the Constituent Assembly. Here is an extract from that speech: "Long years ago we made a tryst with destiny, and now the time comes when we shall resume our pledge, not wholly or in full measure, but very substantially. At the stroke of the midnight hour, when the world sleeps, India will wake to life and freedom. A moment comes, which comes but rarely in history, when we step out from the old to the new, when an age ends, and when the soul of a nation, long suppressed, finds utterance. It is fitting that at this solemn moment we take the pledge of dedication to the service of India and her people and to the still larger cause of humanity".

It is important to note that 15 August was the birthday of Sri Aurobindo. On the same day, Sri Aurobindo too gave a message. Here is an extract from the message: "August 15th, 1947 is the birthday of free India. It marks for her the end of an old era, the beginning of a new age.

But we can also make it by our life and acts as a free nation an important date in a new age opening for the whole world, for the political, social, cultural and spiritual future of humanity. As a mystic, I take this identification, not as a coincidence or fortuitous accident, but as a sanction and seal of the Divine Power which guides my steps on the work with which I began life. Indeed almost all the world movements which I hoped to see fulfilled in my lifetime, though at that time they looked like impossible dreams, I can observe on this day either approaching fruition or initiated and on the way to their achievement.....

India is free but she has not achieved unity, only a fissured and broken freedom.... The old communal division into Hindu and Muslim seems to have hardened into the figure of a permanent political division of the country. It is to be hoped that the Congress and the nation will not accept the settled fact as forever settled or as anything more than a temporary expedient. For if it lasts, India may be seriously weakened, even crippled: civil strife may remain always possible, possible even a new invasion and foreign conquest. The partition of the country must go,—it is to be hoped by a slackening of tension, by a progressive understanding of the need of peace and concord, by the constant necessity of common and concerted action, even of an instrument of union for that purpose.

In this way unity may come about under whatever form—the exact form may have a pragmatic but not a fundamental importance. But by whatever means, the division must and will go. For without it the destiny of India might be seriously impaired and even frustrated.

## INDIA AFTER INDEPENDENCE

Three main problems of the independent India: The newly independent India faced three main problems in the very beginning. They were as follows:

i. The preparation of a constitution of independent India.

ii. The problem of the rehabilitation of the refugees.

iii. The problem of merging of Princely States in the Indian Federation.

Integration of Princely States:

(a) Danger of Independent Princely States after the independence of India.

-When India got independence on August 15, 1947, there existed the Princely States within the territories of India.

-The Princely states had also became independent along with India when the British ended their treaties with them.

-The existence of large number of Princely states became another danger for the newly independent India.

(b) Role of Vallabhbhai Patel: Steps taken by the Indian Government. Vallabhbhai Patel was the first Home Minister and Deputy Prime Minister of the newly independent India.

He was quick to recognise the grave danger of the existence of Princely states within the territorial limits of India. The Indian government drafted an agreement of integration which was to be signed with those Princely states.

Vallabhbhai Patel persuaded most of the Kings, Nawabs and rulers of Princely states to sign the agreement of integration and managed to merge their territories within the Federation of India.

He was helped by the support of the subjects of the Princely states themselves who desired to integrate with the Federation of India.

However, three states namely, Hyderabad, Junagarh and Jammu and Kashmir presented a problem as their ruler resisted the integration with the Federation of India.

## Junagarh

Junagarh was a state in Saurashtra region of Gujarat.

The people of the Junagarh state desired to join with India.

The Nawab of Junagarh however started secret negotiation with Pakistan and kept his people and the Government of India in dark about his real objectives. Pakistan announced to the India that Junagarh was going to join with Pakistan.

When the people of the state learned about it, they arose in strong opposition to the decision of their rulers.

The neighbouring states also denounced the decision of the ruler of Junagarh.

When Nawab and his Diwan found that they were being opposed from all the quarters, they fled India and took shelter with Pakistan.

A referendum was held in Junagarh state and as per the result of the referendum, Junagarh state was integrated with India.

## Hyderabad

a: Nizam of Hyderabad adopted Anti-India stand:

Nizam adopted anti-India stand on the independence of India.

He decided to declare Hyderabad an independent state.

He did not send the representatives of his state to the Constitution Assembly.

In July 1947, he presented before Lord Mountbatten the demand Madhya Prant and part of Berar which Lord Mountbatten refused to accept.

In August 1947, he tried to make a deal with India on conditions but Vallabhbhai Patel refused to listen him before the integration of Hyderabad with India.

Nizam did not accept the proposal of Lord Mountbatten to ascertain the view of public of Hyderabad State on the issue of integration with India under the supervision of English officers.

He tried to dupe India and the Governor General Mountbatten by simultaneously undertaking secret negotiations with Pakistan when he was negotiating with Indian government.

b: Encouragement of Razakar to Nizam:

Kasim Razvi, the leader of fundamentalist group Razakar encouraged Nizam to oppose India.

Kasim Razvi suggested Nizam to continue his anti-Indian activities by advising him that India which was engaged in her own problems could not take any action against him.-Nizam extended the loan of 20 crore to Pakistan under the encouragement of Kasim Razvi.

Nizam also banned the Indian currency in his state.

Kasim Razvi stepped up his anti-Indian propaganda.

Kasim Razvi along with Nizam started oppressing people.

Nizam organised attacks on the India trains.

c: Police Action of September 1948 by India against Hyderabad:

India government was compelled to use force against due to the anti-India activities of Nizam of Hyderabad. (Oct. 01)

On September 13, 1948, Indian government undertook a police action against the State of Hyderabad.

On September 17, 1948, the forces of Nizam of Hyderabad surrendered to the Indian forces.

After that Hyderabad was integrated with the Republic of India. e: Andhra Pardesh and Reorganization of Sates Act of 1956:

In 1956, the Indian Parliament passed the Reorganization of States Act and Andhra Pardesh was created out of the State of Hyderabad.

The Telegu speaking regions were merged with Andhra Pardesh, the Kannada speaking regions were merged with Karnatak and Marathi speaking Marathwada was merged with Maharashtra.

## Death

On 29 March 1949, authorities lost radio contact with a plane carrying Patel, his daughter Maniben and the Maharaja of Patiala. Engine failure caused the pilot to make an emergency landing in a desert area in Rajasthan. With all passengers safe, Patel and others tracked down a nearby village and local officials.

When Patel returned to Delhi, thousands of Congressmen gave him a resounding welcome. In Parliament, MPs gave a long, standing ovation to Patel, stopping proceedings for half an hour. In his twilight years, Patel was honoured by members of Parliament and awarded honorary doctorates of law by the Punjab University and Osmania University.

Patel's health declined rapidly through the summer of 1950. He later began coughing blood, whereupon Maniben began limiting his meetings and working hours and arranged for a personalised medical staff to begin attending to Patel. The Chief Minister of West Bengal and doctor Bidhan Roy heard Patel make jokes about his impending end, and in a private meeting Patel frankly admitted to his ministerial colleague N. V. Gadgil that he was not going to live much longer.

Patel's health worsened after 2 November, when he began losing consciousness frequently and was confined to his bed. He was flown to Mumbai on 12 December to recuperate at his son Dahyabhai's flat — his condition deemed critical, Nehru and Rajagopalacharya came to the airport to see him off. After suffering a massive heart attack (his second), he died on 15 December 1950. In an unprecedented and unrepeated gesture, on the day after his death more than 1,500 officers of India's civil and police services congregated to mourn at Patel's residence in Delhi and pledged "complete loyalty and unremitting zeal" in India's service. His cremation in Sonapur, Mumbai, was attended by large crowds, Nehru, Rajagopalacharya, President Prasad, and many Congressmen and freedom fighters.

## Criticism and Legacy

During his lifetime, Vallabhbhai Patel received criticism of an alleged bias against Muslims during the time of partition. He was criticised by nationalist Muslims such as Maulana Azad as well as Hindu nationalists for readily plumping for partition. Patel was criticised by supporters of Subhash Bose for acting coercively to put down politicians not supportive of Gandhi. Socialist politicians such as Jaya Prakash Narayan and Asoka Mehta criticised him for his personal proximity to Indian industrialists such as the Birla and Sarabhai families. Some historians have criticised Patel's actions on the integration of princely states as undermining the right of self-determination for those states. However, Patel is credited for being almost single-handedly responsible for unifying India on the eve of independence. He won the admiration of many Indians for speaking frankly on the issues of Hindu-Muslim relations and not shying from using military force to integrate India.

His skills of leadership and practical judgement were hailed by British statesmen—his opponents in the freedom struggle—such as Lord Wavell, Cripps, Pethick-Lawrence and Mountbatten. Some historians and admirers of Patel such as Rajendra Prasad and industrialist J.R.D. Tata have expressed opinions that Patel would have made a better prime minister for India than Nehru. Nehru's critics and Patel's admirers cite Nehru's belated embrace of Patel's advice regarding the UN and Kashmir and the integration of Goa by military action.

# 2

# Iron Man of India

Sardar Vallabhbhai Patel, one among the outstanding freedom fighters of India, was born in 1875, in Gujarat. Popularly known as the Iron Man of India, he became immortal by uniting a scattered nation without any bloodshed. He was highly influenced by the ideas of Mahatma Gandhi, the father of the nation. The title 'Sardar' was conferred on him by Gandhiji on account of his powerful movement against the British for the freedom of India, and for keeping the privileges of the poor people of the country.

After completing his law studies from England, he started his practice in Gujarat. He had followed a western life style. Influenced by the ideals of Mahatma Gandhi, he discarded his foreign clothes.

In 1918, Sardar Patel led a revolt against the unjust decision of the British government to collect tax from the farmers of Kaira, though there was a flood in the area. He also led a similar strike against the British in 1928. He was imprisoned for the first time when he participated in the famous Salt Satyagraha with Mahatma Gandhi. With great wisdom and political foresight, he joined several small kingdoms in Indian Union.

After independence, he held the positions of home minister, minister of state and the minister for information and broadcasting. He died in December 1950 in Mumbai.

## OUT OF ALL OF THEM, PATEL IS THE ONLY STRONG MAN

A figure of deep respect for most Indians, Vallabhbhai Patel, given the appellation "Sardar" (leader), is remembered as the "Iron Man" of Indian politics in the Independence struggle era. He is correctly remembered as perhaps the only figure in the Indian National Congress who stayed firm in the face of the intimidation of the British and Muslim League. We have a large part to thank him for the consent of rulers regarding the amalgamation of the princely states of British India into a Greater India.

Vallabhbhai was born in the village of Nadiad in Gujarat. His father was named Jhaverbhai, and had fought in the 1857 Indian War of Independence. Right from the early years of his life, there are anecdotes of Vallabhbhai having demonstrated considerable boldness, valour and firmness. Perhaps the most well-known incident of his early childhood occurred when he was suffering from a boil under his armpit. The cure in his village for such an injury was to have it burnt off with a hot iron. The man with the iron rod hesitated when about to treat him, seeing his tender years. Vallabhbhai was impatient "The iron will go cold. Hurry up, brand the boil." The man with the rod still hesitated. Vallabhbhai picked up the glowing rod and burnt the boil himself, returned the rod to its position, and calmly went about his day! Another occasion demonstrating Vallabhbhai's kshatriya character occurred in the years of his schooling. A teacher of his used to sell the books that the pupils in the class needed, as a business. So far so good, But he used to pressure them into buying books even when they could get it from another source, and even mock and make life difficult for those who procured books from elsewhere, thus overstepping his dharma as a teacher. Vallabhbhai was angered by this. He organised his co-students such that not a single pupil would attend the class until the teacher stopped doing this. Vallabhbhai was successful. This lesson of resisting injustice wherever we find it is deeply enshrined in Hindu teachings, right from the child Krishna's opposition to the unfair and exploitive taxation of the produce of the village Gokul in which he grew up. Unfortunately this value is absent in many of our lives. Vallabhbhai is an example of a person who lived this value from childhood. Vallabhbhai's schooling years contain several other such incidents. In addition, he underwent a character building lifestyle, having to cook for himself, survive on meagre funds, and walk large distances because he couldn't afford a train or bus ticket.

Vallabhbhai later became a barrister. His family did not have enough money to fund his further education. However in those days a candidate could sit for examinations without necessarily being enrolled in a course. With support from his elder brother, he studied books and occasionally visited court where he observed attentively. Vallabhbhai passed the examinations and soon moved to town of Godhra, and set up a small law practice, which soon became widely acclaimed and successful. In his years at Godhra, he got married, and had two children, named Dhayabhai and Manibehn. Unfortunately his married life did not last for long. Vallabhbhai's wife passed away when he was only 33. He did not wish to marry again. In the years that followed, Vallabhbhai steeped himself further into his profession. He went to England for further studies, and set up a practice in Karnavati (more commonly called Ahmedabad), in which he was soon earning 8,000 – 10,000 rupees a month, a very significant sum at that time. For leisure he spent his time at a local club playing cards. He dressed like a Briton, and had a very western way of life, and is reported to have sometimes laughed at the Satyagraha movement of Gandhi. But one day his daughter Mahniben expressed her wish to go to a political conference where Gandhi was present, and Vallabhbhai went with her. His heart was stirred with Gandhi's words, and he joined the movement. His abilities rapidly made him a close compatriot of Gandhiji. His illustrious daughter Mahniben became like his private secretary, helping him through his public life.

Sardar Patel's political career was illustrious. In 1918, a year in which heavy rains severely damaged the crops in Gujarat's countryside, the British added insult to very serious injury by demanding very high taxes. It should be noted that British policies in the countryside were no trifling matter – they caused the death of tens of millions of Indians in famines, (such as which have not recurred in India's independence). The struggle against the British taxation was successfully led by Sardar Patel, who henceforth became a hero in the Gujarati countryside. It was in 1920 that Vallabhbhai ended his occupation as a barrister, and took to the service of India as his only aim in life. Amongst his first endeavours was to set up the Gujarat Vidyapeeth, a school in which children were educated with a view to make them fit to serve India. Vallabhbhai exhorted people to send their children to this school rather than receive the brainwashing, weakening education that the British were promoting. He led the Nagpur flag satyagraha from May to August in 1923 in protest against an order stopping the carrying of the national flag, an order which the British were forced to withdraw. These are just a few of Vallabhbhai's successful campaigns on behalf of the Indian people. He remained a major figure in many agitations, endearing him to the Indian public. He was once jailed for 16 months. One could write many pages about Sardar Patel's achievements in these pre-independence years.

A striking feature of Patel's career is his thoroughly deserved reputation as the 'architect of India's integrity'. There were more than 600 stately divisions in India at the time. Many of these rulers dreamed of their little territories becoming independent states when the British left India. Vallabhbhai undertook a mission to convince all of the rulers of the princely states to throw in their stakes with a united India, employing his renowned skill as a thorough debater (from his time as a barrister). This fateful mission was successful in the majority of cases, winning over even some of the most stubborn Rajas. It is largely due to Patel's extensive diplomatic mission that we have a united India.

Another feature of Vallabhbhai's career is his steadfast and unflinching stand against Muslim aggression. When on August 16th 1946 Muslims in Calcutta launched murderous pogroms against Hindus (called "Direct Action Day"), Patel was one of the few leaders who boldly spoke on behalf of Hindus. When the Hindus finally retaliated, the entire Indian political scene was criticising Hindus and blaming them. Vallabhbhai told them that they should be ashamed of their stance of excusing the Muslim pogroms while blaming the Hindu retaliation, especially because the police force did not intervene on the Hindus' behalf when they were being attacked. Later Vallabhbhai co-ordinated the 'Police Action' which resulted in the annexation of Hyderabad to India. The Nizam of Hyderabad, a Muslim ruler of an 80% Hindu state refused to join India and pledged his support for Pakistan, despite the fact that India surrounded Hyderabad. When Hindus in Hyderabad showed their support for India, the Nizam unleashed gangs called Razakars to harass the Hindus into submission. Unlike the pussy footed attitude of many leaders of India (then and now), Patel ensured that the matter was dealt with firmly. When the Hindus were being persecuted in East Pakistan (now Bangladesh) he suggested the annexing 30% of East Pakistan to India to settle the refugees. Unfortunately there was little he could do without Nehru's permission as Nehru was now the prime minister, therefore Hindus continued to be killed en masse without redress. Another major act that Vallabhbhai will be remembered for is his role in the restoration of Somnath Mandir, together with Jam Saheb and K. M. Munshi. From the 11th century Muslims had destroyed this temple 7 times, and each time it had been rebuilt by Hindus, until its final destruction in the 15th century, when Hindus abandoned the site. The temple was restored, as a symbol of renascent India.

In some ways, Vallabhbhai differed from Gandhi. He was less insistent on absolute nonviolence, yet he regarded Mahatma Gandhi with the utmost reverence. His heart was broken when Nathuram Godse assassinated Mahatma Gandhi. Sardar Patel differed with Nehru on many issues regarding India. Vallabhbhai was set to become Prime Minister of India. 12 out of 15 provinces nominated him as Prime Minister (not even one of the provinces elected Nehru). Yet Nehru blackmailed Gandhiji telling him that unless he could become Prime Minister, he would not participate in the new government. Hence Gandhiji requested Vallabhbhai to step aside to pacify Nehru, who wouldn't have it otherwise. This is regarded by many as Gandhiji's great blunder. India would have faired differently had Sardar Patel been the first Prime Minister. Yet fate willed it otherwise, and it was not to be. Sardar Patel passed away on the 15th December 1950 in Mumbai. His life had been one of tremendous service to the motherland.

Vallabhbhai Jhaverbhai Patel was born on 31 October 1875 at Nadiad in Gujarat in an agriculturist family. After a course in law Vallabhbhai moved to Borsad in 1902, a town in the Kheda district, to set up practice as a defence lawyer. In 1910 he sailed for England and joined the Middle Temple. Here he worked so hard and conscientiously that he topped in Roman law, securing a prize, and was called to the Bar at the end of two years instead of the usual period of three years.

With struggle for freedom being intensified Vallabhbhai left his lucrative legal practice and gave himself up wholly to political work. It was in 1928 that the villagers of Bardoli under the leadership of Vallabhbhai decided to go against the British Government on the issue of the increase of land revenue. The grim struggle drew the attention of the whole country. Ultimately the Government had to bow before popular resolve. It was a triumph not only of the 80 thousand peasants of Bardoli but more particularly of Vallabhbhai, who was given the title of 'Sardar' by the nation for his great leadership.

When India attained Independence Vallabhbhai became the Deputy Prime Minister and was responsible for the Home, States and the Information and Broadcasting portfolios. It was in this capacity that he was called upon to tackle the most intricate and baffling problem of the States' integration into the Union of India. And it is here that his tact, his powers of persuasion and his statesmanship came into full play. He handled it, managing in less than a year's time, to reduce the Princely States from 562 to 26 administrative units. The integration of the States could certainly be termed as the crowning achievement of Vallabhbhai Patel's life. He sorted out the problems of partition, restored law and order and dealt with the rehabilitation of thousands of refugees with great courage and foresight. He reorganised and formed a new Indian Administrative Service, to provide a stable administrative base to the new democracy.

He was thus one of the chief architects and guardians of India's freedom and his contribution towards consolidating the freedom of the country remains unrivalled. On 15 December 1950 the 'iron-man' of India who had fulfilled the duties towards his countrymen passed away. In the week preceding October 31st and on the date itself one had riveted one's attention on the Indian Government machinery and the Indian media as to how much notice they would take and pay service to the memory of independent India's greatest son whose 131st birth anniversary fell that day. It was the birth anniversary of Sardar Vallabhbhai Patel a towering but self-effacing leader on whom the appellation "Sardar" was bestowed by the people of Bardoli in Gujarat where he had led a very determined agitation against the British. While Gandhi had earned the title "Mahatma" about ten years earlier, Patel was bestowed the title of "Sardar" for his sterling qualities of leadership against all odds.

"Sardar" broadly translated from Hindustani carries many meanings: "The Chief", or " The Indomitable Leader" or "The Noble Leader". Patel was all of these and this title continued as a prefix to his name. Jawaharlal Nehru the other freedom movement leader despite his charismatic personality could not earn any title bestowed by the people of India. He had to continue with the prefix "Pandit" which was the common term used by all high class Brahmins. So going by their appellations it was Sardar Patel who was "The Indomitable Leader" amongst the trinity of Gandhi, Patel and Nehru.

Unlike the long line of political dignitaries which make a bee-line to the various "Ghats" and "Samadhis" on such occasions nothing exists of that sort for Sardar Patel in New Delhi except a statue. There are no Memorial Libraries or Bhavans to commemorate his matchless role in India's freedom struggle or his unsurpassable contribution to the building of a stable and modern India in the short time that he had from August 15, 1947 to December 15, 1950 when he passed away. So this October 31 also passed with the public being unaware of Sardar Patel's birth anniversary as there was no conscious effort by the Government to highlight it. It was as if India had a national memory loss on Sardar Patel.

Sardar Patel was the "Iron Man" of India. He was more than India's "Bismarck". Few in India would be able to recall that it was Sardar Patel who by his pragmatic and visionary statesmanship and statecraft welded more than 500 princely states of India into a merger with India. Many of the princely states merged with India voluntarily but not without the impact of the strong persuasive personality of Sardar Patel. Others like Junagadh and the very sizeable Hyderabad State under the Nizam had to face 'Police Action' by Sardar Patel as the country's strong, powerful and assertive Home Minister with the States Ministry under his charge.

If Nehru with his sentimental attachment to his ancestral Kashmir and under what I suspect the influence of Mountbatten had not moved the charge of Kashmir from the Home Ministry to his personal charge in the External Affairs Ministry, India today would not have been saddled with the Kashmir problem and Jihadi Terrorism emanating from Pakistan in the name of Kashmir. Like many other strategic blunders by Nehru jeopardizing India's security his Kashmir and China policies were monumental blunders which plague India till today.

Sardar Patel with his eagle-eyed strategic vision and as a strong votary of political statecraft based on 'political realism' as opposed to 'political idealism' had given many warnings in writing to Nehru as the Prime Minister both on his Kashmir policies and also on his China policies. Only if Mahatma Gandhi had not foisted Nehru as the Prime Minister of India and had let Sardar Patel as the "Indomitable Leader" assume the mantle of Prime Minister the history of India would have been different. But then even the Mahatma was not without frailties and weaknesses.

It is the measure of Sardar Patel's greatness that on his demise that even British leaders and the British media paid glowing tributes. Nothing could be more eloquent than what the British newspaper The Guardian expressed which is as follows:

> *Without Patel, Gandhi's ideas would have had less practical influence and Nehru's idealism less scope., Patel was not only the organizer of the fight for freedom, but also the architect of the new State when the fight was over. The same man is seldom successful both as rebel and statesman. Patel was the exception.*

Sardar Patel was truly an exceptional man and the Indian Nation State needs to do more to honour this architect of Modern India than it has done so far. I had the honour to visit his simple but dignified and austere Memorial at his native place of Karamsad near Anand in Gujarat. But then this Memorial is tucked away in a corner of India leaving the rest of present day India totally unaware of Sardar Patel's magnificent contributions to the solidarity and stability of India.

It is good that the Congress Party does not give too much prominence to Sardar Patel in its political hoardings as Sardar Patel was more than a Congress Party leader. He was India's leader and the architect of Modern India. Sardar Patel was and truly should be the icon of modern India. Sardar Patel always dreamt of a strong and powerful India taking full cognizance of strategic realities as opposed to unwise idealism.

It is my appeal to the people of India to organize a campaign to set up a National Memorial in the hallowed memory of "The Great Sardar" which should incorporate an extensive Memorial Library for research on his political thought and contributions. It should be spread over an area of at least ten acres of land in New Delhi but outside it. The Sardar was never comfortable in post independence New Delhi. A suitable site could be across the road from the Akshardham Temple towards NOIDA side on the banks of the Yamuna River. It should incorporate a giant statue of Sardar Patel gazing over New Delhi as if his paternalistic gaze would protect India for all times to come, auditoriums library and research centers. In size and scale it should match Sardar Patel's towering personality.

In such a memorial the Government should be excluded from any participation as no Government so far in the last 60 years deemed it fit to raise such a memorial to "The Sardar". The cost of land and the Memorial facilities should be raised by public contributions and the project be handled by a Trust with no political or bureaucratic personalities in the Trust. One could even entrust the Akshardham people for the speedy execution of the Sardar Patel National Memorial.

While "The Sardar" belonged to the whole of India and all Indians should contribute to its cost, I am sure the people of Gujarat who have a special claim on his heritage will with their affluent assets and means all over the world and especially in the United States would rise to the occasion and make a Sardar Patel National Memorial in New Delhi a reality.

## THE POONCH REVOLT

In Poonch a rebellion against Dogra rule, based essentially on economic grievances (food prices and taxes), was encouraged to take on a 'Muslim vs Hindu' character a result of the killings in Punjab and Jammu. Further encouragement came from the direction of the North-West Frontier Province (Pashtonkawa).

Pathans angered by reports of Muslim deaths went to Poonch seeking revenge against Hindus and Sikhs. Poonch had come under the direct control of Maharaja Hari Singh in 1935-36, but the former jagir's population had never reconciled themselves to Dogra rule.

Ethnically they had few links with Jammu: they were much closer to Punjab. The Muslims of Poonch, notably the Sudhen tribe, had served widely in both the British Indian army and in the Jammu and Kashmir forces. In 1947, following the end of the Second World War, some 60,000 ex-servicemen had returned to Poonch. These men possessed both military experience and arms.

In June 1947, a revolt broke out over the state government's exorbitant taxes. Some 10,000 Poonchis decided to march on Poonch City in protest at high food prices. Before they reached the city they clashed with state troops at Bagh. The government ordered the inhabitants to surrender their weapons. This was largely ignored.

The situation was exacerbated on August 14, when Muslims attempted to celebrate Pakistan Day (also Kashmir Day) in defiance of a government ban. In addition, with the killings in Punjab after partition and the arrival of a large number of Muslim refugees in Poonch the conflict took on a communal aspect. By September the revolt had acquired a degree of organisation under

Muhammad Ibrahim Khan (the Muslim representative for Poonch in the Praja Sabha and a Muslim Conference member), and had evolved into a secessionist movement. In October 1947, the 'Government of Azad Kashmir' declared the area independent of Dogra rule, and set up its capital in Muzaffarabad.

Once underway, the Poonch rebellion received support from a number of sources: defectors from the Jammu and Kashmir forces, former Indian National Army soldiers, and Punjabi Muslims from Jhelum. Initially most of the support came from Pathans of the North-West Frontier Province. The government of Pakistan was at first very reluctant to become involved. In fact it refused to recognize the Azad Kashmir government. However, by September it was providing unofficial aid to the rebels. Looking at the wider picture, the communal violence in Punjab and later in Jammu and Kashmir generally served to harden the prevalent opinions of the three major groups. The state's Hindu community was even more convinced that it had no future under Muslim rule; if the Maharaja could not retain control, they wanted to accede to India. The Muslim Conference supporters moved closer to joining Pakistan, though some still favoured an independent Muslim state.

## Degeneration of CPI Leaders

The movement in Kashmir was inreality directed against the despotic and brutal rule of the Dogra Maharajas. In other words the class struggle was more prominent in the movement than religious and nationalist sentiments. Had there been a genuine revolutionary Marxist party and leadership, Kashmir could have given a lead to the national liberation struggle that was pulsating throughout British India in the last months of the Second World War. The Communist Party had a modest presence in Kashmir. Unfortunately a position of conciliation with the British imperialists during the later part of the war was adopted by the central leadership of the CPI (Communist Party of India). This was at the behest of the Stalinist bureaucracy in Moscow, which was pursuing its own agenda of compromise with imperialism to forward the "national interest" of the Soviet Union. These policies of the CPI leaders had a drastic impact on the significant forces of communism in all parts of India, including Kashmir. At the beginning of the Second World War, and especially after the Stalin-Hitler pact, the CPI launched an intensive anti-war campaign. It called the war an imperialist war, and the CPI was at the forefront of anti-British agitation.

This was a golden opportunity for the CPI to present itself as a revolutionary alternative to the masses. At the start of the anti-war campaign, the CPI took the courageous step of organising mass strikes against the war.

The first ever anti-war demonstration of workers in the world took place in India on October 22, 1939 with a one-day protest and general strike in which 90,000 people participated.

The main slogans of the demonstration were "Defeat this treachery against the human race", "Down With The Imperialist War", "Long Live The Freedom Of India", etc. The British colonialists increased state repression. Thousands of CPI workers were put in jail during this anti-war agitation. Congress was polarized, and a number of leftist groups, including those around Dr. Subhash Chandra Bose, identified with the CPI. While the process of unity amongst the left on the basis of the anti-war and anti-British posture of the CPI was forging ahead, changes in Moscow's policy struck a devastating blow. On June 22, 1941 Hitler attacked the Soviet Union. The Stalinist bureaucracy made a 180-degree turn on its policies and analysis of the forces in the international arena. The masters of the Kremlin, having completely abandoned a revolutionary international perspective, were totally unaware that Hitler was preparing a devastating blow against them. This is what disarmed the Soviet Union in the face of its terrible foe. From the outbreak of the Second World War right up until June 1941, when Hitler attacked the Soviet Union, Nazi Germany received a large increase in exports from the USSR.

Stalin tried to make a deal with the imperialist powers between 1944 and 1945 at the Big Three Conferences at Tehran, Yalta and Potsdam. His humiliating capitulation at the altar of imperialist diplomacy sealed the fate of several Communist Parties and revolutions in a number of countries. The CPI paid a heavy price for the opportunist turn. Apart from the attitude of appeasement towards the British, it started to develop a conciliatory attitude towards the national bourgeois leadership. In reality, large sections of the CPI were absorbed into Congress.

The CPI cadres should have exposed the real class interests of Nehru, Jinnah and Gandhi to the toiling masses. They should have striven to overcome and eliminate the images of the bourgeois leaders from the minds and consciousness of those who were taking part in the struggle to overthrow the Raj. Their main aim should have been to recruit the socialist youth and militants who were in Congress into the CPI and create a mass movement of the workers and peasants to put an end to imperialist rule.

The change in the CPI's position on the war created disillusionment amongst the masses and confusion and apathy in the party ranks. One of the most prominent Communist leaders of India, E.M.S Namboodripad, admitted the damage done to the Communist Party by its sudden U-turn in its attitude towards war. In his book "B.J.P/R.S.S: In The Service Of Right Reaction", he wrote: "In the first phase of the war the Communists had launched a countrywide movement in demand for total independence. In the second phase they felt a change in the character of the war, the result of the attack of Nazi Germany on the Soviet Union. It had become a 'peoples' war. The CPI leadership opposed the 'Quit India' demand, and isolated themselves from the movement."

The policy zigzags, the wavering and the political ineptitude of the CP leadership at local levels also created a vacuum, which was filled by accidental and populist individuals in the subcontinent, hence we see a plethora of parties and leaders come and go, eventually abdicating the political arena for Congress and the Muslim League.

However, in Kashmir, the National Conference and the Abdullah Dynasty filled the vacuum created as a consequence of this absence of a conscious revolutionary leadership. As we described earlier the oppression and the class antagonisms had reached an explosive level. As history has shown several times, any event can trigger an explosion when the contradictions in society have reached a critical point.

In July 1931 mass anger burst open the accumulated contradictions. The anger that had been simmering and slowly building against the Maharaja exploded through this breach. Given the political vacuum, Sheikh Mohammed Abdullah was able to intervene with a reformist programme for the oppressed Kashmiris. In this intervention he cleverly articulated the problems of the peasants, workers and the artisans. He launched a movement of civil disobedience. Several activists were arrested and jailed in Hari Parbat Fort. The first reforms in Kashmir came as a direct consequence of this movement. Initially the party Sheikh Abdullah had set up was the Muslim Conference in 1930 (which still exists mainly in the Pakistani controlled Kashmir). But the class character of the movement had an impact and the party changed its name to the National Conference in 1939. It adopted a red flag with a white plough in the centre. The slogan given to the peasants was "when the plough moves, it tears apart the enemy".

## Problems of Populism

Since its inception the National Conference was a petit bourgeois populist party with socialist rhetoric. However, to prop-up and expand its mass base, it had to wage a consistent struggle against the despotic rule of the Dogras.

In 1944 Sheikh Abdullah announced his blue print for the future of Kashmir. The clear class character and pressure of the movement amongst the Kashmiri masses is evident from the statement of the NC leaders themselves.

Sheikh Abdullah himself proclaimed, "Wherever I looked I saw a relentless struggle between the oppressor and oppressed. I yearn to become their saviour and sacrifice my life in their cause".

Abdullah described the class-base of the new party in his autobiography: Our movement had been thrown open to all religious groups. It became imperative to develop new political and economic rallying points. We had learnt from experience that the real reason for conflict was not religion but a clash of interests between different classes and groups. The primary objective of our movement was to oppose oppression and support the oppressed.

The aim of the socialist creed was explained in the document titled in "New Kashmir": To perfect our union in fullest equality and self-determination, to raise ourselves and our children forever from the abyss of oppression and poverty, degradation and superstition, from medieval darkness and ignorance, into the sunlit valleys of plenty ruled by freedom, science and honest toil.

Pyare Lal Hindu, Minister of Law under the Sheikh Farooq Abdullah, describes the situation in 1944: The battle for political freedom (had to) mean the battle for economic emancipation.... once he (Sheik Mohammed Abdullah) got this programme adopted as the charter for political and economic emancipation of our state, a swift change swept the countryside till it culminated in the historic slogan of quit Kashmir in 1946...

But in spite of this populist programme they made several compromises and capitulations to the rulers under the Raj. It was later proved that even reforms to this system could not deliver the masses from misery or create social stability. Sir Gopalswami Ayyangar was Prime Minister of Jammu and Kashmir from 1935 to 1943.

The British describe him as 'a strong Hindu and a strong nationalist with not unsympathetic leanings towards the congress.'" Iffat Malik elaborates, In August 1942, Sheikh Abdullah began organizing strikes, processions, etc., in support of the congress movement in India. Through subordinate officials, Ayyangar advised him not to attack the Maharaja or the British. Heeding this advice Abdullah limited his followers' activities to expressing support for Congress. As a result unlike in British India there were no significant arrests in Jammu and Kashmir. In November 1942, Ayyangar held a meeting with Abdullah, the first after several years: 'after which the latter made more protestations of his loyalty to His Highness, and rumours of constitutional reform in Kashmir began to become prevalent...Shortly afterwards the Kashmir Government entrusted the work of issuing Rice ration ticket and permits for fuel in Srianagar to Committees composed almost entirely of non-officials. The National Conference was represented on these committees at the instance of the Kashmir Government but no representative of the Muslim Conference were appointed'.

Although they rejected the religious segregation of the subcontinent and opposed a theocratic state, this was not good enough. They did not understand that post-British India could not achieve genuine democracy, secularism, or "socialism" under the capitalist system. Despite the glaring need for a socio-economic transformation of the subcontinent, the National Conference and its leadership lacked a clear revolutionary perspective and the ideological foundation to carry it through. They were basically radical bourgeois liberals and their programme was restricted to the demands of the national democratic revolution.

The leadership of the National Conference was ideologically closer to the Congress and the Gandhi-Nehru leadership, so they teamed up with them. They were opposed to joining "theocratic" Pakistan .At the same time they were in the struggle against the Dogra Monarchy. According to the Independence Act, the rulers of the princely states were given the right to decide on joining one of the dominions or remaining independent. The Dogra ruler Hari Singh was ambiguous and wavered.

## Intrigues and Treachery

In mid-September, Jinnah instructed his secretary, Colonel William Birnie, to go to Kashmir and arrange for him to spend two weeks of resting and relaxing. Choosing Kashmir for his holiday was entirely natural. To Jinnah, as to most of his countrymen, it seemed inconceivable that Kashmir, with the population over three quarters Muslim, could become any thing but a part of Pakistan.

The British officer, nonetheless, returned five days later with a story that stunned Jinnah. The Maharaja Hari Singh had refused Jinnah permission to set foot on his soil, even as a tourist. This gave Pakistan's leaders their first indication that the situation in Kashmir was not evolving as they had complacently assumed. Forty-eight hours later, Jinnah's government sent a secret agent into Kashmir to evaluate the situation and determine the Maharaja's real intentions. The report he brought back told them that Hari Singh had no intention of acceding to Pakistan. In mid-September, Liaqat Ali Khan, the Prime Minister of Pakistan, arranged a secret meeting of a select group of collaborators in Lahore to decide how to force the Maharaja's hand. The collaborators immediately dismissed the idea of an outright invasion. The Pakistani army was not ready to start a war over Kashmir that could escalate into a war with India. Two other options were considered. Colonel Akbar

Khan, a Sandhurst graduate with a taste for conspiracy, outlined the first. He proposed that Pakistan should supply the arms and money to foment an uprising of Kashmir's dissident Muslim population. The preparation would require several months, but would result in forty or fifty thousand Kashmiris descending onto Srinagar to force the Maharaja to accede to Pakistan.

The second option was far more intriguing. Its sponsor was the chief minister of the Northwest Frontier Province, and it would involve Pakistani tribesmen. The gathering closed with a stern warning from the Prime Minister that the operation must be a complete secret and that the finance would be provided by secret funds from the Prime Minister's office. Neither the officers of Pakistan's army, her civil servants nor the British officers and administrators in the service of the new state were to be given access to this secret. Just before five o'clock on the afternoon of October 24, 1947, Major General Douglas Gracey, who had replaced General Messervy as Commander-in-Chief of the Pakistan army, got his first intimation of what had happen in Kashmir through a secret intelligence report. It gave the raider's strength, armaments, and their location. Gracey did not hesitate. He immediately went to his predecessor's private quarters and communicated precious information to the man who commanded the only force that could deny Kashmir to the raiders... the Commander-in-Chief of the Indian army, Lieutenant General Sir Rob Lockhart, a Scot and Sandhurst classmate of Gracey. Lockhart was stunned by his old friend's report. He in turn communicated it to two more people, both of them British: Governor General Mountbatten, and Field Marshal Auchinleck.

Mountbatten received the news as he was getting ready for a banquet in honour of Thailand's foreign minister. When the last guest had left, he asked Nehru to stay behind. The Prime Minister was shocked by the news. The Governor General was to discover another side of Nehru on Kashmir. The cool detached intelligence, so admired by Mountbatten was replaced by an instinctive, emotional response driven by passions that even the Kashmiri Brahmin could not control. "As Calais was written upon the heart of Queen Marry", Nehru would cry out to him one day to explain his attitude, "so Kashmir is written upon mine".

The following afternoon a DC3 of the Royal Indian Air Force landed on the abandoned dirt strip of Srinagar Airport. It carried VP Menon, the civil servant who had presided over so many princely accessions to India, Colonel Sam Manekshaw of the Indian army, and an air force officer. As soon as they returned to Delhi, V.P Menon and the two officers that had accompanied him to Srinagar made their report to another meeting of the cabinet's Defence Committee. Their words were sombre. The Maharaja was ready at last to present Kashmir to India, but the Pathan raiders were only thirty-five miles from Srinagar and could at any moment seize the only airport in Kashmir on which India could land her troops. While the frenzied preparations for the operation were underway, Lord Mountbatten ordered V.P Menon to fly to Jammu. He carried with him, awaiting only Hari Singh's signature, the Act of Accession, which would provide a legal framework for India's invasion.

V.P Menon was back in his Delhi home late in the evening of that same Sunday, twenty-six October. Alexander Symon, Britain's Deputy High Commissioner joined him for a drink a few minutes after his return. Menon was jubilant. He poured them each a stiff drink . As they sat down, an enormous smile spread across his face. He raised his glass to Symon. Then he pulled a piece of paper from his jacket pocket and waved it gaily towards the Englishman. "Here it is," he said. "We have Kashmir. The bastard signed the Act of Accession and now that we have got it, we will never let it go."

Mehr Chand Mahajan had been a member of the Radcliff Boundary Commission in Punjab. Hari Singh appointed him Prime Minister of Jammu and Kashmir on the recommendation of Sardar Patel. In Alistair Lamb's opinion Mahajan's appointed task was to see through accession to India. This impression is confirmed by Mahajan's visit to New Delhi on 11th October 1947, just before formally taking office as Prime Minister, when he called on Sardar Vallabhbhai Patel, Jawaharlal Nehru and Mahatma Gandhi. "V.P Menon (Sardar Vallabhbhai Patel's right hand man in matters of the accession of states to the India) ensured that Mahajan did not seek an interview with any senior Pakistani politician or official before assuming office."

Lamb writes that the Indian Government was making preparation for military intervention long before the instrument of Accession was signed: The first volume of Sardar Vallabhbhai Patel's correspondence which was published in 1971, makes it clear that both Sardar Vallabhbhai Patel and Baldev Singh were heavily engaged in the planning of some kind of Indian military intervention in Jammu and Kashmir, if only on a contingency basis, by at least 13 September 1947; and that by the third week of October a substantial foundation for such an operation had been laid. Much later in March 1951, Nehru admitted in a statement to Parliament that India would have sent her troops into Jammu and Kashmir even if Hari Singh had not signed the instrument of Accession: 'irrespective of accession we would have had an obligation to protect the people of Kashmir against aggression'.

On March 26, 1935 Maharaja Hari Singh had leased the Gilgit Wazarat, north of the Indus and its dependencies, to the British for a period of sixty years. However, in April 1947, after just twelve years, Mountbatten decided to hand the area back to direct Jammu and Kashmir control before the subcontinent became independent. This handover took effect on August 1, 1947. Hari Singh's Governor, Brigadier Ghansara Singh, reached Gilgit one day before this transfer. The local population, who had not been consulted about the handover, had no desire to return to Dogra rule. The local military force, the Gilgit Scouts, shared these sentiments. Faced with impending mutiny plus a Pathan tribal incursion, the Scouts' British Officer, Major Brown was to put the entire region under Pakistani control. Ghansara Singh was placed under house arrest and, on November 3, 1947 Brown announced Gilgit's accession to Pakistan.

## INDIA AND PAKISTAN 1947-50

The new border that separated India from Pakistan in the Punjab divided the Sikh population of four million in half. Nehru refused to let the British soldiers participate in the Boundary Force, and by August 15, 1947 less than 10,000 troops were in place in the Punjab. In the largest movement of people in world history about ten million Punjabis migrated in 1947. Muslims left East Punjab to go to Pakistan, and the Hindus and Sikhs departed from West Punjab to move to India. Indian intelligence estimated that at least 198,000 people were killed and that 100,000 were forcibly converted to Islam. However, Governor Francis Mudie of West Punjab estimated that half a million Muslims were killed, and the British High Commissioner in Karachi said the total was 800,000. As a result of the disruptions over the partition of India and Pakistan a total of fourteen million people lost their homes. Mountbatten and Jinnah met with the Joint Defense Council on August 29, and they abolished the Punjab Boundary Force. The soldiers went to their regiments in India and Pakistan, and these two dominions were to be responsible for law and order in their own territories. Pakistan formed the Ministry of Refugees and Rehabilitation at the beginning of September. British troops began withdrawing from India on August 17, and the last regiment left on February 18, 1948. The Indian Army was divided by religion with 270,000 soldiers going to India and 140,000 to Pakistan.

On August 15, 1947 Gandhi had fasted and prayed in a Muslim area of Calcutta instead of going to the ceremonies at Delhi. On the first of September he fasted again, and he only broke it three days later after municipal officials assured him that there had been no violence for 24 hours. While he was recovering from this fast, riots broke out in Delhi on September 7. In four days about two thousand people were killed. Gandhi went to Delhi to stop the pogroms against Muslims. When he was asked for a message, he wrote simply, "My life is my message." Meanwhile a caravan of 800,000 people was moving from West Punjab to India. The small state of Junagadh had announced its accession to Pakistan on August 15, 1947; but it is not contiguous with Pakistan, and the tiny states inside Junagadh had already acceded to India and asked for protection. India took over the administration of Junagadh on November 9, and in the plebiscite on February 20, 1948 out of 190,870 votes only 91 favoured joining Pakistan rather than India.

In 1947 the Indian National Trade Union Congress was founded on Gandhian principles, and they represented 577 unions. Women began to be appointed to important positions. Sarojini Naidu became governor of the United Provinces. Vijayalakshmi Pandit was ambassador to Moscow and Washington.

Most of the people in Jammu and Kashmir were Muslims; but the Sikh conqueror Ranjit Singh had annexed it in 1819, and from 1846 it had been ruled by Hindu kings from the Dogra tribe. Their laws respected Hindu religion, and Muslims suffered discrimination. Maharaja Hari Singh began ruling in 1925, and he kept his capital at Jammu without going north to the summer centre at Srinagar. In 1931 the school-teacher Sheikh Muhammad Abdullah began asking for more state services for Muslims. In April 1932 the Glancy Commission reported that real grievances needed redress. A new constitution enabled Hindus and Muslims to be elected to the legislature, but the Maharaja still held autocratic power. In his presidential address to the Muslim Conference on March 26, 1938 Sheikh Abdullah called for an end to communalism, hoping that all the communities would fight for freedom. They endorsed the political struggle in June 1939 and changed their name to the National Conference.

Ghulam Abbas revived the Muslim Conference in 1941 with the support of the religious leader Yusuf Shah. Jinnah visited Kashmir for two months in the summer of 1944, and the Congress party held a conference a year later with Nehru, Azad, and Abdul Ghaffar Khan attending. The Maharaja refused to give up power and arrested the leaders of the National Conference. In 1946 Sheikh Abdullah demanded the abrogation of the 1846 Treaty of Amritsar that had established the Dogra dynasty, but the Congress party policy was not to displace Indian princes but to allow them to head constitutional democracies. The Muslim Conference did not support the Quit Kashmir campaign of the National Conference; but when they defied a ban on holding a conference in Srinagar, the Maharaja had their leaders arrested on October 25. The Government called an election for January 1947, and the National Conference with its leaders in jail boycotted the election. Only 182,000 voted out of the 707,400 who were eligible. The Muslim Conference participated and won 16 of the 21 Muslim seats. Congress party president Acharya Kripalani visited Kashmir in May. He pleaded for the release of Sheikh Abdullah and warned the Maharaja that he would have trouble if he did not join the Indian Union. Abdullah and most of the National leaders remained in jail until late September after India's Independence.

Pakistani leaders complained that Gurdaspur, which had the only road connecting India to Kashmir, had been awarded to East Punjab, and they believed that the Border Commission chairman Radcliffe was unfairly influenced by the Indians through Mountbatten. Sikhs were also upset that they lost some of their shrines to Pakistan. Sikhs and Hindus fled from West Punjab to the Kashmir Valley, and Muslims refugees went from East Punjab to Jammu. Maharaja Hari Singh signed standstill agreements with Pakistan and India, and a minister visited Delhi. The usual methods of repression by the Maharaja of Kashmir could not control the communal violence, and Muslim peasants in Poonch began a revolt. Then armed raiders from Pakistan crossed the border near Jammu, attacked villages, and stole cattle. Patel persuaded the Maharaja to release Sheikh Abdullah, and on October 3 Abdullah urged Kashmir to join India. He considered Nehru his best friend, and he revered Gandhi. Meanwhile the Muslims formed the Azad Kashmir government with the local barrister Muhammad Ibrahim as president.

Mehr Chand Mahajan replaced General Janak Singh as prime minister of Kashmir on October 15, and on that day he held a press conference and sent a telegram to Pakistan protesting the raids. One week later about five thousand tribesmen in British trucks and jeeps from the Pakistan army sacked Muzaffarabad and began pillaging and raping inside Kashmir. The Maharaja's army of 8,000 was defeated and fled. British officers in Pakistan informed their British counterparts in India of the raids. The deputy prime minister of Kashmir went to Delhi, and on October 25 he asked the Indian Defense Committee for help. That day the Pakistan army notified New Delhi that "tribal volunteers" had entered Kashmir. Sheikh Abdullah went to Nehru's house and also asked for aid. V. P. Menon flew to Jammu and persuaded the Maharaja to sign a letter of conditional accession to India; a plebiscite was to be held when conditions returned to normal. Kashmir Prime Minister Mahajan returned with Menon to New Delhi and met with Nehru and Patel. Menon later wrote that Kashmir had signed the accession papers before India sent troops, but Mahajan's report contradicted this. Nehru telegraphed Liaquat Ali Khan on October 26 that India was sending troops to Kashmir.

Governor-General Mountbatten wrote a letter to accept Kashmir's accession. More than a hundred planes carried troops and supplies from

India, and 329 soldiers arrived on October 27 just in time to save Srinagar. By the end of October they had been joined by three battalions, and the raiders retreated. Jinnah ordered General Gracey to move Pakistani troops into Kashmir, but he refused to do so without the approval of Field Marshal Claude Auchinleck, who flew to Lahore on October 28 and persuaded Jinnah to withdraw his invasion order. The next day Nehru and Patel refused to go to Lahore, and Mountbatten went only with his chief of staff Ismay and met with Liaquat and Jinnah. Meanwhile Gandhi was telling his prayer meetings that the kings and maharajas of the Indian states had been puppets of British imperialism, but now the people had become the real rulers.

In a broadcast on November 2 Nehru asked how the tribesmen crossing the frontier had been "armed so effectively," but Pakistani prime minister Liaquat Ali Khan condemned the "illegal ownership" of Kashmir by the infamous Amritsar Treaty. Sheikh Abdullah inspired the popular resistance to the raiders, and by November 8 they had taken Baramulla. Pakistan refused to withdraw its forces and suggested the United Nations. Patel decided to stop honoring India's financial commitments to Pakistan until they stopped supporting the raiders. On December 22 the Indian cabinet demanded that Pakistan stop aiding the raiders and warned that they would appeal to the UN Security Council. By the end of 1947 the Indian army had cleared the invaders out of the Kashmir Valley. India's appeal to the UN on the first day of 1948 mentioned that their forces were opposed by 34,000 raiders. At a press conference the next day Nehru asked Pakistan to withdraw their personnel from Kashmir. Pakistan replied on January 15, accusing India of genocide against Muslims in East Punjab. Two days later the UN Security Council adopted a resolution establishing the UN Commission for India and Pakistan (UNCIP). India wanted the Security Council to recognize Pakistani aggression in Kashmir; but Pakistan believed the accession was not legally valid, and they would not withdraw unless India did so too.

Gandhi was criticized for approving India's action in Kashmir; but he believed it was justified because not to stand one's ground to defend oneself against an aggressor would be cowardice. Although he may not help one retaliate, Gandhi believed that he must not let a coward find shelter behind the guise of nonviolence. However, he advised that India should transfer the money due to Pakistan. Gandhi began a fast on January 13, 1948 and said he would continue until people stopped killing each other or he died. On the third day Patel and the Indian cabinet gave in and agreed to pay the £40 million from India's assets that they had withheld from Pakistan because of Kashmir. Hindu refugees outside the gate chanted "Let Gandhi die," and the visiting Nehru angrily challenged them to kill him first, causing them to disperse. Azad learned from the physically weakened Gandhi his demands that Muslims be allowed to move freely, live where they want with no economic boycott, and that 117 mosques should be returned to them. Gandhi's kidneys were not functioning well. A Congress committee got 130 leaders that included Hindus, Muslims, Sikhs, Christians, and others to sign a peace agreement, and 200,000 people took a written pledge to protect Muslims. So on January 18 he ended his fast. Although this religious hatred saddened Gandhi, India had gained independence, accomplishing the greatest nonviolent revolution in the history of the world.

Gandhi held open prayer meetings in Delhi for all faiths, and anyone could attend. A small conspiracy of Hindus in the extremist Rashtriya Swayam Sewak Sangh (RSSS) plotted to assassinate him, but their first attempt with a bomb on January 20 failed. Nehru and Patel urged Gandhi to accept police protection, but he refused, saying that he trusted God and would not submit to anger or fear. Police learned the names of those who would carry out the assassination, but they were unable to stop them. On January 30 at a prayer meeting Nathuram Godse shot Gandhi three times at close range; with his last breath the Mahatma chanted the name of God. More than a million people attended his funeral. Because the assassin was a Maharashtrian Brahmin, assaults in Maharashtra were made against the Brahmin and Bania communities; but most of the communal violence stopped. After a trial the assassin Nathuram Godse and one accomplice were hanged, and five other conspirators were sentenced to life imprisonment. The RSSS and other organizations of communal violence were banned.

The Eastern States merged into the provinces of Orissa and the Central Provinces. In March and April 1948 many of the smaller states were integrated into Mataya, Kathiawar, Rajasthan, and Vindhya Pradesh. In May, the Madhya States Union was formed from Gwalior, Indore, and Malwa. The Patiala and East Punjab States Union began in July. Junagadh and some adjoining states joined Kathiawar on the last day of 1948. The Greater Rajasthan Union was inaugurated as the largest union of states with 13 million people in March 1949. Baroda merged into Bombay in May, and Bhopal, Cooch Behar, Tripura, and Manipur joined the Central administration. By November all the states had become integrated except for Hyderabad and Kashmir. A total of 554 states were dissolved and integrated into the Union of India.

Hyderabad had a population of 16 million, who were mostly Hindu, but since the Mughal reign of Aurangzeb they had been ruled by the Nizam and elite Muslims. The seventh Nizam, Mir Usman Ali Khan, wanted to remain independent. When India withheld Pakistan's Rs. 550 million share of the treasury in September 1947, the Nizam approved a Rs. 200 million loan to Pakistan. Hyderabad made a standstill agreement with the Indian Union in November to maintain its status quo before independence. The Nizam's private force of Razakars were led by Kasim Razvi, and they caused border incidents with Madras, the Central Provinces, and Bombay. The Government of India demanded that the Nizam disband them, but he refused and appealed to the United Nations. Two days after a final letter of warning on September 11, 1948, Indian troops entered Hyderabad. Major-General El Edroos surrendered Hyderabad to Major-General J. N. Chaudhury of the Indian Army on September 18. Kasim Razvi was arrested, and the Nizam withdrew his case from the UN Security Council. Chaudhury became the military governor, and Hyderabad acceded to the Indian Union on January 26, 1950.

The Kashmir Maharaja appointed Sheikh Abdullah prime minister in March 1948. He was a socialist and proposed radical land reform without compensating land-owners. Pakistan's military leaders allowed soldiers to desert their army in order to raid in Kashmir, and in April their British commander-in-chief approved their sending in troops for "self-defense." India also launched an offensive in the spring, and neither side was able to advance much. On April 21 the UN Security Council resolved to send five commissioners to oversee the withdrawal by Pakistani and Indian troops. A Plebiscite Administration was to be set up to supervise the police. However, both Pakistan and India refused to accept the resolution. Mountbatten left India in June 1948, and Rajagopalacharya became the first Indian governor-general.

Mediation efforts in Kashmir failed, and the UNCIP commission did not arrive in Kashmir until July. UNCIP learned on the first day that Pakistan had sent in regular troops, but they did not inform the Security Council nor India until much later. The Commission told Pakistan that they had violated international law. Sheikh Abdullah agreed with Nehru that the best solution was to partition Kashmir, but Pakistan rejected this. On August 13 the UN Security Council proposed a cease fire. India agreed with minor modifications, but Pakistan demanded conditions that the Commission would not accept. On October 12 delegates of Kashmir passed a National Conference resolution recommending permanent accession to India. At the very end of 1948 a cease-fire agreement was signed, and US Admiral Chester W. Nimitz was appointed UN Administrator for the plebiscite.

The Maharaja passed on restricted power to his son Karan Singh when he left Kashmir for health reasons in June 1949. UNCIP invited the two governments to meet at Karachi in July, and the cease-fire line was established.

The Commission proposed an arbitrator, and Pakistan accepted; but India refused, fearing they would be at a military disadvantage if Pakistan invaded again with Azad Kashmir forces. On December 17 the UN Security Council appointed the Canadian General McNaughton to mediate, but India's B. N. Rau argued that Pakistan made the plebiscite problematic by sending troops into Kashmir, occupying the northern areas, and building up the Azad forces. Pakistan's representative Zafrulla Khan pointed out that Muslims made up 77% of Kashmir. The UN Security Council appointed the Australian Owen Dixon the next mediator on April 12, 1950, but he concluded that only bilateral talks between India and Pakistan could solve the problem of Kashmir.

In January 1948 a food shortage caused the refugee camps in West Punjab to become more permanent, and in April the camps had 750,000 people. Jinnah made a broadcast to the United States in February and said that Pakistan would not be a theocratic state but would have a democratic constitution with equal rights for all religions. On February 28 Pakistan's finance minister Ghulam Muhammad presented an annual budget to the Karachi assembly calling for £27.8 million in military spending out of total expenditures of £39.4 million. A deficit of £25.1 million was expected. India also allocated more than half its budget for defense and projected a deficit of £20 million. In March the governments of India and Pakistan declared each other foreign nations in regard to customs and excise duty. Governor-General Jinnah only visited East Pakistan once, and he made his last major public address at Dacca on March 21 in English. His audience spoke Bengali, but he announced that Pakistan's official language would be "Urdu and no other language." East Pakistan was much smaller in area than West Pakistan, but it had a larger population. It would become Bangladesh in 1971.

On March 7, 1949 the Constituent Assembly of Pakistan adopted the Objectives Resolution that called for a constitution that would allow the state to exercise its power through the people's chosen representatives with principles of democracy, freedom, equality, tolerance, and social justice in accord with the teachings of Islam with provisions to protect minorities and depressed classes by guaranteeing equal rights with freedom of thought, expression, belief, faith, worship, and association, with the independence of the judiciary secured, and the rights of the Federation's territories safeguarded.

The canals in the divided Punjab were a source of dispute. When Pakistan did not renew the agreement, on April 1 the East Punjab Government cut off the water supply from the canals going into Pakistan from the Ravi and Sutlej rivers. Pakistan made another agreement on May 4; but later they complained that they had accepted it under duress. India believed that Pakistan had enough water from their rivers, and at the Inter-Dominion Conference in August 1949 they pressed for a joint survey of the water resources of the Indus rivers.

India followed the British government in devaluing the pound sterling by 30% in September, but Pakistan declined to do so. So the Indian Government refused to recognize the Pakistani rupee, and trade between the two countries stopped for seven months.

In the first three months of 1950 a half million refugees went from East Pakistan to India. The prime ministers Nehru and Liaquat Ali Khan met, and on April 8 they made a general agreement on minorities and trade-related issues. The problem of evacuee property had not been solved yet because Hindu refugees had left behind property worth 14 billion rupees, while Muslims had left property valued at only 2 billion rupees in India. The Pakistan Ministry of Refugees calculated that West Pakistan had 7,900,000 Muslim refugees. An agreement was made at the fifth Inter-Dominion Conference at Karachi in January 1949, but the next month Pakistan ordered rent slashed on urban evacuee property by up to 80%. The Indian Government considered this a subtle way of undermining the agreement, and Pakistan accused India of not implementing the agreement. By the end of 1950 they still could not agree. That year 600,000 more refugees entered Pakistan from India.

India adopted a new constitution on November 26, 1949, and it came into force on January 26, 1950. The Constitution established a democratic republic to secure justice, liberty, equality, and fraternity and to guarantee all citizens equality before the law and freedom of speech, expression, assembly, conscience, and worship regardless of religion, race, caste, sex, and place of birth. English would continue to be the official language for fifteen years, but thereafter the official language would be Hindi. A president and vice president are elected for five-year terms. The Council of States is elected by the legislators in each state, but voters elect the House of the People directly. Governors of the states are appointed by the President for five-year terms, and the chief ministers in each state are appointed by the governors. The Supreme Court has jurisdiction over disputes between states and hears appeals from any High Court in a state. The first elections were conducted without major difficulties, and the Congress party was victorious. On January 24, 1950 Rajendra Prasad was elected the first President of India. Socialists had left the Congress party and formed their own party in March 1948. Their policy statement in October 1949 explained that they stood for democratic socialism and individual rights while they rejected totalitarian Communism. After the conservative Deputy

Prime Minister Patel died in December 1950, Nehru's influence became even greater.

In a speech on foreign policy on December 4, 1947 Nehru affirmed that India stands for peace as well as freedom from imperialistic control. He began the policy that led the non-aligned movement when he stated that they avoid foreign entanglements by not joining either power bloc of the US or the USSR. He wrote in his 1949 book *Independence and After* that India's long history is significant. Although India had little military power he argued that India could have much influence because of the "world situation in which force as a factor in international affairs will be reduced to the absolute minimum." On January 18, 1950 Prime Minister Nehru wrote a letter to the Prime Minister of Pakistan proposing a joint declaration by their governments "for the avoidance of war," but the Government of Pakistan rejected his terms as "too vague.

## PAKISTAN RESOLUTION: FROM CONCEPT TO REALITY

It is a historical fact that after the events of 1857 and the subsequent consolidation of the British Raj in India, the political thinkers and intellectuals of the Subcontinent started to think about the political, religious cultural and social future of India. As a result, many ideas, plans, proposals and schemes were put forward for the partition of India and the formation of a separate Muslim state. Apart from indigenous proposals, British parliamentarians, writers and others were also thinking in terms of the bifurcation of India.

The first such scheme for the partition or division of India was voiced by a British Parliamentarian John Bright in June 1858. Addressing the House of Commons he suggested "five or six large presidencies with complete autonomy, ultimately becoming independent States." After two decades, in December 1877, he again reiterated that "he is seeing several independent and sovereign states in India when British withdrawal had been affected."

After 1857, since the Muslims of India were grossly marginalised in the social, religious and political fields, they were not inclined to accept the demand for partition of India into two independent and autonomous states. Although the actual struggle for the establishment of a proposed Muslim state started in March 1940 from the platform of the All India Muslim League (AIML), it nonetheless has a long historical background. Sir Syed Ahmed Khan was the first Muslim thinker who stressed that Hindus and Muslims are two different nations, hence any attempt to fuse them into one nation would fail. Accordingly in 1867, before the Divisional Commissioner of Banaras, he very clearly said "I am convinced both these nations will not join whole heartedly in any thing. At present, there is no hostility between the two communities, but on account of the so-called educated it will increase immediately in future. He who lives will see." After the establishment of the Indian National Congress in 1885, his conviction became firmer when he said "Indian National Congress is a Hindu organisation and it can not provide safeguard to the interests of Muslims."

Although Sir Syed Ahmad Khan did not present in principle, any plan or proposal for the partition of India, yet he provided a basis to the Indian Muslims for thinking about their future.

From to 1940, more than one hundred proposals and schemes for the partition of India were presented by different quarters. In these proposals, the principal of partition was presented mostly on administrative and communal grounds; however, these proposals not only popularised but also paved the way for the vivid description and elucidation of the Two Nation Theory.

It is amazing that the first scheme for the partition of India was presented by John Bright in 1858, a Britisher. On the 4th of June 1858, while participating in a discussion in the British Parliament concerning the Government of India, he was of the opinion, "A great country like India cannot be administered by Britain for a long time, one day we will have to let them rule. Hence it is necessary to abolish the Governorship and instead of keeping a colony, and for administrative purposes, India should be divided into five presidencies." It is however strange that in 1947, the last scheme after some 90 years, was also presented by Viceroy Lord Mountbatten- a British.

In 1887, Theodore Beck, educated at Cambridge and the Principal of M. A. O. College at Aligarh, after reviewing the political and social condition of India observed that "Muslims are a separate nation, rule of majority is impossible; Muslims will never agree to be ruled by the Hindu majority."

The second scheme for the partition of India was proposed by a renowned Muslim Scholar Jamaluddin Afghani who in 1879, proposed a broader Muslim state. He was of the opinion that there should be a Muslim State incorporating the northwest Muslim majority provinces of India, Afghanistan and Muslim Central Asia.

During the tenure of Viceroy Lord Ripon, in 1883 a British writer Wilfred Scawen Blunt, visited India and held negotiations with different leaders. He wrote in his book Ideas about India that "practically India is to be divided as such that all Northern provinces under the Muslim Government while the South provinces under a Hindu government".

A great Muslim journalist and novelist Maulana Abdul Haleem Sharar, after analysing the deteriorating conditions of the Indian Muslims and the chances of future Hindu-Muslim riots, felt that if the current problems were to be solved, the partition of India was a must.

In 1899, another British intellectual and the principal of MAO College Aligarh, Theodore Morison proposed that the only solution to the Indian political uncertainty was to centralise the Indian Muslims in one province or tract of the country, for instance, the north of India from Peshawar to Agra.

From 1899 to 1913, no clear proposal for the partition of India came out, although some political and communal incidents and events took place which strengthened the faith of the Muslims in the Two Nation Theory. Amidst all this, the Governor of United Provinces Sir Anthony MacDonald's order to replace Urdu as the official language was a main event which permitted the use of the Devnagri language in place of Persian and Urdu in government offices. This order was very perturbing for the Muslims of India. At this stage a companion of Sir Syed, Nawab Mohsinul Mulk founded the Urdu Defence Council and protested against the Governor's order. In 1901, another organisation was formed by Nawab Wiqarul Mulk named "Muhammadan Political Organisation"; the main objective of the organisation was to voice the Muslim grievances and demands before the Indian Government. In the same year Viceroy Lord Curzon after bifurcating Punjab established northern frontier area as a province.

But the most shocking event was revealed on October 16, 1905, when Lord Curzon decided to divide the province of Bengal into two. This was a blessing for the Muslims of India but was against the interests of the Hindus.

In 1906, the All India Muslim League (AIML) came into being. In 1908, the Muslims of India achieved more successes through the efforts of AIML; with the help of new reforms, the right for separate electorate for the Muslims was accepted. The Minto-Morley Reforms in 1909 ensured that the Muslims would be free to choose their own candidates. According to the same reforms, the Administrative Council of Viceroy was expanded and changed into Imperial Legislative Council. Almost simultaneously, on December 12, 1911, at his coronation ceremony, King George V announced the cancellation of the division of Bengal. This was a painful moment for the Muslims, while the Hindus who were continuously raising voices against this decision, celebrated joyously. These events forced the Muslims of India to struggle for their rights as a separate community.

On 10th May, 1913, a newspaper called Comrade published a comic column written by a journalist named Wilayat Ali Bambooq where he said, "to solve the Hindu-Muslim problem, Hindus and Muslims must be separated from each other. North India must be handed over to Muslims, while the rest may be handed over to Hindus". From 1913 to June 1917 five proposals came out about India's constitutional and administrative future but in September 1917 the two Khairi Brothers, Abdul Jabbar and Abdul Sattar, played a prominent role in advancing the idea of a Muslim state in India.

During the period 1913 to 1917, a vital change occurred in the political scenario of the Subcontinent through the efforts of M A Jinnah, who was actively participating in politics from the platform of the Indian National Congress and the Legislative Council. He joined the AIML in 1913 and made efforts to create communal harmony between Hindus and Muslims. He was gaining popularity on both sides but some ideologies were not in favour of Jinnah's efforts.

In 1918, Sir Aga Khan in his book "India in Transition" proposed a plan of a huge federation of South Asia with India as its nucleus and centre.

From 1919 to 1923, some other politicians and social scientists proposed schemes. Prof. Muhammad Sarwar in his book Afadat wa Malfuzat-i-Hazrat Maulana Ubaidullah Sindhi, wrote that in 1924 an anti-British personality Ubaidullah Sindhi in his manifesto issued from Istanbul in 1924, observed that each region of India was to be called "Swarajiya Republic" and the collection (India) was to be known as the Indian Federal Swarajiya Republican State". The Federal Capital was to be at Delhi.

Apart from Sindhi's observation, Maulana Hasrat Mohani, a renowned poet and politician was the first Indian who moved a resolution demanding, "Complete independence" for India from the Congress platform during its 1920 annual session and again in his presidential address delivered before the ML's annual session at Ahmadabad in Dec 1921. Three years later, Maulana Hasrat presented a slightly amended proposal in his meeting with the Hindu leaders in 1924. Mohani proposed his scheme on two grounds: that no country could be really free under dominion status and that the Muslims would receive a better deal under the independent Federal structure. In the same year Lala Lajpat Rai a Congress leader, founder of the Hindu Mahasabha and a journalist, wrote several articles on the Hindu-Muslim problem and on Pan-Islamism. In May 1925, Khilafat leader Maulana Muhammad Ali Jauhar, while commenting on Sardar Gul Khan's proposal in his journal Comrade, said "Muslims have no desire to rule over Hindu areas". Maulana Muhammad Ali never gave any concrete suggestion about the partition of India but from his writings and speeches it is indicated that he had a very clear idea about the partition of India.

Apart from Patric Fagan's assumption that Muslims will fight for their domination in north India, few other opinion came forward in 1925 which are on record. In the same year some teachers and students of the Aligarh Muslim University prepared a scheme of partition in which they suggested that India should be rearranged on the basis of a new theory of nationality. The scheme was published in the form of a pamphlet and distributed on the occasion of jubilee celebration of the Aligarh Muslim University.

Journalist Murtaza Ahmad Khan Maikash, Syed Sardar Ali Khan and Nawab Zulfiqar Ali Khan, Sir Ross Masud also presented their proposals but all were superseded by the proposal made by Allama Iqbal in his presidential address. Allama Iqbal proposed that "I would like to see the Punjab, North-West Frontier Province, Sindh, and Balochistan amalgamated into a Single state. Self-government within the British Empire or without the British Empire, the formation of a consolidated North-West Indian Muslim appears to me to be he final destiny of the Muslims, at least of North-West India." In the same address, Iqbal also said "the principal of European democracy can not be applied to India without recognising the fact of communal groups. The Muslim demand for the creation of a Muslim India within India is, therefore, perfectly justified" The proposal of Iqbal was not only welcomed by the Muslim circles but also gained popularity and importance even in non-Muslim circles.

In 1933, a very thought provoking declaration was made by Choudhary Rahmat Ali, a student of Cambridge University. After passing the examination of Law, during the Round Table Conferences in January 1933, Rahmat Ali issued a declaration entitled "Now or Never: Are we to live or perish forever?" In his declaration, Rahmat Ali demanded a Muslim homeland. The homeland of the Muslims of the Subcontinent was named in the first sentence of the declaration as 'Pakistan', according to which "...we mean the five Northern units of India, *viz.*, Punjab, North-West Frontier Province (Afghan Province), Kashmir, Sind and Balochistan." Choudhary Rahmat Ali's proposal embodied in his declaration, gained significance and importance due to two reasons: first, he issued this declaration at a time when the Round Table Conferences were in session in London; second, that Rahmat Ali was the only person who suggested a name "Pakistan" for his proposed Muslim homeland. After Rahmat Ali's declaration, a flood of opinions and suggestions burst forth in India and internationally. The word "Pakistan" became immensely popular.

In August 1933, the Joint Parliamentary Select Committee of British Empire discussed the said declaration with the visiting deputation of the Indian Muslims. From 1933 to 1936, no clear proposal came forward.

In April 1934, Jinnah was elected the president of the AIML again. He reorganised the League with the purpose to participate in the elections which were due to be held under the India Act of 1935.At this crucial stage Allama

Muhammad Iqbal extended his full support to Jinnah. During 1936 and 1937 he was in touch with Jinnah and was continuously writing to him on the issues which the Muslim India was facing. In his letter on 28, May 1937, Iqbal commenting and elucidating the seriousness of the Muslim India's situation wrote that to solve these problems it is necessary to redistribute the country and to provide one or more Muslim states with absolute majorities. 1937 to early 1940 were the years when many a proposal, suggestion, scheme and observation came forward about the partition of India on Hindu Muslim basis from all the corners of the country.

1940 was the landmark of the demand for partition because in that year AIML in its annual session held in March 1940 at Lahore in the supreme leadership of the Quaid-i-Azam Muhammad Ali Jinnah presented its separate Muslim homeland plan. The plan was embodied in a resolution, which was initially called Lahore Resolution, which later became famous as Pakistan Resolution. The entire struggle of All India Muslim League after March 1940 was concentrated around this Resolution till the creation of Pakistan in August 1947.

Syed Sharifuddin Pirzada, Professor Sharif al Mujahid and K K Aziz in their research work summarised these proposals and schemes with authentic sources and came to the conclusion that the historic Pakistan Resolution was not the end but the beginning which led to the creation of Pakistan.

## PATEL AND 1946 EPISODE

Waves of anti-imperialist struggle rose one after another in different parts of India – from North to South, from East to West and lashed at the regime of the imperialists. The most spectacular and most significant among them was the uprising in Bombay which began on 18 February 1946. The ratings of the Royal Indian Navy (R.I.N.) rose in revolt first in Bombay and then in Karachi, Calcutta and Madras. The rebel navymen, who had various grievances – bad food, racial discrimination, insults meted out by British officers and so on – were inspired by the deeds of Subhash and the example of the I.N.A.

By 22 February 1946 the rebel sailors were in control of about 22 vessels in Bombay, including the flagship of the British Vice-Admiral. A total of 78 ships of the R.I.N., 20 shore establishments and 20,000 ratings were involved in the struggle. Over a thousand men in the Royal Indian Air Force camps in Bombay came out on a sympathy strike. When ordered, Indian soldiers refused to fire on the R.I.N. ratings in Bombay as well as in Karachi. On 21 February the strike by the navymen developed into a pitched battle between them and British troops who had been called in as Indian soldiers refused to fire. And Bombay's workers and youth, irrespective of the community to which they belonged, stood by the heroic men of the navy, carried food to them, erected barricades and fought pitched battles with armed policemen and several British battalions equipped with armoured cars and tanks. On 22 February, Bombay observed a general strike in the teeth of the opposition from big Congress and Muslim League leaders.

Ignoring the Congress and League leaders, the entire working class of Bombay came out at the call of the Naval Central Strike Committee, which was supported by the CPI. For two days there were pitched battles on the city's streets, in which, according to official estimates, there were about 1,500 casualties including more than 200 dead. "The British tanks could clear the streets", wrote B. C. Dutt, one of the leaders of the revolt, "only after hundreds had been shot down. This was the first time in the turbulent history of India's freedom movement that the rulers were forced to use tanks to battle with unarmed and leaderless people.... February 21 had been the ratings' day. February 22 belonged to the workers of Bombay." In his 'Foreword' to Dutt's book, S. Natarajan wrote: "What was impressive among the ratings was their complete freedom from communal or sectarian prejudices and their staunch loyalty to each other." To quote Dutt, "The R.I.N. mutiny was the one conspiracy against the crown in which there was no king's witness. They tried their best. They drew blank".

Besides Bombay, Karachi was the scene of actual fighting between navymen and British soldiers. Gurkha soldiers refused to obey orders to fire on the *Hindustan*, an old sloop, which put up a brave fight. The Gurkha soldiers had to be replaced by British soldiers. Not only did the Indian army units refuse to obey orders to fight the navymen, they went on strike in several places in sympathy with the rebel navymen. We have noted that one thousand men of the Indian Air Force went on sympathy strike in Bombay. So did the men of the Air Force in Poona, Calcutta, Madras and Ambala. To quote Dutt, "An R.I.A.F. squadron, which had been ordered to proceed to Bombay, was grounded at Jodhpur; every aircraft had mysteriously developed engine trouble." Hallett, then Governor of the U.P., informed Wavell on 19 November 1945 that soldiers of the Air Force stationed in Allahabad, Bamrauli and Cawnpore had sent their contributions to the I.N.A. Defence Fund. The Indian Air Force stationed in Calcutta opposed the court martial of the I.N.A. men. It sent its subscription to the I.N.A. Defence fund with the words: "for the defence of the brave and patriotic sons of India." Penderel Moon noted: "There was also unrest at this time in the R.I.A.F. and in some of the technical units of the Indian Army." Not only was there unrest in some technical units of the army but army units, as pointed out before, disobeyed orders in Bombay and Karachi.

In the Jabalpur cantonment soldiers staged a revolt in March 1946 and in Dehradun Gurkha soldiers went on strike. In some places the police also rose in revolt. In March 1946 the police in Allahabad and Delhi went on hunger-strike. In April 10,000 policemen struck work. In September the military police went on strike in Patna and Begusarai. There was a widespread strike by policemen in Bihar in March 1947. The wall sedulously erected by the British Raj to segregrate the armed forces from the people crumbled down. At no time since the First War of Indian Independence in 1857-8 did the regular armed forces come out to defend the cause of freedom as they did now.

The brave men of the navy refused to be cowed by any threat – not even the threat of Admiral Godfrey (who had flown in bombers) to sink the navy. They appealed to political parties to lead them, promised to hand over to them the navy which they had renamed the Indian National Navy. But no political party, not even the CPI, responded to their appeal though they could have access to the rebel men of the navy.

Jinnah's appeal to them, *especially the Muslims among them*, to surrender came in the early hours of 23 February when their representatives were meeting to decide their future course of action. Dutt wrote: "... the overwhelming majority were for a fight to death and not for surrender." The Naval Central Strike Committee ultimately took the decision to surrender, stating that they were surrendering not to the British Raj but to the Congress and the League. In their last message to the people, they said: "For the first time the blood of the men in the services and the people flowed together in a common cause. We in the services will never forget this. We also know that you, our brothers and sisters, will never forget. Long live our great people. Jai Hind." After the surrender the manhunt began. More than two thousands of the rebels were arrested and kept in detention camps; about five hundred were sentenced to prison terms to serve as common criminals. The top Congress leaders, who had given the pledge that "no disciplinary action" would be taken, did little to keep their pledge. What role did the Congress leaders play during the historic naval revolt? Sardar Patel, Abul Kalam Azad, S.K. Patil (secretary of the Bombay Provincial Congress Committee, and later, minister of the central government), Jinnah and Chundrigar of the Muslim League openly opposed the call for a strike on 22 February issued by the Naval Central Strike Committee and advised the navymen to surrender to the British. Patil had secret confabulations with the Bombay governor and the

Congress and the League placed 'volunteers' at the service of the Raj to "assist the police" and British army units to fight the people. Colville wrote to Wavell that on 22 February he "saw several of these volunteers... and they did useful though limited work".

Bombay observed a successful general strike in the teeth of the bitter opposition of the Congress and the League leaders. Workers and students of Bombay fought pitched battles in the streets with British army units and the armed police, who were assisted by Congress and League volunteers.

At a mass meeting held in Bombay with the permission of the Bombay government on 26 February, Nehru and Patel strongly condemned "the mass violence in Bombay", that is, the resistance of the navymen and workers who had dared to raise the banner of anti-imperialist revolt. Addressing the press next day, Nehru thundered: 'The R.I.N. Central Strike Committee had no business to issue such an appeal [to the city of Bombay to observe a sympathy strike]. *I will not tolerate this kind of thing*." The Nehrus alone had the right to issue calls for strikes!

Gandhi, the prophet of nonviolence, condemned the rebels for their thoughtless orgy of violence – not the real orgy of violence by the Raj, of which the people were victims. To him the "combination between Hindus and Muslims and others for the purpose of violent action is unholy..." He went on denouncing those who disbelieved in British professions that they would grant freedom to India. It was a country-wide anti-imperialist revolt. Wavell noted in his diary on 7 March 1946 that the victory parade that was organized in Delhi was boycotted and crowds of men burnt down the Town Hall.

Workers were on the march everywhere despite the opposition of Congress and League leaders. The number of workers who went on strike in 1946 was 1,961,984 and in 1947, 1,840,784. There was an unprecedented upsurge of anti-imperialist struggle throughout the country, in which workers, peasants, students, other youths, office employees, navymen and sections of the Indian army, air force and police and lower rungs of the bureaucracy took part, and armed confrontations were frequent. Peasant revolts took place in different parts of India. In the Thana district in Maharashtra the struggle of the Warlis broke out. In the Alleppey district of the native state of Travancore (now a part of Kerala) peasants and workers launched a united struggle. In several districts of Bengal, especially in North Bengal, the Tebhaga struggle broke out under the leadership of the Communist Party. It was a struggle of the peasantry, mainly sharecroppers (who bore the expenses of cultivation) for a two-thirds share of the produce. Peasants fought heroically. In the undivided district of Dinajpur, forty peasants became martyrs. In 1946 began the historic struggles of the peasants in Telangana districts of the native state of Hyderabad (Telangana, now a part of Andhra Pradesh) under the leadership of the Andhra State Committee of the CPI. It developed into a struggle for land and power. Large areas were liberated. The struggle continued even after the march of troops of the Indian government in 1948 to suppress it, until it was withdrawn unconditionally by the CPI leadership in 1951. In several other native states ruled by princes, puppets of the British Indian government, there were revolts of the people, especially in Travancore and Kashmir.

## SARDAR PATEL-BUILDER OF A STEEL STRONG INDIA

The history of India would have been different had Sardar Patel not been the Deputy Prime Minister when India became independent in 1947. The triumvirate-Gandhiji, Nehru and Sardar Patel were responsible for giving direction to the destiny of the country. Sardar Patel consolidated the country into one united whole in a unique manner.

### Formative Years

Born on October 31, 1875 at Nadiad, in the Kaira district of Gujarat, Vallabhbhai Patel was the son of Zaverbhai Galabhai Patel, a Leva Patidar. This class of cultivators was known for their simple character, industrious habits and straightforward dealings. Vallabhbhai possessed an ingenous mind as a school boy. He was a rebel whose exceptional organisational abilities were recognised by his schoolmates and teachers. Patel passed the matriculation examination from the Nadiad High School in 1897.

Patel had two ambitions to fulfil, first to become a pleader and later a barrister. During those days a matriculate could become a lawyer by taking the pleaders examination. He became a pleader in 1900, and started practising in Godhra. In 1902 he shifted to Balsad, a taluka headquarter, where he practised as a criminal lawyer for nearly eight years, during which period he had built a name for himself as a most successful criminal lawyer. In 1910, he left for London and joined the Middle Temple, where he took an examination in Roman Law and stood first. He returned to India in 1913 and started practising as a barrister in Ahmedabad, fulfilling his second ambition.

### Gandhiji's Disciple

The impact of Gandhiji's personality on Vallabhbhai was tremendous. It gave him a new mission in life. The Champaran struggle waged by Gandhiji had a sweeping effect on Patel's mind. In Gandhiji's Champaran victory Patel saw the beginning of a new agrarian revolution. His interest in politics had been kindled, as became abunduntly clear in the Provincial Political Conference organised by the Gujarat Sabha and presided by Gandhiji at Godhra. The conference appointed a permanent committee with Gandhiji as the President and Patel as one of the secretaries. He became a staunch follower of Gandhiji. From then on there was no looking back. Blessed with rare qualities of fortitude, integrity and an iron determination, Patel played an important role in the freedom movement.

## Indomitable Personality

It was due to his sterling leadership and practical vision that the peasant movement in Gujarat became a success. It was in this struggle that the organisational capacity for which Sardar Patel was famous in the whole country became visible. He took over as the nascent nation's Home Minister at a very crucial juncture in history and devoted himself whole heartedly to ensure that the country which was already partitioned, remained intact and united.

## Building a Union

On the eve of their departure, the British government announced that its paramountcy would lapse not only over the British territory but even over the native States . This meant that as many as 625 small and big native States would become independent like India and Pakistan. Consequently, the country would be divided into a number of small and big units.

Before embarking on this mammoth task, Sardar sought to ensure the stability of administration by forging a bridge of faith and confidence with the"Steel Frame". Most of the I.C.S. officers suspected that the Congress leaders, particularly Sardar in view of his past experiences with them, would have no faith in the I.C.S. But Sardar rose to the occasion and reposed total trust in their capability to serve the nation. He was, thus, able to win their unstinted support in the endeavour of nation building.

Attempts were afoot for finalising the standstill agreement with the States. It provided that the Central Government will be vested with powers of defence, foreign policy and communications even over the States. Travancore, Hyderabad and some other States declared themselves sovereign States and created hurdles in the agreement. On the other end, Jinnah with a view to tempt Jodhpur, Jaisalmer and other border States made them an unconditional offer to align with Pakistan on their terms.

## Political Sagacity

To find an amicable solution to this complicated situation, Sardar issued a statement to the princes wherein he appealed to their sense of patriotism and reiterated that the new States department in no way, desire to have supremacy over them. "If at all, any sense of supremacy is required, it would be with common understanding and for common good. We are at a momentous stage in the history of India. By common endeavour, we can raise the country to new greatness, while lack of unity will expose us to unexpected calamities. I hope the Indian States will realise fully that if we do not cooperate and work together in the general interest, anarchy and chaos will overwhelm us all great and small, and lead us to total ruin". The statement which amply reflected his statesmanship and political sagacity, removed whatever doubts lurked in the minds of the princes.

There was a popular agitation in Travancore and the State acceded to India. The Nawab of Bhopal could not take all this but when he realised that there was no alternative, he sent the instrument of accession duly signed to Sardar.

A man of iron will and absolute fearlessness, Sardar Patel tackled the question of 550 and odd State territories and principalities in such a strategic manner which left even his wildest critics in complete amazement. Almost within a year he redrew the map of India with every princely State joining the Indian union and thus, forming part of the political stream of life that was endowed with cultural unity and harmony.

## Intricate Situation

The intricacy of the situation can perhaps be gauged by the fact that there were 26 small States in Orissa and 15 in the Chattisgarh area of present Madhya Pradesh. It required skilful diplomacy on the part of Sardar Patel to persuade them to merge into bigger, more viable units. Even more ticklish was the case of Saurashtra where there were 14 big States, 119 small States and other units under different administrations totalling 860.

The herculean task of merging all of them into the Saurashtra union was also accomplished by Sardar Patel. Soon, State after State started acceding to the Indian Union. One after the other, Gwalior, Indore, Dhar, Dewas all accepted the advice of Sardar. Rajputana States followed the same. The Sikhs of Punjab also cooperated with the merger.

Even by August 15, Hyderabad kept aloof. Hence, Lord Mountbatten himself started negotiations. At one stage, it appeared that there was a settlement but Nizam found himself helpless against the pressures of Razakars. The Razakars started harassing the local public. Thus, when the situation went out of control, Sardar with the consent of the Governor General initiated police action. In 108 hours, the Nizam surrendered and Hyderabad acceded and merged with India. The Nawab of Junagadh accepted an accession with Pakistan. Sardar solved this complex problem in his own inimitable way and the Nawab and his Diwan left Junagadh for Pakistan.

Thus, the 'Yagna' for establishment of a united India undertaken by Sardar was completed with the merger of Hyderabad. Politically, India became one and united. In the history of India stretched over ages, India became one and united for the first time and that too without shedding a drop of blood. That was the marvel of the personality of Sardar. The sterling qualities of leadership he had shown as leader of Satyagraha, flowered in greater way in the administration of the country, maintenance of law and order and ensuring stability of the country and making it invulnerable.

## THE DAY OF DESTINY

The All India Muslim League played a vital role in the creation of Pakistan in the year 1940. Muslim league had become a stronger political party for the Muslims of Indo-Pak Subcontinent, under which the Muslims were struggling for a separate homeland for them. The great leader of the Muslims, Muhammad Ali Jinnah by the time had become the lining symbol of Muslim unity and Muslim politics and the Muslims had so completely centred on him that he had become almost an institution in himself.

In the year 1940, the annual session of the Muslim league opened at Lahore, on the 22nd of March amidst scenes of great enthusiasm. Thousands met in the League Pandal which was tastefully decorated. This was a great moment and thousands of lovers of Muhammad Ali Jinnah were waiting for the historical speech. Muhammad Ali Jinnah arrived in the afternoon and was led directly to the Pandal. Nawab of Mamdot, welcomed the participants and pointed that the greatest achievement of the League was the suspension of the Federal part of the Government of India Act of 1935.

In the presidential address delivered by Muhammad Ali Jinnah, he explained the position of the Muslims and the criticized the Hindus and the Britishers and their diplomacy role against Muslims. He observed thus:

> *"As soon as circumstances permit or immediately after the war at the latest, the whole problem of India as future constitution must be examined de novo and the Act of 1935 must go once for all. We do not believe in asking the British Government to make declarations. These declarations are really of no use. You cannot passably succeed in getting the British Government out of this country by asking them to make declarations."*

Jinnah also criticised the attitude of the Congress towards the constitutional problem and various Hindus suggestions for the establishment of a Constituent

Assembly. Finally, he outlined the Muslim demand in most emphatic terms. "The problem in India is not of an inter-communal but manifestly of an international character and it must be treated as such. So long as this basic and fundamental truth is not realised, any constitution that may be built will result in disaster and will prove destructive and harmful, not only to Muslims but the British and the Hindus also.

If the British Government is really in earnest and sincere to secure peace and happiness of the people of this subcontinent, the only course open to us all is to allow the major nations separate homelands by dividing India into Autonomous National States. There is no reason, as to why these states should be antagonistic to each other. On the other hand, the rivalry and the natural desire and efforts on the part of one to dominate the social order and establish political supremacy over the other in the government of the country will disappear. It will lead more towards natural goodwill by international pacts between them, and they can live in complete harmony. This will lead further to a friendly settlement all the more easily with regard to minorities by reciprocal arrangement and adjustments between Muslim India and Hindu India, which will far more adequately and effectively safeguard the rights and interests of the Muslims and various minorities".

***On 23rd March 1940, the Chief Minister of Bengal, Moulvi Fazalul - Haque moved the following Resolution:*** " Resolved that It is the considered view of this session of the All India Muslim League that no Constitutional Plan would be workable in this country or acceptable to the Muslims, unless it is designed on the following basic principle, namely that geographically contiguous units are demarcated into regions which should be so constituted, with such territorial readjustments as may be necessary, that the areas in which the Muslims are numerically in majority as in the North Western and Eastern Zones of India would be grouped to constitute 'Independent States' in which the constituent units shall be autonomous and sovereign."

***The Impact:*** The Lahore Resolution was indeed a landmark in the history of India and of the Muslims. Before this, the Muslims of India had no goal and no future in view and Muslim politics remained in the hands of the individuals with conflicting interests and inclinations. As soon as Lahore Resolution was passed by the Muslim League, the Hindu press started criticising the Muslim League and declared this resolution as Pakistan Resolution. The personality of Muhammad Ali Jinnah was also criticised by the Hindus and their prominent leaders. Muhammad Ali Jinnah got nationwide popularity after Lahore Resolution, because the Muslims of India had a lot of expectations from him and he was the only source of inspiration for the Muslims.

***Conclusion:*** Slowly and gradually, Muslim were moving towards their goal and in a short span of seven years of their struggle, the Muslims of Indo-Pak Subcontinent finally succeeded in getting Pakistan, on 14th of August, 1947. The dream of Muhammad Ali Jinnah and thousands of other Muslim workers came true on this day. Every year on 23rd of March, the country celebrates this day with great joy and enthusiasm.

## TOWARD PARTITION

Congress predictably opposed all proposals for partition and advocated a united India with a strong centre and a fully responsible parliamentary government. To many, notably to Jawaharlal Nehru, the idea of a sovereign state based on a common religion seemed a historical anachronism and a denial of democracy. From 1940 on, reconciliation between Congress and the Muslim League became increasingly difficult, if not impossible.

During World War II, the Muslim League and Congress adopted different attitudes toward British rule. British priorities were driven by the expediencies of defense, and war was declared abruptly without any prior consultation with Indian politicians. Congress ministers in the provinces resigned in protest. As a consequence, Congress, with most of its leaders in jail for opposition to the Raj, lost its political leverage over the British. The Muslim League, however, followed a course of cooperation, gaining time to consolidate. The British appreciated the loyalty and valour of the British Indian Army, many of whose members were Punjabi Muslims. The Muslim League's success could be gauged from its sweep of 90 percent of the Muslim seats in the 1946 election, compared with only 4.5 percent in the 1937 elections. The 1946 election was, in effect, a plebiscite among Muslims on Pakistan. In London it became clear that there were three parties in any discussion on the future of India: the British, Congress, and the Muslim League.

Spurred by the Japanese advance in Asia and forceful persuasion from Washington, British prime minister Winston Churchill's coalition war government in 1942 had dispatched Sir Stafford Cripps to India with a proposal for settlement. The plan provided for dominion status after the war for an Indian union of British Indian provinces and princely states wishing to accede to it, a separate dominion for those who did not, and firm defense links between Britain and an Indian union. Cripps himself was sympathetic to Indian nationalism. However, his mission failed, and Gandhi described it as "a postdated check on a crashing bank."

In August 1942, Gandhi launched the "Quit India Movement" against the British. Jinnah condemned the movement. The government retaliated by arresting about 60,000 individuals and outlawing Congress. Communal riots increased. Talks between Jinnah and Gandhi in 1944 proved as futile as negotiations between Gandhi and the viceroy.

In July 1945, the Labour Party came to power in Britain with a large majority. Its choices in India were limited by the decline of British power and the necessity of retaining Indian links in imperial defense. General unrest in India spread, and, when a naval mutiny in Bombay broke out in 1945, British officials came to the conclusion that independence was the only alternative to forcible retention of control over an unwilling dependency. The viceroy, Lord Wavell, met with Indian leaders in Simla in 1945 to decide what form of interim government would be acceptable. No agreement was reached.

New elections to the provincial and central legislatures were ordered, and a three-man team came from Britain to discuss plans for self-government. The Cabinet Mission Plan, proposed by Cripps, represented Britain's last, desperate attempt to transfer the power it retained over India to a single union. The mission put forward a three-tier federal form of government in which the central government would be limited to power over defense, foreign relations, currency, and communications; significant other power would be delegated to the provinces. The plan also prescribed the zones that would be created: northeastern Bengal and Assam would be joined to form a zone with a slight Muslim majority; in the northwest, Punjab, Sindh, North-West Frontier Province, and Balochistan would be joined for a clear Muslim majority; and the remainder of the country would be the third zone, with a clear Hindu majority. The approximation of the boundaries of a new Pakistan was clear from the delineation of the zones. The mission also suggested the right of veto on legislation by communities that saw their interests adversely affected. Finally, the mission proposed that an interim government be established immediately and that new elections be held.

Congress and the Muslim League emerged from the 1946 elections as the two dominant parties, although the Muslim League again was unable to capture a majority of the Muslim seats in the North-West Frontier Province. At first, both parties seemed to accept the Cabinet Mission Plan, despite many reservations, but the subsequent behaviour of the leaders soon led to bitterness and mistrust. Nehru effectively quashed any prospect of the plan's success when he announced that Congress would not be "fettered" by agreements with the British, thereby making it clear that Congress would use its majority in the newly created Constituent Assembly to write a constitution that conformed to its ideas. The formation of an interim government was also controversial. Jinnah demanded equality between the Muslim League and

Congress, a proposal rejected by the viceroy. The Muslim League boycotted the interim government, and each party disputed the right of the other to appoint Muslim ministers, a prerogative Jinnah claimed belonged solely to the Muslim League.

When the viceroy proceeded to form an interim government without the Muslim League, Jinnah called for demonstrations, or "Direct Action," on August 16, 1946. Communal rioting broke out on an unprecedented scale, especially in Bengal and Bihar. The massacre of Muslims in Calcutta brought Gandhi to the scene, where he worked with the Muslim League provincial chief minister, Hussain Shahid Suhrawardy. Gandhi's and Suhrawardy's efforts calmed fears in Bengal, but rioting quickly spread elsewhere and continued well into 1947. Jinnah permitted the Muslim League to enter the interim government in an effort to stem further communal violence. Disagreements among the ministers paralyzed the government, already haunted by the specter of civil war.

In February 1947, Lord Mountbatten was appointed viceroy with specific instructions to arrange for a transfer of power by June 1948. Mountbatten assessed the situation and became convinced that Congress was willing to accept partition as the price for independence, that Jinnah would accept a smaller Pakistan than the one he demanded (that is, all of Punjab and Bengal), and that Sikhs would learn to accept a division of Punjab. Mountbatten was convinced by the rising temperature of communal emotions that the June 1948 date for partition was too distant and persuaded most Indian leaders that immediate acceptance of his plan was imperative.

On June 3, 1947, British prime minister Clement Attlee introduced a bill in the House of Commons calling for the independence and partition of India. On July 14, the House of Commons passed the India Independence Act, by which two independent dominions were created on the subcontinent; the princely states were left to accede to either. The partition plan stated that contiguous Muslim-majority districts in Punjab and Bengal would go to Pakistan, provided that the legislatures of the two provinces agreed that the provinces should be partitioned—they did. Sindh's legislature and Balochistan's *jirga* (council of tribal leaders) agreed to join Pakistan. A plebiscite was held in the Sylhet District of Assam, and, as a result, part of the district was transferred to Pakistan. A plebiscite was also held in the North-West Frontier Province. Despite a boycott by Congress, the province was deemed to have chosen Pakistan. The princely states, however, presented a more difficult problem. All but three of the more than 500 states quickly acceded to Pakistan or India under guidelines established with the aid of Mountbatten.

The states made their decisions after giving consideration to the geographic location of their respective areas and to their religious majority. Hyderabad, the most populated of the princely states, was ruled by a Muslim but had a Hindu majority and was surrounded by territory that would go to India, and Junagadh (a small state with a Muslim prince but a Hindu majority) presented a problem. Both hesitated but were quickly absorbed into India. The accession of the third state, Jammu and Kashmir, could not be resolved peacefully, and its indeterminate status has poisoned relations between India and Pakistan ever since.

Throughout the summer of 1947, as communal violence mounted, preparations for partition proceeded in Delhi. Assets were divided, boundary commissions were set up to demarcate frontiers, and British troops were evacuated. The military was restructured into two forces. Law and order broke down in different parts of the country. Civil servants were given the choice of joining either country; British officers could retire with compensation if not invited to stay on. Jinnah and Nehru tried unsuccessfully to quell the passions of communal fury that neither fully understood. On August 14, 1947, Pakistan and India achieved independence. Jinnah the first governor general of the Dominion of Pakistan.

# 3

# Patel and Political Integration

## POLITICAL INTEGRATION

The term integration, as pointed out by Myron Weiner, "covers a vast range of human relationships and attitudes - the integration of diverse and discrete cultural loyalties and the development of a sense of nationality; the integration of political units into a common territorial framework with a government which can exercise authority; the integration of the rulers and the ruled; the integration of citizens into a common political process; and, finally, the integration of individuals into organisations for purposive activities." Myron Weiner gives five broad definitions of the term integration. According to him integration may refer to:

...the process of bringing together culturally and socially discrete groups into a single territorial unit and the establishment of a national identity, the problem of establishing national central authority over subordinate political units or regions which may or may not coincide with distinct cultural or social groups, the problem of linking government with the governed, the process in evolving a minimum value consensus necessary to maintain a social order, the "integrative behaviour", referring to the capacity of people in a society to organise for some common purpose (Weiner1965: 53-54).

Integration is, as maintained by most scholars, a matter of degree and the national state representing only a more or less stable balance of centripetal and centrifugal forces (Harrison 1956: 141).

The term integration is defined in two senses, sometimes as a process and sometimes as a condition. Ernst B. Haas uses it in the former sense and defines political integration as the "process whereby political actors in several distinct national settings are persuaded to shift their loyalties, expectations, and political activities toward a new centre, whose institutions possess or demand jurisdiction over the pre-existing national states" (Haas1958: 16).

Karl W. Deutsch uses the term integration both as a process and a condition and defines political integration as "the attainment of a sense of community, accompanied by formal or informal institutions or practices, sufficiently strong and widespread to assure peaceful change among members of a group" (Deutsch 1954: 33). Such an integrated community, which Deutsch terms it as "security-community", may or may not be a sovereign state and called it an "amalgamated" community.

Philip E. Jacob and Henry Teune describe political integration as a "relationship of community among people within the same political entity" who are held together by "mutual ties...which give the group a feeling of identity and awareness" (Jacob and Teune1964: 4). In these two definitions it can be pointed out that political integration is the uniting of distinct national entities.

James S. Coleman and Carl G. Rosberg, jr., define political integration as "the progressive bridging of elite-mass gap on the vertical plane in the course of developing a participant community" (Coleman and Rosberg, jr. 1964: 9). Political integration also means the existence of one political entity having some form of jurisdiction over both areas. A strict definition of political integration is the predicted change in political relations between communities by a movement toward ultimate union into a new, more comprehensive and coherent political community. All the above definitions are attempts to define "what is which holds a society and a political system together" (Weiner, 1965: 54).

In simple words, political integration is the integration into the government, the political parties and the pressure group life of a country (Goldman, 1964: 28). In the theoretical treatment of political development and political stability, the concept of political integration is usually employed in a sense that approximates Deutsch's definition (Lijphart 1971: 3), where the focus of interest is on integration within states, or, in other words, on the question whether an amalgamated community is integrated or not ( Mye 1968: 871). Political integration is said to occur "when the linkage consists of joint participation in regularised, ongoing decision-making" (Lindberg, 1970: 649).

## NATIONAL INTEGRATION OF INDIA

The euphoria of independence was short-lived as partition brought disastrous consequences for India in the wake of communal conflict. Partition unleashed untold misery and loss of lives and property as millions of Hindu and Muslim refugees fled either Pakistan or India. Both nations were also caught up in a number of conflicts involving the allocation of assets, demarcation of boundaries, equitable sharing of water resources, and control over Kashmir.

At the same time, Indian leaders were faced with the stupendous task of national integration and economic development. When the British relinquished their claims to paramountcy, the 562 independent princely states were given the option to join either of the two nations. A few princely states readily joined Pakistan, but the rest—except Hyderabad (the largest of the princely states with 132,000 square kilometres and a population of more than 14 million), Jammu and Kashmir (with 3 million inhabitants), and Junagadh (with a population of 545,000)—merged with India. India successfully annexed Hyderabad and Junagadh after "police actions" and promises of privileges to the rulers.

The Hindu maharajah of predominantly Muslim Jammu and Kashmir remained uncommitted until armed tribesmen and regular troops from Pakistan infiltrated his domain, inducing him to sign the Instrument of Accession to India on October 27, 1947. Pakistan refused to accept the legality of the accession, and, as a result, war broke out Kashmir remains a source of friction between the neighbors.

The assassination of Mahatma Gandhi on January 30, 1948, in New Delhi, by a Hindu extremist opposed to Gandhi's openness to Muslims ended the tenuous celebration of independence and deepened the hatred and mutual suspicion in Hindu-Muslim relations. Economic backwardness was one of the serious challenges that India faced at independence. Under three successive five-year plans, inaugurated between 1951 and 1964 under Nehru's leadership, India produced increasing amounts of food.

Although food production did not allow self-sufficiency until fiscal year 1984, India has emerged as the nation with the seventh largest gross national product in the world Linguistic regionalism eventually reached a crisis stage and undermined the Congress' attempts at nation building.

Whereas in the early 1920s, the Congress had deemed that the use of regional vernaculars in education and administration would facilitate the governance of the country, partition made the leaders, especially Nehru, realize how quickly such provincial or subnational interests would dismantle India's fragile unity. However, in the face of widespread agitation for linguistic separation of states, beginning with the Telangana Movement in 1953, in 1956 Nehru reluctantly accepted the recommendations of the States Reorganisation Commission, and the number of states grew by reorganization along linguistic lines.

The states became the loci for democratization of political processes at district levels, for expression of regional culture and popular demands against a national culture and unity, for economic development at strategic localities in the rural areas, and for proliferation of opposition parties that ended the possibility of a pan-Indian two-party system.

## Remembering Sardar Patel

31st October is a very important day for most Indians, especially Gujaratis. We make sure that we are in London on that day. It is the birthday anniversary of Bharat Ratna Sardar Vallabhbhai Patel, which is celebrated on a grand scale in London every year, organized by the Sardar Patel Memorial Society, normally at the prestigious venue of Kadwa Patidar Samaj Hall in Harrow.

But this year (2004) we were expecting to celebrate this grand occasion at even more prestigous location, at none other than India House, as Shri Ronan Sen, the previous High Commissioner and Shri P.C. Haldar, Minister for Coordination at the time, a true friend of the Indian community, promised the members of the Sardar Patel Memorial Society (UK) that in future Sardar's Birth Celebration will be held at India House. It was done openly in a speech at last year's celebrations at Kadwa Patidar Samaj hall, in the presence of some six hundred people. But with the change of government in New Delhi, it did not take long for the Congress led UPA government to show their antipathy towards Sardar and as expected by some of us, the permission to hold the celebration at India House was denied at the eleventh hour. What surprises me is that the SPMS did not anticipate this attitude, especially in view of the treatment Sardar received at the hands of the Nehru dynasty in the past.

Sardar Vallabhbhai Patel, born in a tiny sleepy village, rose to become a right-hand man of Gandhiji and a frontline warrior, a freedom fighter of the Quit India Movement, the freedom struggle that ultimately freed Bharat from the clutches of the British Raj and gave Bharat her independence in 1947.

Sardar's great achievement of the political integration of some 665 princely Indian states into the Indian Union, welding India into the proud and a powerful nation that she is today has been almost ignored by successive Congress governments.

In fact Sardar's immense contribution was only recognised when the Congress party was liberated from the clutches of the Nehru dynasty. Shri P. V. Narsimaha Rao awarded the title of Bharat Ratna to Sardar posthumously in 1991, some 40 years after the death of Sardar, which was in the possession of his grandson Bipinbhai Patel who recently presented it to the Sardar Memorial Trust museum in Gandhinagar.

## Sonia Ist Member of Nehru-Gandhi Family to Visit Sardar's Home

Congress President Sonia Gandhi today became the first member of the Nehru-Gandhi family to visit ancestral house of Sardar Patel after India's Independence, which is seen here as a huge gesture on the part of the family to win over the Patel community.

The visit comes amidst a tirade launched by the BJP against the Congress that like always the party continued to ignore the immense contribution of Sardar Vallabhbhai Patel, the first Home Minister and contemporary of Jawaharlal Nehru, to the country.

### *Congress has Constantly Ignored the Iron Man of this Country*

In the allocation of budget for the celebration of 150th anniversary of the First War of Independence, the Congress-led UPA Government has allocated Rs 30 crore for Nehru but not a single paise for Sardar," Gujarat Chief Minister Narendra Modi had said on the Iron Man of India's birth anniversary on 31st October.

Gandhi paid floral tribute to the statue of Patel and his elder brother Vitthalbhai Patel (first speaker of Lok Sabha) during her visit.

"It is for the first time since the country's Independence that a member of Nehru family has visited the ancestral house of Sardar Patel," said Ullas Patel, a trustee of the Sardar Patel Memorial Trust which maintains it.

"Nehru, Indira Gandhi and Rajiv Gandhi had never ever visited the place after independence," Patel added.

The visit by Sonia Gandhi to Karamsad is aimed at winning over the politically powerful Patel community, which falling away from the ruling BJP and is in the forefront of the rebellion under Keshubhai Patel, Congress sources said.

Sonia was welcomed into the ancestral house by a 90-year-old freedom fighter Shantaben Patel. A large group of people who had assembled outside the house greeted the Congress leader.

Sonia later spent about 15 minutes looking at the photographs of Sardar Patel and other freedom fighters, including Jawaharlal Nehru.

On her way out, Sonia wrote in the visitor's book, "it is a matter of pride and privilege for me to pay respect to the native house of Sardar Vallabhbhai Patel, our freedom fighter, who contributed so much to national politics and in building of our free nation".

"So far four former Presidents Shankar Dayal Sharma, V V Giri, Gyani Zail Singh and Fakruddin Ali Ahmed and five Prime Ministers—Morarji

Desai, V P Singh, Deve Gowda, Chandrasekhar and Atal Bihari Vajpayee—have visited the house," Ullas Patel remarked.

Another trustee Harshad Patel said that the Sardar Patel Memorial Trust has requested Sonia Gandhi to sanction an amount of Rs 10 crore for the upkeep of the memorial at Karamsad. Other Congress leaders, including Union Textile Minister Shankersinh Vaghela, Gujarat Congress incharge B K Hariprasad, GPCC chief Bharat Solanki and others had accompanied Sonia on her visit to Karamsad.

I would like to urge the trustees of Sardar Patel Memorial Trust to start a fund in this country and to acquire and refurbish Sardar's bungalow in New Delhi to rival that of Nehru and to create a grand memorial monument, a national treasure house in Gujarat's capital Gandhinagar, where Sardar's meagre but valuable belongings, such as his spinning wheel or Charka, shawl, tea set presented to him by Lord Mountbatten, his writing desk and chair, diaries, letters and photographs should be displayed for the public to view.

Such a building should be surrounded by a vast garden and lakes, a floating restaurant and butterfly house, a bird aviary, in the surrounding ground for the public to enjoy, a picnic area and a funfair for the children and a rural heaven for the wildlife.

With BJP government in Gujarat, it is time to give Sardar his rightful place in the history books. I understand that the Sardar Patel Trust, under the presidency of Shri Ashok Patel, has already been created in Gandhinagar to perpetuate the memory of the late Sardar Vallabhbhai Patel and the late Veer Vithalbhai Patel. We the NRI can provide the funds and the administration to assist such a project. I would be the first to make a small donation if someone takes the initiative to start such a fund.

While celebrating Sardar's 129th birthday anniversary, Modiji said that "To my mind, even Gandhiji would have been incomplete without Sardar at his side." That is the best compliment one can give to Sardar.

The 129th birthday anniversary of the Sardar was celebrated at the National Association of Patidar Samaj Hall in Tooting. HE Mr. Kamlesh Sharma garlanded a large portrait of Sardar Patel and Mr M. T. Patel lighted the Deep. National songs were sung by Maya Panchal and Surendra Chudasama. Mr Kanoobhai Desai welcomed the guests. Praveen Amin briefly described the achievements of the Sardar. Tributes were paid by the High Commissioner who said that the Sardar had the unique skill of negotiation which forged the unity of India.

## About IMC

Indian Merchants' Chamber took birth on September 7,1907 to wrest economic Swaraj for people under the inspiration of great leaders like Lokmanya Tilak, Justice Ranade, Dadabhoy Naoroji and Mohandas Karamchand Gandhi. Mahatma Gandhi noticed the singular role played by the Chamber and agreed to become its honorary member, thereby bestowing upon it a unique honour.

The patriotic fervour churned up by the chamber roused the business community to work towards liberating Indian industry, trade and commerce from foreign domination. The spirit of Swaraj possessed the chamber, a long succession of its presidents turned fighters for economic freedom.

The chamber lent full support to the hardcore political struggle led by the congress and engaged itself in organising nationalist businessmen. The Indian economy suffered violent disturbances under the impact of two world wars, a series of global depressions, famines that took millions of lives, recurring epidemics of banks insolvency, sporadic eruption of communal riots and political upheavals. Against this backdrop, the British government was quietly tightening its stronghold on vital parts of the Indian economy-industry, trade, commerce, banking and transport through a plethora of legislative measures.

The chamber waged historic battles against every one of these measures and dispelled wrong impressions, if any, that the chamber was constituted to safeguard only traders' interests. Pre-independence, IMC functioned as the nation's watchdog on the economic front, keeping vigil on the colonial masters' exploitative moves.

Post-independence, the IMC continued its association with eminent personalities who shaped India as we know it today-Jawaharlal Nehru, Sardar Vallabhbhai Patel, Dr. Rajendra Prasad, Dr. S. Radhakrishnan, Lal Bahadur Shastri, Smt. Indira Gandhi and Rajiv Gandhi, to name a few. Such stalwarts often graced the Chamber by their presence and thought-provoking addresses.

## Indian Independence Day—August 15

As India celebrates its Independence day,lets remember the great Patriots who laid down their lives for our Independence:

***Tatia Tope:*** Tatia Tope was a hero of the fight for freedom in 1857. His very name made the mighty English Generals tremble. Deceived by his friend, he faced death like a hero, for the sake of his country. He was the Supreme commander in the War of Indian Independence, which in 1857, had challenged the hold of the British over India. It was he who, more than anybody else, shook the mighty British Empire to its foundations. Holding aloft the flag of freedom, he sought to break the chains of slavery and fought the military might of the English heroically. His name had become a household word for bravery.

***Jhansi Lakshmi Bai:*** Lakshmi Bai was the great heroine of the First war of India Freedom. She lived for only 22 years. She became a widow in her eighteenth year. Jhansi, of which she was the queen, was in the grip of the cunning, cruel British. She was the embodiment of patriotism, self-respect and heroism. She was the queen of a small state, but the empress of a limitless empire of glory. She led her troops to battle against the British in the Revolt of 1857. She was one of the first women martyrs of the country.

***Bal Gangadhar Tilak:*** Bal Gangadhar Tilak was a great Sanskrit scholar and astronomer. He fixed the origin and date of Rigvedic Aryans, which was highly acclaimed and universally accepted by Orientalists of his time. His role in Congress and advocating Home Rule for India were enormous. His newspaper (Kesari) founded in 1881 is going strong even today. He was Guru to V.D. Savarkar and hundreds of nationalists and thousands of Indians. He led the Indian Freedom Movement, till 1920, his death. After him Gandhiji took over. Although Gandhi accepted Gokhale as his mentor, in practice, he adopted all of Tilak's ideas of Swadeshi and of social reform.

His words, "Swaraj is my birthright and I shall have it!" roused a sleeping nation to action, making Indian people aware of their political plight under a foreign rule. Tilak did not question the British Sovereignty nor his demands were rebellious or revolutionary. All he was asking was favorable conditions in India, to enable people to learn to govern themselves.

***Surendranath Banerjee:*** Surendranath Banerjee was one of the early leaders in the history of the Indian freedom movement. He was a great leader and at the same time professor, newspaper editor and social reformer. Due to his refusal to accept defeat he was known as 'Surrender Not'. He served as the President of the Indian National Congress twice, in 1895 and 1902. He became the editor of a paper called "Bengali" from 1878 and wrote fearlessly on patriotism, freedom, unity and culture

***Bhagat Singh:*** Bhagat Singh was born in September 27, 1907 in the village Banga of Layalpur to Mata Vidyavati and Sardar Kishan Singh. Bhagat Singh grew up in a patriotic atmosphere as his father and uncle, were great freedom fighters and were put in jail many times by the British.

Bhagat Singh, along with the help of Chandrashekhar Azad, formed the Hindustan Socialist Republican Army. The aim of this Indian revolutionary movement was defined as not only to make India independent, but also to create "a socialist India."

In February 1928, the Simon Commission visited India. The purpose of its visit was to decide how much freedom and responsibility could be given to the people of India.

Indian freedom fighters started an agitation called "Simon go back". It was in this agitation that during a police lathicharge, Lala Lajpat Rai was hurt and died. To avenge the death of Lala Lajpat rai, Bhagat Singh and Rajguru shot and killed the British Officer who had hit Lala Lajpat Rai. Bhagat Singh became "Shaheed Bhagat Singh" or Martyr at the age of 24.

***M.K.Gandhi:*** Mohandas Karamchand Gandhi became one of the most respected spiritual and political leaders of the 1900's. Gandhi helped free the Indian people from British rule through nonviolent resistance, and is honored by his people as the father of the Indian Nation. Gandhiji stayed in South Africa for 21 years working to secure rights for Indian people. He developed a method of direct social action based upon the principles of courage, nonviolcncc and truth called 'Satyagraha.' He believed that the way people behave is more important than what they achieve. 'Satyagraha' promoted nonviolence and civil disobedience as the most appropriate methods for obtaining political and social goals. In 1915 Gandhi returned to India. Within 15 years he became the leader of the Indian nationalist movement. Using the tenets of 'Satyagraha' he led the campaign for Indian independence from the British rule.

***Subhash Chandra Bose:*** Subhash Chandra Bose was the most visionary and fierce activist in the pre-independence era. Known as Netaji, he followed the path, which no one even could have thought of. Bose advocated complete freedom for India at the earliest. He was elected president of the Indian National Congress twice in 1937 and in 1939, the second time defeating Gandhiji's nominee. Later he resigned from the Congress and formed a progressive group known as the Forward Block. An unparalleled example of the declaration of Independent Indian government with a cabinet and its own army was seen in form of the Indian National Army under the leadership of Subhash Chandra Bose. It literally had a military attack on British India and had confronted them up to Imphal. With the help from Germany and active support from Japan, they shook the very foundation of the British Empire.

***Vallabhbhai Patel:*** Vallabhbhai Patel, the iron-man of India, was born on 13th October, 1875, in a small village Karamsadh of Bombay region. The British government declared to confiscate all the lands of farmers. Patel forced the government to amend the rules. He brought together the farmers and encouraged them and hence got the title of 'Sardar' and thus became famous. With great wisdom and political foresight, he consolidated the small kingdoms. The public was with him. He tackled the Nizam of Hyderabad and the Nawab of Junagarh who initially did not want to join India. There were a lot of problems connected with the reunion of the numerous states into India. Sardar Patel's untiring efforts towards the unity of the country brought success. Due to the achievement of this massive task, Sardar Patel got the title of 'Iron Man'.

*Maulana Abul Kalam Azad:* Independent India's first Education Minister. He was given the chrono-grammatic name of Firoz Bakht (of exalted destiny) but commonly called Muhiyuddin Ahmad. He was imprisoned several times by the British. From 1920-1945, Abul Kalam Azad was in and out of prison a number of times. He was twice elected President of the Indian National Congress in 1923 and in 1940. He was the the youngest person to be elected the President of the Congress. He continued as President of the Congress till 1946 and when India became Independent. He started Urdu weekly, "Al-Hilal". The paper was amazingly forceful. It was a patriotic weekly. This antagonized the Britishers.

*Jawaharlal Nehru:* Jawaharlal Nehru was a leader of the socialist wing of the Indian National Congress during and after India's fight for independence from the British empire. He became the first Prime Minister of India when the country became a independent in 1947 and remained Prime Minister until his death in 1964. Nehru embodied a synthesis of ideals: politically an ardent nationalist, ideologically a pragmatic socialist, and secular in religious outlook, Nehru possessed a rare combination of intellect, breadth of vision, and personal charisma that attracted support throughout India. During the freedom struggle, he courted arrest many a times, and had been jailed 14 years in all. He was elected Congress President five times, and it was under his influence in Lahore, that the Congress adopted complete freedom as its goal.

The Bardoli Satyagraha drew Munshiji into its vortex. He felt impelled to give up his style of living in Bombay and visit the peasants in revolt. He witnessed in Bardoli the self-respecting dignity of the peasants who, under Gandhiji's and Vallabhbhai Patel's leadership, were prepared to risk their all in the fight against injustice. Deeply stirred, he placed his time and his legal talents at the disposal of the Satyagraha, marking him out as an invaluable recruit for both Gandhiji and Sardar Vallabhbhai Patel. Writing to Gandhiji in April 1930, Munshiji said: "When the whole of Gujarat and with it India has started on a glorious march to martyrdom, I, who dreamt of their greatness through my literary efforts, cannot stand by and look on." The die had been cast. With Gandhiji as Guru and General, Sardar Patel as Counsellor and Captain, Munshiji became a soldier in the nonviolent army of freedom fighters. If Sri Aurobindo had initiated Munshiji into jnanayoga, Gandhiji initiated Munshiji into karmayoga. Munshiji became thereby an example of wisdom through action, and action through wisdom. Sir C. P. Ramaswami Aiyar rightly described him once as "a philosopher in action".

Munshiji was invited in 1937 to join the first popular Ministry in the Bombay Presidency under B.G. Kher. His own preference was for the Departments of Law and Education, but it fell to Munshiji's lot to take up the onerous Department of Home. A student of the Gita does not flinch from duty. Munshiji's stewardship of the Home Ministry was memorable. We must remember that those were times when the British were only too keen to prove that Indians were incapable of rising to the occasion, particularly in the matter of handling the growing communal problem. Munshiji made it clear that he and his Ministry would be totally impartial instruments and would admit of no disorder.

It was only natural that Munshiji's political insight and legal acumen should be harnessed for framing free India's Constitution by the Constituent Assembly. He became one of the Assembly's most active members. The framing of the new nation's supreme statute called for the gift of idealism as well as realism. Munshiji was possessed of both. Small wonder that as a Member of the Constituent Assembly he became a member of as many as eleven Committees-the largest tally for any single Member of the Constituent Assembly. The Drafting Committee headed by Dr. B. R. Ambedkar was one of the important Committees of which Munshiji was a member and he made invaluable contributions to its deliberations. I cannot but refer to the fact that the principle of guaranteeing to every person equal protection of the laws was the result of a draft written jointly by Munshiji and Dr. Ambedkar. Munshiji's sense of equality did not confine itself to mere legal protection. He was a great champion of women's rights to social, economic and legal equality.

Aided by his talented wife Lilavati Munshi, he carried on a crusade for raising the status and dignity of women. The struggle for freedom directed itself not merely to shedding the foreign yoke but also towards emancipation of Harijans, women, labour-agricultural and industrial. Everyone of the oppressed section of the community found a glimmer of hope and joined the movement enthusiastically. And the women of India played a notable part in the national movement for freedom.

The main thrust of Munshiji's work in the Constituent Assembly was, however, towards the making of a strong Centre. A student of the history of the subcontinent that he was, Munshiji knew that a weak Centre had always led to a weakening of the nation as a whole. Munshiji saw the history of India not as a record of dynasties or battles but rather as a record of the progress of our people in time. He saw that periods of strength, confidence and self-reliance alternated with periods of decline, weakness, subjugation and drift. He regarded 1947 as an opportunity for India to begin an ascent once again. He believed that we had it in us to climb up into a new millennium. He wrote:

> *"The Egypt of the Pharaohs, the Greece of Pericles, the Iran of Darius and the Rome of the Caesar are all dead; their life and culture are mere materials for scholarly research. But India has stood the shocks of time. Manu, Buddha, Panini, Bhasa and Kautilya are still living influences operating on life; Sri Krishna's exhortation to Arjuna still inspires the thought, hope and conduct of millions."*

Munshiji's palpable devotion to the concept of a strong and unified motherland must definitely have weighed with the Government when it appointed him as Agent-General of the Government of India in Hyderabad. The Nizam's province was trying hard to fly in the face of history and become a Third Dominion. That step would have been not merely retrograde but disastrous. Fortunately for us, our leadership did not allow personal ambitions to trifle with destiny in Hyderabad. If Sardar Patel was the architect of Hyderabad's accession to India, Munshiji was surely the engineer in the field. Acknowledging Munshiji's role, the Sardar wrote: "On behalf of the Government, I wish to say that we are deeply conscious of the high sense of public duty that induced you to accept this office and the very able manner in which you discharged the duties entrusted to you which contributed in no small measure to the final result."

Back in Delhi, Munshiji was soon called upon to fill the seat in the Council of Ministers vacated by Dr. Rajendra Prasad on his election to the office of President. Munshiji's services as Union Minister for Food and Agriculture between 1950 and 1952 saw him in yet another nation-building role. Munshiji showed that a man with pride in the past could also have a faith in the future through the instruments of science and technology. It was Munshiji who laid the foundations of a self-reliant agricultural economy, through an interlocking of agricultural research and extension. My friend Sri C. Subramaniam, who later heralded the Green Revolution, vouched for this. Today when we are all so conscious of the environment and of ecological factors, it is instructive to note that as much as half century ago, as Union Agriculture Minister, Munshiji said in a letter to Prime Minister Nehru:

> *"I find that trees are being cut down thoughtlessly by the villagers and the process practically connived at by the authorities. (I wish) ecological studies*

*and the relation of our national existence to our land, water, rivers and forests, is more closely studied."*

The original impulse for preserving ecology came with Munshiji's Vanamahotsava scheme. The Governorship of Uttar Pradesh, which Munshiji held from 1952 to 1957 saw him establish the healthiest of conventions. Munshiji's relationship with the Council of Ministers headed by Pantji and later by Sampurnanandji was, by any standards, exemplary. Respect was reciprocated by trust. The Ministers valued his erudition and turned to him, as to an elder, for advice. He, in turn, strove to discharge his due constitutional role with maturity combined with a becoming modesty. Where others, out of office, are known to flounder like flightless birds, Munshiji flew out of public office for the last time in 1957. The 'release' from government gave him more time than ever for public service.

With the solidarity and support of Smt Lilavati Munshi, he toured extensively, wrote and lectured. His canvas was wide; the paints on his palette many. Culture, literature, the arts, legal issues and of course politics continued to interest him. Whether in Gujarati or in Hindi or English, he expressed himself prodigiously. Even those who did not always agree with him admired him. His integrity, his patriotism, his scholarship and his vision of India were what mattered. The foremost vehicle of Munshiji's expression was the Column 'Kulapati's Letter' in the Bhavan's Journal. Like Rajaji's 'Dear Reader' column in Swarajya, 'Kulapati's Letter' covered a wide range of subjects, with a vitality that was almost exuberant.

As M. C. Chagla had observed, a silver thread of continuity ran through all his scintillating comments. And that thread was a passion for India's greatness, be it in the past, present or future. Munshiji built the Bharatiya Vidya Bhavan with the devotion of one engrossed in raising a temple. The Bharatiya Vidya Bhavan is a Somnath of Learning. For sixty-four years, people have sought it out from far and near in what has verily been a pilgrim's progress.

Of this Somnath, Kulapati Munshi was the sthapati (sculptor-architect) no less than the Kulapati. He conceived of the Bhavan, raised it brick by brick, combining as he did so, both breadth of vision and a grasp of detail. Naturally, both the design and its execution turned out to be masterly. It would be instructive to remember that Kulapati Munshi, founded the Bharatiya Vidya Bhavan a full decade before the advent of Independence. He foresaw that Independent India would need the binding force of a pan-Indian movement, a pan-Indian spirit and a pan-Indian ethos which would present to contemporary Indians, a glimpse of the composite magnificence of ancient times. Kulapati Munshi knew that a Government and a Constitution are one thing, the people's own inner vision is another. And so the Bhavan was launched to supplement the political unity of India with the cultural and spiritual unity of India.

## PROBLEMS OF POLITICAL INTEGRATION

With the gaining of independence by countries of Asia and Africa during the middle of the twentieth century, the task of nation-building has been left with these countries. The first and foremost problem encountered by them was the issue of integrating the vast chunk of people who had been loosely administered with varying degrees by the colonial powers.

In large and multi-national nation-states, the problem of integrating people inhabiting different regions with varied language, religion, culture and ethnic communities, the task is an arduous one. As Leonard Binder, while analysing the crisis of political development in new nation-states, pointed out: "the greatest task facing the new nation will be to build a nation out of a collection of tribes or of isolated communities" (Binder 1971: 46).

The problem of integration has been faced by most nation-states in one form or the other. The problem of political integration, according to Myron Weiner, is the "process of bringing culturally and socially discrete groups together into a single territorial unit, and the establishment of a sense of loyalty to that unit" (Weiner, 1968: 27).

Claude Ake broadly defines the problem as follows: "how to build a single coherent political society from a multiplicity of 'traditional societies'; how to increase cultural homogeneity and value consensus; and how to elicit, from the individual, deference and devotion to the claims of the state" (Ake 1967: 486-499). Historically, the problem of integration has been "restricted to the determination of the nature and diffusion of nationalism in a particular transitional polity and the impact that nationalism had on the developmental process" (Alam 1981: 2).

The emergence of nation-states with a fixed territory is a relatively new phenomenon. The sovereignty of these states is generally marked by an exclusive control over their territory. The control over territory is usually accompanied by a movement to infuse the feeling of a common nationality. However, there needs to be first of all territorial integration before any other forms of integration can possibly take place. There are instances where "nation" precedes "state" formation as in the case of Israel. But most of the modern nation-states in Asia and Africa are a by-product of colonial rule, where the emergence of territorial nation-state precedes the emergence of a nation.

There are serious problem of territorial integration, where the new governments tries to take control over border areas which were loosely administered by colonial governments. Moreover, "there are also areas occupied by recalcitrant tribes who forcefully resisted efforts toward their incorporation in the larger nation-state" where "the colonial rulers generally did not establish a central authority over the entire territory under their *de jure* control" (Weiner 1965: 52-56). Thus, the areas under indirect control by colonial governments have been placed under the direct control of the new governments. In the establishment of most new nations, the establishment of a territory precedes the establishment of loyalties from the subjects.

The problem of integration faced by each nation-state differs from others in nature as well as in degree. It varies from country to country "because of the ambiguity as to what constitutes a nation which is to be integrated" and also because of the "differences between the countries in their history and ethnic composition" (Emerson 1966: 96). Even developed countries of the west face the continuing resurgence of such integrational problems and there are instances of the break-up of multi-national nation-states.

Therefore, the solution to the problem of integration cannot be uniform even among the developing countries. Some of the most common problem in integration involves the "problems of national identity, territorial control, the establishment of norms for the handling of public conflict, the relationship between the governors and the governed, and the problems of organising individuals for the achievement of common purposes" (Weiner 1965: 52). Nonetheless, students of comparative politics develop some theoretical framework, where much of the theories developed out of concern for nation building in pluralistic societies.

## Theoretical Considerations

The primary prerequisite of political integration is the existence of political culture. According to Sidney Verba, political culture "consists of the system of empirical beliefs, expressive symbols, and values which defines the situation in which political action takes place" (Verba 1965: 513). Verba pointed out that not all beliefs about political culture are relevant to the concept of political culture; but the concept refers to only those beliefs which affect politics in a fundamental way. In almost all the theories of political integration cultural homogeneity, especially a homogeneous political culture is often regarded as a prerequisite for political integration, which in turn is a prerequisite for political stability, especially in democracies (Lijphart 1971: 4-5). It is also further argued that shared culture may not be a prerequisite for unification but a requirement that has to be fulfilled before the process can be advanced.

Claude Ake stresses the requirement from the members of the political system to identify with and trust one another. He said that "without some basic mutual trust among members of a civic body there can be no stable expectations about the modes of acquisition and exercise of political power, no coherence and predictability in political life" (Ake 1967: 487). He further argues that if the different cultural entities within the political system are so profoundly dissimilar that they cannot communicate with one another, mutual trust and a sense of collective identity cannot develop. Therefore, one of the essential preliminary requisite for political integration is the broadening and intensifying of "social communication". The improvement of the communicative facilities of a new state depends, in turn, on social mobilisation- "the process in which major clusters of old social, economic, and psychological commitments are eroded or broken down and people become available for new patterns of socialisation and behaviour" (Deutsch 1961: 494). Social mobilisation involves a huge change of an old way of life and therefore generates tensions.

Claude Ake hypothesise that, "the political system driving for integration maximises its chances for achieving a high degree of integration and remain stable, in spite of short-run destabilising effects of the drive for integration, if it is an authoritarian, consensual, 'identific', and paternal." Ake said that the pursuit of integration underscores the need for authoritarianism as the quest for integration aggravates political instability by attempting to make people relate to national symbols rather than to tribal ones. Thus, in order to maintain a minimum of political stability it is crucial that the government be strong enough to deal with the centrifugal forces that the drive for integration will activate and the government must also be able to decide and act quickly (Ake 1967: 489).

Ake further theorise that leaders of a new state must not concentrate power in their own hands but father social transformation and be innovative as they are committed to integration of their culturally pluralistic societies. They must destroy or modify certain habits of mind and undermine certain traditional symbols of collective identity; they must induce the people to accept new norms, new goals, new motivations; they must readjust patterns of social and economic relationship and to this effect they must supply the initiative for relising it. As socio-cultural gap between the elite and the masses is one of the most striking features of the newly independent state which poses the threat of mutual alienation between them, the political style and the way of life of the ruling elite must be calculated to dramatise its concern for and identity with the masses so as to lessen this threat. Political leaders need to eschew corruption, conspicuous consumption, and social snobbery and give their politics a distinctly "populistic' one. Ake believes that "the ultimate cure for the inherent instability of the new states lies mainly in the modification of the political behaviour of its elites." He argues that the "government should be a coalition of the leaders of the major social, religious, professional, and ethnic groups...Consensus is sought not at the grass-roots level but at the leadership level by enlisting the support of leading personalities from all major social groups." Political integration is said to occur "when the linkage consists of joint participation in regularised, ongoing decision-making" (Lindberg1970: 649).

John Wood criticise Verba and Ake's equation of political integration with the achievement of national identity or a value consensus. He said that these psychological phenomena are no doubt important to the "making whole" that integration connotes, but they are dependent aspects insofar as the fundamental political process is concerned (Wood 1984: 68). Wood further pointer out that Verba and Ake wrongly suggest that integration implies a homogenisation of political values, conformity of political purposes. Etzioni also views that homogeneity of political values among subunits does not guarantee political integration anymore than heterogeneity precludes it (Etzioni, 1965 25-27). Political integration cannot be assessed by measuring sameness. Rather, some measure of political interaction and exchange among the integrating units must be devised.

Deutsch's communication theory stress on communication among persons, cities, ethnic groups, language communities, and countries. To him the success or failure of political integration depends in part upon the compatibility of autonomous responses as well as ... on the distribution and balance of range of social transaction, and of the streams of experiences to which they give rise (Deutsch 1954: 4). As political integration does not just happen anywhere a core area of "larger, stronger, more politically, administratively, economically, and educationally advanced" political units is usually present to lead the process (Deutsch, *et al*1957: 58). In their study of the North Atlantic area, Deutsch and others found that "mutual compatibility of main values" was an essential condition for both amalgamated and pluralistic security communities. They conclude that political communities occur whenever groups not only exchange a high proportion of communications but also share a superordinate goal and a "we-feeling".

Referring to Deutsch's approach as too broad, Ernst Haas excludes transactional and institutional criteria from his initial formulation, though he considers them as potentially helpful factors (Haas 1966: 20). Haas specifies that integration is a process which takes place in a period of time "between the establishment of common economic rules and the possible emergence of a political entity", and which must consist "of increasing politicisation, of shifting loyalties, of adaptation by the actors to a new process of mutual accommodation" (Haas & Schmitter 1966: 266). Thus, the goal of the political community is "a condition in which specific groups and individuals show more loyalty to their central political institutions than to any other political authority, in a specific period of time and in a definable geographical space" (Haas 1958: 5). Whereas the functional theory of David Mitrany stresses the role of non-political international organisations as promoters of integration whenever experts replace politicians as key actors, Haas refines Mitrany's functionalism by arguing that there is a need for both political and nonpolitical actors, since technical organisations can only expand in number and in scope so long as they have political support (Haas 1964: Chapter 2). According to Haas, political integration is a process where the goal is the eventual formation of a political community.

William Riker, on his work on federalism and coalition formation, propound the "bargain" concept, a tool with which to analyse the exchange of rewards and loyalties between political actors of the core and the periphery (Riker 1964: 42). Political bargains may be public or secret, explicit or undefined, confirmed or anticipated. They may be amicably negotiated or arrived at under stress. In integrational terms, the bargains forge new links among hitherto separate units, and facilitate the building of new loyalties to a larger system. The term "counterbargain" implies competition among bargain-offers and alternative integrational formulas. The later may appear at the onset of the integrational process or at the later stage if, in the view of at least one bargainer, the initial bargain has been debased or broken. Marxist conceive successful political integration as a method of state-building has performed two critical state functions: provision of the political infrastructure for the expansion of productive forces in protocapitalist and capitalist societies; and an appropriate means for legitimating the power necessary to maintain the social relations integral to these societies (Cocks1980: 4).

The bulk of integration theorists have dealt with only the contemporary world. They argue at some length about the appropriate definition of their dependent variable, whether there is more or less integration, how one is to measure it, whether different dimensions of integration change at different speeds, and whether some measures are better predictors of the future of the phenomenon than others. Michael Haas has summarised the objectives of the various approaches as an: attempt to discern preconditions for the achievement of higher levels of integration, variables that account for the maintenance of existing levels of integration, and factors that promote increases from present to future levels of integration. Key variables in all three research avenues, when reversed, may tell us about factors accounting for backsliding in integration (Haas1958).

According to Ernst Haas, integration theories are "becoming obsolete because they are not designed to address the most pressing and important problems on the global agenda of policy" (Haas 1976: 178). Rapid changes in technology and communications have thrown the process of integration itself into doubt. Growing international interdependence has created a turbulent world with crucial problems whose solutions are international rather than regional, global rather than European (Haas1975: 18-20).

## POLITICAL INTEGRATION IN ASIA AND AFRICA

Most of the nation-states in Asia and Africa had been under colonial subjugation. In the post-independence years these countries inherited a vast array of problems which needs to be tackled and among one of them which needs to be solved at the outset was the problem of political integration. These countries also inherited from the colonial rule certain features of administrative and legal system, forms of government and fixed territory, which help in their efforts to build their state and nation.

Several approaches to the problem of political integration were followed in Asia and Africa. One of them is avoiding the problem altogether by retaining the essential "steel frame" feature of colonialism - open or disguised (Coleman 1955: 46). This process has been followed in the Belgian and Portuguese territories. A similar result has been achieved in federation of Rhodesia and Nyasaland by means of the wide devolution of power from imperial government in the United Kingdom to the European settlers in Africa. Another approach is found in the role played by powerful political leaders, nationalist movements and political parties, and territorial political institutions, as an instruments and new modes of integration. Charismatic leadership exercised by Kwame Nkrumah, Jawaharlal Nehru, Mahatma Gandhi, Sardar Vallabhai Patel, etc. were a factor in the successful transition from a British colony to a stable parliamentary democracy. The political movements of the Indian National Congress, Northern Rhodesia National Congress, Sierra Lone People's Party, etc. have been instrumental in enlarging the scale of political activity. Moreover, territorial assemblies and legislatures, centralised bureaucracies, and other territory-wide institutions have been structures that have fostered, indeed, forced progressive integration.

Common language, which is the one of the most important factors favouring political integration, is absent in most of the countries of Asia and

Africa. Linguistic regionalism remains a formidable obstacle in the path toward integration in Asian countries. Although these countries lack a common language efforts were made to introduce a national language in the interests of integration, and in order to counteract "linguistic regionalism" (Harrison 1956: 143-144). There are instances of the introduction of English as a second language in some countries of Southeast Asia. Language as a key factor in the integration of Southeast Asian societies naturally features prominently in educational policies, which are themselves virtually concerned with integration-political, social and cultural.

The impact of British conquest and occupation has resulted in bringing into the open the issue of minorities where it has "left a difficult legacy by accentuating the distinctions and differences between various groups". They also "left a valid tradition of effective political hegemony with control" from the centre of administration and "a sketchy but uniform system of statewide education and modern communications network which ultimately should prove to outweight the difficulties they created and left" (Thet 1956: 161-162).

## The Indian Experience

The British rule significantly brought about an enduring political consolidation in India. The effect of the British rule, plus modern innovations in transport and communications, in promoting a working sense of Indian unity was of vital importance. The maintenance of law and order, administrative unity, the introduction of a common body of social and political concepts and values, the appearance of English as a lingua franca, fiscal and economic integration, all served to link together the disparate elements which made up the Indian society as did the common national struggle against British rule (Emerson 1960:12).

The imminent withdrawal of the British from India after the end of the Second World War led to the appearance of different plans for autonomy by most of the princely states. On the eve of British withdrawal from India two forces operated: pan-Indian nationalism seeking an integrated independent India, and the separatists seeking its independent existence. At first, the Indian National Congress leaders were not against giving the Right to Self-determination and even the Right to Secession to the aggrieved components and agreed to prepare a federal constitution with residuary power vested in the units. However, alarmed by the rising number of claims the Congress did not agree to any proposal by any unit to secede from the Indian Union. Even though the Congress conjured that it cannot think in terms of compelling the people in any territorial unit to remain in the Indian Union against their will, the post-independent India wanted to inherit as much as the British India.

With the imminent lapse of paramountcy, a number of schemes were envisaged, demanding sovereign homelands, responsible governments, a state within the Indian union and threat to join Pakistan or Burma. The task of the new government was to prevent the disintegrative forces, integrate them with the mainland and protect the territory handled to them by the British. A States Department was created which was headed by Sardar Vallabhai Patel and V.P. Menon as secretary, to carry out the arduous task of integrating the princely states and all dissident groups. Sardar Patel said that: "Our first task was to prevent the balkanisation of the country and to stop any possible inveiglement of the States by Pakistan was to bring the States into some form of organic relationship with the Centre" (quoted in Menon 1956: 485).

British India was granted independence on August 15, 1947 as the separate dominions of India and Pakistan. The British Government dissolved its treaty relations with more than six hunderd princely states, which means that, "The rights of the States which flew from their relationship to the crown will no longer exist and that all rights surrendered by states to the paramount power will return to the states" (Menon 1956: 83). The vaccum which arises from the lapse of political arrangements between the States and the Crown was to be filled in either with the states entering into federal relationship with succeeding Government or Governments in British India or enter into particular political arrangements with or without them. The states were given freedom whether to associate with India or Pakistan or to stand alone. The British Government did not put any pressure on the states in deciding which dominion they desire to accede. Most of the states acceded to India, and a few to Pakistan. Hyderabad and Manipur opted for independence, although the armed intervention of India brought Hyderabad into the Indian Union and the coerced tactics led Meitei Maharaja into signing a merger agreement with India.

The integration of Indian states took place in two phases, with a skilful combination of baits and threats of mass pressure in both. The primary "bait offered was that of very generous privy purses, while some princes were also made into Governors or Rajpramukhs" (Sarkar 1983: 451). One of the most difficult in the process of integration was that of the integration of states with the neighbouring provinces or into new units. By August 15, almost all states has agreed to sign an Instrument of Accession with India acknowledging central authority over the three areas of defence, external affairs and communications. The gaining of independence was "a culmination of long-drawn, multi-stream process of transformation, unification and integration of the Indian people into one political entity" (Nag 1999: 74). By January 26, 1950 when the Constitution of Indian Republic came into force all states and outlying areas were fully integrated.

Many princely states were merged with the neighbouring Governors' provinces of British India to form Part A states under the 1950 Constitution. A large number of princely states which were governed by a rajpramukh were combined into "states union"; and together with the three biggest principalities, Hyderabad, Jammu and Kashmir and Mysore, they acquired a separate existence as Part B states for a while. For strategic and other reasons, former Chief Commissioners' Provinces and other centrally administered areas, except Andaman and Nicobar Islands, were Part C states. The Part C states were Ajmer-Merwara, Bhopal, Bilaspur, Coorg, Delhi, Kutch, Himachal Pradesh, Manipur, and Tripura. With linguistic reorganisation the distinctions between Part A, B, and C states ended, and a complex recombination of ex-princely and ex-British territory was carried out.

Therefore, the ultimate geographical, political and economic integration of India was achieved. Great credit can be given to Sardar Patel for the rapid integration of Indian states. The Indian nationalism of the freedom struggle was responsible for the integration of people belonging to different religion, languages, and cultures into a single political entity.

## Conclusion

The mode of political integration in India involved negotiations, promises, baits and even force. In the formation of a new and sovereign India, the integration of more than six hunderd princely states and other loosely administered areas enjoying varying degrees of autonomy, was a great challenge to the new government and it pose serious obstacle to the unity, cohesion and stability. While some princely states willingly joined the union, most of them made a stiff opposition to the integration process. As hypothesised by Claude Ake, in most of the process the Indian state adopted an authoritarian approach in integrating the Northeastern states, where different techniques was used to coerce the constituent units to come to terms.

In the context of the history of political integration in Northeast India, it is found that the integration with the Indian union politically remained a serious issue of concern for the people. These attempts at assimilation of the region and its people with the Indian mainstream have resulted in resentments amongst different ethnic communities. Some areas like Manipur and Naga Hills refused to merge with India and expressed desire for withdrawal from the Union. The manner in which the merger was brought about has left a residual bitterness that the insurgent groups successfully tap into. A number of insurgent groups regarded the merger as illegal and unconstitutional, and many among the Manipuri intelligentsia are bitter about the way it was effected (Baruah, 2000). The Meitei and Naga insurgent groups resented the forceful integration of their land and continued their armed struggle. The Kukis in the hill areas of Manipur, who are known to have fought the British (1917-1919) to secure their freedom, too resented the forceful integration of their land.

In previously separate principalities like Manipur, political integration should involve overcoming parochial loyalties and residual loyalties (Wood 1984: 66); however the transitional government's approach failed to overcome these loyalties. As in the case of Gujarat, political integration in stages could have been adopted in Nagaland so as to permit the time for adjustment to the constraints and opportunities to the new system and develop a homogeneous political culture. The late realisation that such integrationist policy was erroneous has led the government to concede autonomy demands of ethnic groups, which led to creation of separate states. However the formation of new states had a cascading affect leading to new demands from other smaller ethnic groups vying different levels of autonomy.

Since the eve of India's independence smaller ethnic groups in the hills of Northeast India too asserted their desire for separated administrative units. The Kukis were fully aware of the various aspects of the vexing problems of the hills and the valley, and therefore pledge to be under Manipur if only conditions are satisfactory. After independence the Kuki National Assembly (KNA) demanded a separate state for the Kukis within India. In this regard the KNA submitted several memoranda to the Central Government. The dormant political demands were revived as an insurgent movement in the late 1980s due to the intolerable atrocities committed by the Naga rebels and what the Kukis termed it as the policy of "ethnic cleansing".

# 4

# Patel and Freedom Struggle

## SUPPRESSION OF THE MOVEMENT

### Picketing in Front of Medical School at Bangalore

The British, already alarmed by the advance of the Japanese army to the India/Burma border, responded the next day by imprisoning Gandhi at the Aga Khan Palace in Pune. All the members of the Congress Party's Working Committee (national leadership) were arrested and imprisoned at the Ahmednagar Fort.

Due to the arrest of major leaders, a young and till then relatively unknown Aruna Asaf Ali presided over the AICC session on August 9 and hoisted the flag. Later, the Congress party was banned. These actions only created sympathy for the cause among the population. Despite lack of direct leadership, large scale protests and demonstrations were held all over the country. Workers remained absent *en masse* and strikes were called. However, not all the demonstrations were peaceful. At some places bombs exploded, government buildings were set on fire, electricity was cut, and transport and communication lines were severed.

The British swiftly responded by mass detentions. A total over 100,000 arrests were made nationwide, mass fines were levied, and demonstrators were subjected to public flogging. Hundreds of resisters and innocent people were killed in police and army firings. Many national leaders went underground and continued their struggle by broadcasting messages over clandestine radio stations, distributing pamphlets, and establishing parallel governments. The British sense of crisis was strong enough that a battleship was specifically set aside to take Gandhi and the Congress leaders out of India, possibly to South Africa or Yemen, but such a step was ultimately not taken out of fear of intensifying the revolt.

The entire Congress leadership was cut off from the rest of the world for over three years. Gandhi's wife Kasturbai Gandhi and his personal secretary Mahadev Desai died in a short space of months, and Gandhi's own health was failing. Despite this, Gandhi went on a 21-day fast and maintained a superhuman resolve to continuous resistance. Although the British released Gandhi on account of his failing health in 1944, Gandhi kept up the resistance, demanding the complete release of the Congress leadership.

By early 1944, India was mostly peaceful again, while the entire Congress leadership was incarcerated. A sense that the movement had failed depressed many nationalists, while Jinnah and the Muslim League, as well as Congress opponents like the Communists and Hindu extremists, sought to gain political mileage, criticizing Gandhi and the Congress Party.

## Contributions towards Indian Independence

The successes and failures of the Movement are debated. Some historians claim it failed. By March 1943, the movement had petered out. Even the Congress, at the time saw it as failure. Analysis of the campaign obtained by Military Intelligence in 1943 came to the conclusion that it had failed in the aim of paralysing the government. It did however cause enough trouble and panic among the War administration for General Lockhart to describe India as an "Occupied and hostile country." However, much as it might have disconcerted the Raj, the movement may be deemed to have ultimately failed to bring the Raj to its knees and the negotiating table for immediate transfer of power, as it aimed to. It came to all but a close within five months of its inception, and was nowhere near its grandiose aim of toppling the Raj. The primary underlying reason, it seems, was the loyalty of the army, even where the local and native police came out in sympathy. This certainly, was also the view of the British Prime Minister at the time of transfer of power, Clement Atlee. Atlee deemed the contribution of *Quit India* as minimal, ascribing stupendous importance to the revolts and growing dissatisfaction among Royal Indian Armed Forces during and after the war as the driving force behind Britain's decision to leave India.

Some Indian historians, however, argue that, in fact, the movement had succeeded. In support of the latter view, without doubt, the war had sapped a lot of the economic, political and military life-blood of the Empire. Also, although at the national level the ability to galvanize rebellion was limited, the movement is notable for regional success especially at Satara, Talcher, and Midnapore. In Tamluk and Contai subdivisions of Midnapore, the local populace were successful in establishing parallel governments, which continued to function, until Gandhi personally requested the leaders to disband in 1944.

At the time, from intelligence reports, the Azad Hind Government under Netaji Subhash Bose in Berlin deemed these an early indication of success of their strategy of fomenting public rebellion.

It is uncertain whether it was ultimately the Quit India Movement or unrest in the British Indian Armed Forces that allowed the post-War Labour government to negotiate a swift transfer or power to India after WWII. However, what is certain is that a population of millions had been motivated as it never had before to claim independence as a non-negotiable goal, and every act of defiance and rebellion only reinforced the nationalist sentiment. In addition, the British people and the British Army seemed unwilling to back a policy of repression in India and other parts of the Empire even as their own country lay shattered by the war's ravages.The INA trials in 1945, the resulting militant movements, and the Bombay mutiny had already shaken the confidence of British rule in India. By early 1946, all political prisoners had been released and Britain adopted a political dialogue with the Indian National Congress for the eventual transfer of power. On August 15, 1947, this transfer was complete, and the states of India and Pakistan came into being.

A young, new generation responded to Gandhi's call. Indians who lived through *Quit India* came to form the first generation of independent Indians-whose trials and tribulations may be accepted to have sown the seeds of establishment of the strongest enduring tradition of democracy and freedom in post-colonial Africa and Asia-which, when seen in the light of the torrid times of Partition of India, can be termed one of the greatest examples of prudence of humanity. Quit India Movement, 1942 an important event of the Indian freedom struggle, was the outcome of a compound of anti-white fury. The cripps mission, with its vague proposals of a post-war Dominion Status for India, a constitution making body elected by provincial legislatures and the native states, provincial opt out clause, the immediate participation of Indian leaders in war effort but the retention of the control of Indian defence by the British, satisfied none and threatened to Balkanise the Indian subcontinent.

The retreat of the British from Malay, Burma and Singapore, leaving their dependants to fend for themselves, the indescribable plight of the Indians trekking back home from these places, the racial ill-treatment meted out to Indians by white soldiers stationed here and there in India, the 'scorched earth' policy pursued by the British in Bengal to resist probable Japanese invasion which resulted in the commandeering of all means of communicating, war-time price rise, black-marketeering and profiteering-all these contributed to the creation of an anti-white fury. Above all, there was the attempt of the

British bureaucracy right from the outbreak of the war for a wholesale crackdown on the Congress on the pattern of 1932.

The early morning round up of Congress leaders on 9 August 'unleashed an unprecedented and country-wide wave of mass fury'. And the wave engulfed the Bengal cities, particularly the bigger ones. There were three broad phases of the movement. The first was predominantly urban and included *hartals*, strikes and clashes with the police and army in most major cities. All these were massive and violent but quickly suppressed.

The second phase of the movement started from the middle of August. Militant students fanned out from different centres, destroying communications and leading peasant rebellion in Northern and Western Bihar, Eastern UP, Midnapore in Bengal, and pockets in Maharastra, Karnataka and Orissa. A number of short-lived local 'national governments' were also set up.

The third phase of the movements started from about the end of September and was characterised by terrorist activities, sabotage and guerrilla warfare by educated youths and peasant squads. Parallel national governments functioned at Tamluk in Midnapore, Satara in Maharasfra, and Talcher in Orissa. All the three phases of the movement were crushed by brutal atrocities including the use of machine guns from the air.

A good deal of controversy exists about the nature of the movement-whether it was a 'spontaneous revolution' or an 'organised rebellion'. The famous 'Quit India' resolution passed by the Bombay session of the AICC on 8 August 42 followed up its call for 'mass struggle on non violent lines on the widest possible scale', 'inevitably' under Gandhi, with the significant rider that if the Congress leadership was removed by arrest, every Indian who desires freedom and strives for it must be his own guide...'. The Wardha working committee resolution of 14 July had also introduced an unusual note of social radicalism-'the princes', '*jagirdars*', 'zamindars' and propertied and moneyed classes derive their wealth and property from the workers in the fields and factories and elsewhere, to whom eventually power and authority must belong.

At the crucial working committee session of 27 April-1 May, Gandhi's hard-line was backed by a combination of Right-wingers like Patel, Rajendra Prasad and Kripalni and the socialists like Achyut Patwardhan and Narendra Dev. Jawaharlal was initially hesitant, but ultimately joined the queue and only the Communists opposed the Quit India resolution.

During and after the Quit India upsurge, the British in documents like Tottenhams' Report painted the whole outburst as a 'deliberate fifth columnist conspiracy', intending to strengthen the Axis powers. This interpretation not only ignored the consistent anti-fascist international stance of the Congress throughout the 1930s, but also made a historical travesty of the facts that being arrested in the early morning of 9 August the Congress leaders could hardly lead the outburst and that the Quit India resolution was also remarkably vague about the details of the coming movement. Far from ruling out further negotiations, the whole thing may conceivably have been an exercise in brinkmanship and a bargaining counter which was followed by an explosion only because the British had decided on a policy of wholesale repression. Despite strenuous efforts, the British failed to establish their case that the Congress before 9 August had really planned a violent rebellion.

The movement was, in reality 'elemental and largely spontaneous'. It was sparked off by a variety of factors and of an expectation that British rule was coming to an end. Bureaucratic high-handedness and provocation worsened the situation. Financial losses incurred in Malay and Burma induced sections of Indian business community to give some covert support to a movement (even if violent) for a short while.

The real picture was that the removal of established leaders left younger and more militant cadres to their own initiative and gave greater scope to pressure from below. Amery's slander that the Congress had planned attacks on communications and sabotage boomeranged with a vengeance, for many believed that this really had been the Working Committee's plan. In any case, in a primary hegemonic struggle as the Indian National Movement was, preparedness for struggle cannot be measured by the volume of immediate organisational activity but by the degree of hegemonic influence that the movement has acquired over the people.

The participation of labour was short-lived and limited but there was certainly considerable covert upper-class and even Indian high official support to secret nationalist activities in 1942. Such support enabled activists to set up a fairly effective illegal apparatus, including even a secret radio station under Usha Mehta for three months in Bombay. Unlike in the Civil Disobedience days, middle class students were very much in the forefront in 1942, whether in urban clashes, as organisers of sabotage, or as motivators of present rebellion. What made the movement so formidable, however, was the massive upsurge of the peasantry in certain areas, particularly in Bihar.

Indeed, that 1942 clearly surpassed all previous Congress led movements in its level of anti-British radicalism possibly reduced internal class tensions and social radiation. The characteristic feature of this movement was that private property was less attacked and even no-revenue was not as comprehensive as in 1930-34.

The paradox why the people turned violent when the Congress insisted on nonviolence may be solved in the following manner. In the struggle there were many who refused to use on sanction violent means and confined themselves to the traditional weaponry of the Congress. But many of those, including many staunch Gandhians, who used 'violent means' in 1942 felt that the peculiar circumstances warranted their use. Many maintained that the cutting of telegraph wires and the blowing up of bridges were all right as long as human life was not taken but others admitted that they could not square the violence they used, with their belief in nonviolence, although they did resort to it in most trying circumstances and in self-defence.

Gandhi refused to condemn the violence of the people because he saw it as a reaction to the much bigger violence being perpetrated on the state. It is held that Gandhi's major objection to violence was that its use prevented mass participation in a movement. For in 1942, Gandhi had come round to the view that mass participation would not be restricted as a result of isolated violence. Gandhi had come to realise that the kind of nonviolence he had wanted his country men to inculcate and practise, could not be achieved and so towards the end of his career he had kept some amount of space for the participants to follow their own line of action.

His patience had been dragged to such extremes that he felt that even at the cost of some risks, he should ask his people to resist slavery. Although Gandhi was now in an unusually militant mood, at no stage was he prepared to forsake his faith in nonviolence. He would have liked the movement to be nonviolent but was prepared to run the risk of unrestricted mass action even if that meant civil war. He thus said, 'Let them entrust India to God or, in modem parlance, to anarchy'.

The Quit India movement was thus not a controlled volunteer movement like Gandhi's previous movements of 1920-22 and 1930-34. It was not conceived as a traditional *Satyagraha*. It was to be a 'fight to the finish', an 'open rebellion', 'short and swift' which could very well plunge the country into a 'conflagration'. Foreign domination was to be ended whatever the cost.

Scholars have analysed the questions of 'spontaneity' and 'preparedness' in terms of action and reaction. The arrest of the leaders made the people aghast and took them completely unaware. Strikes and demonstrations followed and 'the very size of the crowds made the Government nervous'. Tension bred tension and led to confrontation. The people had no guidance, the leaders were either behind the bars or underground.

Passions were ranging high. Individuals and groups interpreted the situation to the best of their understanding and acted, as they thought best.

The continuing police repression and 'Ordinance Raj' further inflamed the feelings of the people. There had been no Congress call for civil disobedience. 'Therefore what started as individual acts of angry defiance, soon swelled into a movement, and the movement into a revolt'.

The gravity and extent of the Quit India movement by LINLITHGOW's own admission may be compared to those of the Revolt of 1857. It failed because an unarmed people without leaders and proper organisation could not stand for long before the mighty strength of an imperial government in power.

Yet, the significance of the great movement lay in the fact that it placed the demand for independence on the immediate agenda of the national movement. After Quit India, there could be no turning back. Any future negotiations with the British government could only be on the manner of transfer of power. Independence was no longer a matter of bargain and this became amply clear after the war.

## FARMERS' MOVEMENTS IN INDIA

The farmers in India had to undergo great struggle in all the states to stop exploitation by the Jagirdars and Zamindars. Some of the movements were successful, but others failed. The farmer movements in 1907 under the leadership of Sardar Ajit Singh and in 1921 under Sardar Vallabhbhai Patel were successes, but others, such as the revolts in Chauri Chaura, Avadh and Mopla, were great losses.

At the global level the French Revolution had changed the course of history, as it was the working class which became the vanguard of revolution in Europe. During the first half of the 20th century, national liberation struggles started against colonisation. In these colonies, very little industry was present and their working class, if it existed at all, was still in infancy, making the impetus for these rebellions have to come from somewhere else. It was Mao's peasant revolution in China which became a catalyst for national liberation movements in many colonies, including India.

It was in Punjab that India's first farmers' movement emerged. The role played by Ghadar party, led by Raja Mahendra Pratap, in the political awakening of India was an important step. The Sikhs of Punjab were the first to migrate to the United States and Canada in the 19th century. They financed and helped the formation of Ghadar party which when gave the call to Indians abroad to return home and fight British imperialism, had its call immediately heeded to. The majority of those who did return, 8000 of them comprised Punjab's Sikhs. Despite its apparent failure, the Ghadar Movement was to have a powerful impact on Punjab politics and especially on the peasants. It established a tradition of militant and secular anti-imperialism, enriched in subsequent years by social radicalism, which was to continue to inspire subsequent generations.

The peasant conferences were held in Lahore, Faisalabad, Lyallpur and other places of West Punjab—the most famous of them being 1938-39 Long Morcha in Lahore when peasants from all over Punjab courted arrests for nine months in front of the assembly building.

The slogan of *Pagri Sambhal O jatta* (Hold your head high, O peasant) was first raised at a mass gathering in Lyallpur in 1907. Ten Thousand people—the Hindus, the Muslims and the Sikhs alike—attended this gathering.

## Bardoli Satyagraha

Bardoli Satyagraha of 1925 in the state of Gujarat, India during the British Raj was a major episode of civil disobedience and revolt in the Indian Independence Movement. In 1925, the taluka of Bardoli in Gujarat suffered from floods and famine, which hurt the crop produce, leaving farmers facing great financial troubles. However, the Government of the Bombay Presidency had raised the tax rate by 30% that year, and despite petitions from civic groups, refused to cancel the rise in face of the calamities. The situation for the farmers was grave enough, that they barely had enough property and crops to pay-off the tax, let alone for feeding themselves afterwards.

The Gujarati activists Narhari Parikh, Ravi Shankar Vyas and Mohanlal Pandya talked to village chieftains and farmers, and solicited the help of Gujarat's most prominent freedom fighter, Vallabhbhai Patel. Patel had previously guided Gujarat's farmers during the Kheda struggle, and had served recently as Ahmedabad's municipal president. He was widely respected by common Gujaratis across the state. Patel and Gandhi decided that the struggle be left entirely to the people of Bardoli taluka.

Governor of Bombay ignored the request made by Patel to reduce taxes but reciprocated by announcing the date of collection. Patel instructed all the farmers of Bardoli taluka to refuse payment of their taxes. Aided by Parikh, Vyas and Pandya, he divided Bardoli into several zones-each with a leader and volunteers specifically assigned. Patel also placed some Gujarati activists close to the government, to act as informers on the movements of government officials. Patel instructed the farmers to remain completely nonviolent, and not respond physically to any incitements or aggressive actions from officials. He reassured them that the struggle would not end until not only the cancellation of all taxes for the year, but also when all the seized property and lands were returned to rightful owners.

The Government declared that it would crush the revolt. Along with tax inspectors, bands of Pathans were gathered from northwest India to forcibly seize the property of the villagers and terrorize them. The Pathans and the men of the collectors forced themselves into the houses, took all property, including cattle. The government began to auction the houses and the lands. But not a single man from Gujarat or anywhere else in India came forward to buy them. Patel had appointed volunteers in every village to keep watch. As soon as he sighted the officials who were coming to auction the property, the volunteer would sound his bugle. The farmers would leave the village and hide in the jungles. The officials would find the entire village empty. They could never find out who owned a particular house.

Members of the legislative councils of Bombay and across India were angered by the terrible treatment of the protesting farmers. Indian members resigned their offices, and expressed open support of the farmers. Even many in the Raj's offices heavily criticized the Government. In 1928, an agreement was finally brokered by a Parsi member of the Bombay government. The Government agreed to restore the confiscated lands and properties, as well as cancel revenue payment not only for the year, but cancel the 30% raise until after the succeeding year.

While Patel credited Gandhi's teachings and the farmers' undying resolve, people across the nation recognized his vital leadership. Gandhi and his fellow satyagrahis called him *Sardar* for the first time, which in Gujarati and most Indian languages means *Chief* or *Leader*. It was after Bardoli, that Sardar Patel became one of India's most important leaders.

## Farmer Movements in Rajasthan

Rajasthan is known as the land of kings and palaces and whose history is replete with encomium of their kings, the land known for "Sati", the land known for its vast tracts of deserts was witness to a history in making, the successful agitation of farmers and peasants for their right to livelihood.

The twenty-two princely states of erstwhile Rajputana state did not form a common political collectivity which can be termed as a unified political action model. Each state had its own territorial area, which was exclusive politically in that it had its separate administration nag and army. Each state retained its cultural and linguistic distinctiveness. Political authority varied from ruler to ruler depending upon the terms of contract or covenant with the paramount power dating back to the period of subsidiary alliance of Lord Wellesley. Obviously in a state like this, the freedom movement was bound to be divided and segmented, depending upon the degree of unity and cohesiveness among political players in each state. The two states of Jaipur and Jodhpur provided differential patterns of political movements. Justice Kan Singh Parihar, the retired Judge of High Court of Rajasthan, has written about exploitation of farmers by Jagirdars prior to Independence as under:

> *"Every thing that the Kisan had, never treated as his own. In Jagir areas all cultivators were really landless. There was no tenancy law and one could be thrown away from the land one cultivated at the pleasure of Jagirdar, his "malik". In most of the Jagirs a Jagirdar would in the first instance be taking fifty percent of the produce. This would be taken by actual division of the produce on the thrashing floor or by appraisal of the standing crop (*kunta*). Then over and above the share of the produce the Kisan had to pay numerous "lags" or cesses.*
>
> *Together with the share of the produce known as "Hasil" these cesses meant that the Kisans had to part with more than eighty percent of their produce. The findings of the Sukhdeonarain Committee in the years 1940-42 bear this out. If a Kisan had to marry his daughter he had to pay "Chavri Lag", if he held a dinner then a "Kansa Lag"; if members of the family separated then "Dhunwa Lag" and so on. If the Jagirdar had a guest then fodder for his mount had to be supplied. Then there was "begar" that is forced labour, for tilling the personal lands of the Jagirdar. The homestead in which the Kisan lived in the Abadi had to be vacated in case he ceased cultivating the land. He could not alienate the plot to anyone."*

Shri Kan Singh Parihar played a great role in drafting and enactment of Marwar Tenancy Act of 1949 and Marwar Land Revenue Act of 1949. Shri Parihar's idea of fixing all tenants in cultivatory possession as Khatedars thus making all of them almost the proprietors of all their fields, wells etc. without paying any premium or compensation and further being relieved from paying any lag bag (Cesses) etc., impacted these documents. This Marwar Tenancy Act of 1949 and Marwar Land Revenue Act of 1949 became a role model for the Rajasthan Assembly in 1955 and similar laws were passed based on these Acts, thus greatly benefiting the farmers of Rajasthan.

## Shekhawati Farmers' Movement

The farmers of the Sekhawati region are considered to be the most advanced in the state of Rajasthan. The Shekhawati region has the highest literacy in the state. The most dominating farmer community in the rural areas of Shekhawati is Jat. The Jats are politically and economically very sound. The major land holdings in the present times are with Jats. Then comes the Rajput community who were the jagirdars before independence. The farmers of the region have done great struggle to come to the present status.

Before independence the conditions of the farmers were worst. The farmers of the Shekhawati region were exploited and oppressed by the Jagirdars during British Raj. They were deprived of fundamental rights. They were given inhuman treatment when the Jagirdars did not get cesses known as *lag* (tax) or *begar* (unpaid work) in time, they were given hard punishments and their crop used to be destroyed. There were 37 kinds of *begars* (work without pay) prevalent in Shekhawati. A newly married bride was forced to go first to Jagirdar.

The Shekhawati Jat farmers' movement had its genesis in the Jat Praja Pati Maha-Yagna a socio-religious festival held in January, 1934. It lasted ten days and was the biggest of its kind in Rajputana. It facilitated a widespread involvement of Jats in a community festival. Each Jat household attending it was to contribute some cash and an unspecified quantity of ghee. A total of two hundred maunds of ghee were used in the sacrificial flame. The function concluded with a triumphal elephant ride hitherto prohibited by the rules of Sikar Thikana. The success of this movement encouraged the Jats to hold more meetings on local levels and print literature to glorify Jat history.

The Yagna became a dominant symbol of folklore which glorified it as the beginning of an anti-feudal struggle. The peasants demanded remissions in taxes and finally a Jat-Sikar Thikana Agreement was signed on August 23, 1934, by which the Thikana authorities conceded to abolish various lags (taxes) and agreed to provide for a mobile dispensary. The following year, the Kisan Sabha formally came into existence and under its aegis the famous Sikar Andolan of 1935 was launched. With outside mediation efforts of Jamnalal Bajaj, Sir Chhotu Ram-a renowned Jat leader of Punjab and Ratan Singh of All India Jat Mahasabha, a settlement was arrived at and the Jats were promised remissions of rent, abolition of internal cesses and an introduction of fixed rent tenure. The Jats were also promised equal opportunities in Thikana administration and were permitted to ride elephants and horses and to construct schools for their children.

The formation of a Jat Kisan Panchayat was officially sanctioned and the right to agitate for redressal of grievances in non-Khalsa areas was conceded. Much however, could not be made out of these agreements for two reasons. First, the subordinate Thikanedars of Sikar did not fully cooperate with Sikar authorities to ensure compliance with the terms of these agreements. Secondly, the beginning of settlement operations and reform of revenue administration was a time-consuming process which entailed enormous delay. This was interpreted by the Jats as a breach of agreement and hence, they indulged in acts of disorder and violence, which were perceived by Thikana authorities as signs of bad faith. In the meanwhile two unsavoury incidents led to a termination of agreements. The first, occurred at Khudi village, where the sight of Jat bridegroom riding a horse incensed the local Rajputs and the two sides readied themselves for an armed combat. The state authorities asked the two parties to disperse but the Jats refused. The state police charged and in the melee that followed, several people were injured. The second incident took place at Kudan village, where about one hundred armed Jats attacked Sikar revenue officials. The police fired upon the armed mob, which resulted in several casualties and injuries. A total of 104 Jats were arrested.

Farmers of the Shekhawati, mainly the Jats, united against oppression of Jagirdars by forming 'Sikar Jat-Kisan-Panchayat' and stopped giving "lags" or cesses to the Jagirdards. The 'Jaipur Praja-Mandal' also supported the Shekhawati farmers' movement against abolition of Jagirdari system. The leaders of 'Bijoria-Kisan-Movement' of 1922, 1931, and 1932 supported the movement of Shekhawati farmers. The Jagirdars tried to suppress the movement in many ways. Many farmers were killed and a large number were sent to jail. A Jat farmer was beaten to death in the market of Sikar town; his dead body was thrown and insulted. This movement got support from famous Kisan leaders like, Baldev Ram Mirdha, Nathuram Mirdha and Kumbharam Arya. After a long struggle the farmers got rid of oppression and got the ownership right over the land they were cultivating.

The leading Jat farmers of Shekhawati region, who played important role in the movement for abolition of the Jagirdari system, were:

- Sardar Har Lal Singh, Mandasi
- Iswar Singh Bhamu Bhairupura,
- Hari Singh Burdak and Hardeva Palthana,
- Prithvi Singh Gothra,
- Ganeshram Kudan,
- Panne Singh Bataranau,
- Goru Singh Katrathal,
- Deva Singh Bochalya,
- Chandrabhan Singh,
- Hardev Singh Nehra Harsawa.

Shekhawati farmers' movement against abolition of Jagirs got great support from outside Kisan leaders like Sir Chhotu Ram from Haryana, Kunwar Ratan Singh and Thakur Deshraj from Bharatpur, Kunwar Hukum Singh from Aangai.

## Marwar Farmers' Movement

The farmers of the Marwar region are considered to be the most simple in the state of Rajasthan. The most dominating farmer community in the rural areas of Marwar is Jat. The Jats are politically and economically very sound. The major land holdings in the present times are with Jats.

Though the position of *Kisan* (farmer) in what was *Khalsa* (under the direct control of the state) was better in comparison to a Kisan of the Jagir areas, he was only a little above a beast of burden. In Jagir areas of Marwar state before independence all cultivators were really landless. There was no tenancy Law and one could be thrown away from the land one cultivated at the pleasure of Jagirdar, his "malik".

In most of the Jagirs a Jagirdar would in the first instance be taking fifty percent of the produce. This would be taken by actual division of the produce on the thrashing floor or by appraisal of the standing crop (*kunta*). The latter method proved at times more onerous as the appraisal depended on the whims of the *Kamdar*.

Then over and above the share of the produce the farmer had to pay numerous "lags" or cesses. There were 64 kinds of *begars* (work without pay) prevalent in Marwar. Then the bigger Jagirdars had judicial powers including magisterial powers. Further they had their own police force besides the revenue staff. This enabled them to keep their stronghold on the farmers. Over and above this policy of divide and rule was fully practiced. By offering the temptation of giving better land for cultivation one farmer would be set against another. There were no schools worth the name in rural areas and the masses were steeped in ignorance.

The oppression of the public by traditional Samantas (chiefs) and Jagirdars (feudatories) of Marwar state made their life difficult, which led to a class war. In urban areas, Jaynarayan Vyas started agitation against oppression, under the banner of "Marwar Lok Parishad" founded on 16th May 1938. This movement was supported by National Congress. The persons who played important role in "Marwar Lok Parishad" were: Shiv Dayal Dave and Jorawar Singh Oswal of Nagaur, Rajpurohit Manji Jagarwal of (Bagra, Jalore), Kishanlal Sahu, Manak Chand Konari and Sari Mal of Kuchaman City, Tulsiram of Didwana, Srikishan Pandit of Kolia and Sukhdev Dipankar of Ladnu.

Rural masses of Marwar were united by Kisan Kesari-Baldev Ram Mirdha under the banner of "Marwar Kisan Sabha" founded in 1940. After the formation of Rajasthan, Baldev Ram Mirdha who had by then retired from Government service formed the "Rajathan Kisan Sabha" and unified the *Kisans* of Rajasthan under its banner.

He was its first president. Since the broad objectives of the *Kisan Sabha* and the congress were identical the congress leaders approached Baldev Ram Mirdha to unite the Rajasthan *Kisan Sabha* with the Congress. Baldev Ram Mirdha was a visionary and he realized that the two could not and should not remain separate. Therefore, he just made one demand from the national leaders that the Jagirs be abolished forthwith in Rajasthan. This was agreed to by the Congress high command with the result that the Jagirs were soon abolished. A tenancy law was passed and the cultivating farmers were made the owners of the land.

## Gharsana Farmers' Movement

The tehsil town of Gharsana and the neighbouring Raola in Sriganganagar district of Rajasthan is currently site of clashes between the police and the farmers agitating for irrigation water. The farmers, and their leaders who led the agitation under the banner of Kisan Mazdoor Vyapari Sangarsh Samiti, were either nursing their injured or in hiding. About 20 injured have been admitted to the Gharsana hospital and the district hospital in Sriganganagar. The authorities said curfew was clamped in Raola as a precautionary measure as in the previous agitation by the farmers on the same issue in October-November 2004 both Raola and Gharsana had witnessed serious violence.

Earlier in October 2004, Defying prohibitory orders, hundreds of farmers had gheraoed the SDM's office at Gharsana town in Sriganganagar district, reviving their agitation for irrigation water after the October 27, police firing which claimed five lives. With a view to appeasing the agitating farmers, the Vasundhara Raje Government ordered the removed of the Divisional Commissioner of the region, Mr Ramavtar Raghuvanshi, and Superintendent of Police, Mr Sunil Dutt, while two officers of the Rajasthan Administrative Service, Mr Indra Singh Rao and Mr Hitesh Kumar, have been placed under suspension. The farmers' agitation led the Government to impose curfew in July 2005 also.

Farmers of Gharsana, at Ganganagar in Rajasthan, are on path of confrontation with the BJP government for the release of water from Pong Dam to the Phase I areas of Indira Gandhi Canal, the lifeline of farmers in the Gharsana-Raola agriculture belt. At a juncture when India is importing wheat from other countries, the state government is dissuading farmers in the region from cultivating wheat during the rabi season. The farmers have been told to sow barley or mustard, rather than wheat, which is a water-intensive crop. The movement has gained momentum with the Kisan Mazdoor Vyapari Sangharsh Samiti, the committee of farmers, labourers and agro-traders of the region deciding to go ahead with sowing wheat. The strife over water has seen the peasants and the state administration clash often in the past three years. Seven farmers were killed and many were injured when police fired at protesters in 2004.

## SUCCESS AND LEGACY

Gandhi's resulting fame spread like fire all over the nation. He had become a defining influence on Indian Nationalism. People in Gujarat still revere Gandhi and Sardar Patel, and their role in the freedom struggle. Gujarat is the most industrialized and progressive state in India today. In Bihar, poverty and social conflict pervades what was the founding of the Satyagraha movement. The Naxalite insurgency is centred around the same age-old problem of class struggle between poor farmers and rich landlords, now involving terrorism.

### The Issue

In the district of Kaira, the crops for the year 1917-18 have, by common admission, proved a partial failure. Under the revenue rules, if the crops are under four annas, the cultivators are entitled to full suspension of the revenue assessment for the year ; if the crops are under six annas, half the amount of assessment is suspended. So far as I am aware, the Government have been pleased to grant full suspension with regard to one village out of nearly 600, and half-suspension in the case of over 103 villages. It is claimed on behalf of the ryots that the suspension is not at all adequate to the actuality. The Government contend that in the vast majority of villages, crops have been over six annas. The only question therefore at issue is, whether the crops have been under four annas or six annas, as the case may be, or over the latter figure.

### Tyrannical Talatis

Government valuation is in the first instance made by the Talatis assisted by the chief men of the villages concerned. As a rule, no check on their figures is considered necessary, for it is only during partial failure of crops that Government valuation of crops may have to be challenged. The Talatis are as a class obsequious, unscrupulous and tyrannical. The chief men are especially selected for their docility. The Talatis, one aim is naturally to collect full assessment as promptly as possible. We sometimes read accounts of assiduous Talatis having been awarded 'pugree' for making full collection. In applying to the Talatis the adjectives I have given, I wish to cast no reflection on them as men. I merely state the fact. The Talatis are not born; they are made; and rent-collectors all the world over have to cultivate a callousness without which they could not do their work to the satisfaction of their masters. It is impossible for me to reproduce the graphic description given by the ryots of the rent-collectors which the Talatis chiefly are.

## Government Estimate Biased

My purpose in dealing with the Talatis is to show that the Government's valuation of the crops is derived in the first instance from the tainted source and is presumably biased against the ryots. As against their valuation, we have the universal testimony of ryots, high and low, some of whom are men of position and considerable wealth, who have a reputation to lose and who have nothing to gain by exaggeration except the odium of Talatis and possibly higher officials. I wish to state at once that behind this movement there is no desire to discredit the Government, or an individual official. The movement is intended to assert the right of the people to be effectively heard in matters concerning themselves.

## Careful Inquiry

It is known to the public that the Hon'ble Mr. G. K. Parekh and Mr. V. J. Patel, invited and assisted by the Gujarat Sabha, carried on investigations, as also Messrs. Deodhar, Joshi and Thakkar of the Servants of India Society. Their investigation was necessarily preliminary and brief and, therefore, confined to a few villages only. But the result of their inquiry went to show that the crops in the majority of cases were under four annas. As their investigation, not being extensive enough, was capable of being challenged, and it was challenged, I undertook a full inquiry with the assistance of over 20 capable, experienced and impartial men of influence and status. I personally visited over 30 villages and met as many men in the villages as I could, inspected in these villages most of the fields belonging to them and after a searching cross-examination of the villagers, came to the conclusion that their crops were under four annas. I found that among the men who surrounded me there were present those who were ready to check exaggerations and wild statements. Men knew what was at stake if they departed from the truth. As to the rabi crops and the still standing kharif crops, I was able by the evidence of my own eyes to check the statements of the agriculturists. The methods adopted by my co-workers were exactly the same. In this manner 400 villages were examined and with but a few exceptions, crops were found to be under four annas, and only in three cases they were found to be over six annas. The method adopted by us was, so far as the kharif crops were concerned, to ascertain the actual yield of the whole of the crops of individual villages and the possible yield of the same village in a normal year. Assuming the truth of the statements made by them, this is admittedly an absolute test, and any other method that would bring about the same result must be rejected as untrue and unscientific; and as I have already remarked, all probability of exaggeration was avoided in the above-named investigation. As to the standing rabi crops, there was the eye estimate and it was tested by the method mentioned above.

## The Government Method

The Government method is an eye estimate and, therefore, a matter largely of guess-work. It is moreover open to fundamental objections which I have endeavoured to set forth in a letter to the Collector of the District. I requested him to treat Vadthal—a well-known and ordinarily well-to-do village of the district with the railway line passing by it and which is near a trade centre—as a test case and I suggested that if the crops were in that village proved to be under four annas, as I hold they were, it might be assumed that in the other villages less fortunately situated, crops were not likely to be more than four annas. I have added to my request a suggestion that I should be permitted to be present at the inquiry. He made the inquiry but rejected my suggestion and, therefore, it proved to be onesided. The Collector has made an elaborate report on the crops of that village which, in my opinion, I have successfully challenged. The original Government valuation, I understand, was twelve annas, the Collector's minimum valuation is seven annas. If the probably wrong methods of valuation to which I have drawn attention and which have been adopted by the Collector are allowed for, the valuation according to his own reckoning would come under six annas and according to the agriculturists it would be under four annas.

## Need for Impartial Inquiry

Both the report and my answer are too technical to be of value to the public. But I have suggested that, as both the Government and the agriculturists hold themselves in the right, if the Government have any regard for popular opinion, they should appoint an impartial committee of inquiry with the cultivators' representatives upon it, or gracefully accept the popular view. The Government have rejected both the suggestions and insist upon applying coercive measures for the collection of revenue. It may be mentioned that these measures have never been totally suspended and in many cases the ryots have paid simply under pressure.

The Talatis have taken away cattle and have returned them only after the payment of assessment. In one case I witnessed a painful incident—a man having his milch buffalo taken away from him; and it was only on my happening to go to the village that the buffalo was released; this buffalo was the most valuable property the man possessed and a source of daily bread for him. Scores of such cases have already happened and many more will no doubt happen hereafter, if the public opinion is not ranged on the side of the people. Every means of seeking redress by prayers has been exhausted. Interviews with the Collector, the Commissioner and His Excellency have taken place. The final suggestion that was made is this :

## Proposals to the Government

Although in the majority of cases, people are entitled to full suspension, half suspension should be granted throughout the district except for the villages which show, by common consent, crops over six annas. Such a gracious concession may be accompanied by a declaration that the Government would expect those who have already means voluntarily to pay up the dues, we, the workers, on our part undertaking to persuade such people to pay up the Government dues. This will leave only the poorest people untouched. I venture to submit that acceptance of this suggestion can only bring credit and strength to the Government. Resistance of popular-will can only produce discontent which, in the case of fear-stricken peasantry such as of Kaira, can only find an underground passage and thus demoralize them. The present movement is an attempt to get out of such a false position, humiliating alike for the Government and the people.

## Law Abused

And how do the Government propose to assert their position and so-called prestige? They have a Revenue Code giving them unlimited powers without a right of appeal to the ryots against the decisions of the Revenue Authorities. Exercise of these powers in a case like the one before us, in which the ryots are fighting for a principle and the authorities for prestige, would be a prostitution of justice, of a disavowal of all fair-play. These powers are :

1. Right of summary execution.
2. Right of exacting a quarter of the assessment as punishment.
3. Right of confiscation of land, not merely Royatwari but even Inami or Sanadi.
4. Right of keeping a man under lock-up.

These remedies may be applied singly or all together, and unbelievable though it may seem to the public, it may be mentioned that notices of the application of all these remedies but the last have been issued.

Thus a man owning several hundred acres of land in perpetuity and valued at thousands of rupees, paying a small assessment rate, may at the will of the authority lose the whole of it, because for the sake of principle he respectfully refuses voluntarily to pay the assessment himself and is prepared meekly but under strong protest to penalities that may be inflicted by law.

Surely vindictive confiscation of property ought not to be the reward for orderly disobedience which, properly handled, can only result in progress all round and in giving the Government a bold and a frank peasantry with a will of its own.

### Appeal to the Public

I venture to invite the Press and the public to assist these cultivators of Kaira who have dared to enter on a fight for what they consider is just and right. Let the public remember this also that unprecedentally severe plague has decimated the population of Kaira. People are living outside their homes in specially prepared thatched cottages at considerable expense to themselves. In some villages mortality has been tremendous. Prices are ruling high of which, owing to the failure of crops, they can but take little advantage and have to suffer all the disadvantages thereof. It is not money they want so much as the voice of a strong, unanimous and emphatic public opinion.

## BARDOLI SATYAGRAHA

The Bardoli Satyagraha of 1928, in the state of Gujarat, India during the period of the British Raj, was a major episode of civil disobedience and revolt in the Indian Independence Movement. Its success gave rise to Vallabhbhai Patel as one of the greatest leaders of the independence struggle.

### Background

Mahatma Gandhi had led two great revolts of communities of poor Indian farmers against the tyranny of the British government and allied landlords in Champaran, Bihar, and Kheda, Gujarat. Success in both struggles had helped win the farmers economic and civil rights, and electrified India's people.

In 1920, the Indian National Congress under Gandhi's leadership launched the Non-Cooperation Movement. Millions of Indians revolted against the British, boycotting the courts, government services, schools and disavowing titles, pensions and British clothes and goods. The freedom fighters, known as *Satyagrahis*, peacefully protested authoritarian British laws, and called for India's independence. Many thousands were beaten, tortured and arrested.

In 1922, however, a mob of protestors killed some policemen in Chauri Chaura. Fearing a slide into violence and anarchy, Gandhi called for the struggle to be suspended. He was arrested in the same year and sentenced to be imprisoned for six years, but released in 1924. In this struggle, many considered Sardar Patel as the Lord of Bardoli.

## The Crisis

In 1925, the taluka of Bardoli in Gujarat suffered from floods and famine, causing crop production to suffer and leaving farmers facing great financial troubles. However, the Government of the Bombay Presidency had raised the tax rate by 30% that year, and despite petitions from civic groups, refused to cancel the rise in the face of the calamities. The situation for the farmers was grave enough that they barely had enough property and crops to pay-off the tax, let alone for feeding themselves afterwards.

## Considering the Options

The Gujarati activists Narhari Parikh, Ravi Shankar Vyas, and Mohanlal Pandya talked to village chieftains and farmers, and solicited the help of Gujarat's most prominent freedom fighter, Vallabhbhai Patel. Patel had previously guided Gujarat's farmers during the Kheda struggle, and had served recently as Ahmedabad's municipal president. He was widely respected by common Gujaratis across the state.

Patel told a delegation of farmers frankly that if they should realize fully what a revolt would imply. He would not lead them unless he had the unanimous understanding and agreement of all the villages involved.

Refusing payment of taxes could lead to their property being confiscated, including their lands, and many would go to jail. They could face complete decimation. The villagers replied that they were prepared for the worst, but definitely could not accept the Government's injustice.

Patel then asked Gandhi to consider the matter. But Gandhi merely asked what Patel thought, and when the latter replied with confidence about the prospects, he gave his blessing. But Gandhi and Patel agreed that neither the Congress nor Gandhi would directly involve themselves, and the struggle left entirely to the people of Bardoli taluka.

## The Struggle

Patel first wrote to the Governor of Bombay, asking him to reduce the taxes for the year in face of the calamities. But the Governor ignored the letter, and reciprocated by announcing the date of collection.

Patel then instructed all the farmers of Bardoli taluka to refuse payment of their taxes. Aided by Parikh, Vyas and Pandya, he divided Bardoli into several zones – each with a leader and volunteers specifically assigned. Patel also placed some Gujarati activists close to the government, to act as informers on the movements of government officials.

Above all, Patel instructed the farmers to remain completely non-violent, and not respond physically to any incitements or aggressive actions from officials. He reassured them that the struggle would not end until not only the cancellation of all taxes for the year, but also when all the seized property and lands were returned to their rightful owners.

The farmers received complete support from their compatriots in Gujarat. Many hid their most precious belongings with relatives in other parts, and the protestors received financial support and essential supplies from supporters in other parts. But Patel refused permission to enthusiastic supporters in Gujarat and other parts of India from going on sympathetic protest.

The Government declared that it would crush the revolt. Along with tax inspectors, bands of Pathans were gathered from northwest India to forcibly seize the property of the villagers and terrorize them. The Pathans and the men of the collectors forced themselves into the houses, took all property, including cattle.

The government began to auction the houses and the lands. But not a single man from Gujarat or anywhere else in India came forward to buy them. Patel had appointed volunteers in every village to keep watch. As soon as he sighted the officials who were coming to auction the property, the volunteer would sound his bugle. The farmers would leave the village and hide in the jungles. The officials would find the entire village empty. They could never find out who owned a particular house.

However, some rich people from Bombay came to buy some lands. There was also one village recorded that paid the tax. A complete social boycott was organized against them, wherein relatives broke their ties to families in the village.

Members of the legislative councils of Bombay and across India were angered by the terrible treatment of the protesting farmers. Indian members resigned their offices, and expressed open support of the farmers. The Government was heavily criticized, even by many in the Raj's offices.

## Resolution

In 1928, an agreement was finally brokered by a Parsi member of the Bombay government. The Government agreed to restore the confiscated lands and properties, as well as cancel revenue payment not only for the year, but cancel the 30% raise until after the succeeding year. The farmers celebrated their victory, but Patel continued to work to ensure that all lands and properties were returned to every farmer, and that no one was left out. When the Government refused to ask the people who had bought some of the lands to return them, wealthy sympathizers from Bombay bought them out, and returned the lands to the rightful owners.

## Commemoration

The momentum from the Bardoli victory aided in the resurrection of the freedom struggle nationwide. In 1930, the Congress would declare Indian independence, and the Salt Satyagraha would be launched by Gandhi.

While Patel credited Gandhi's teachings and the farmers' undying resolve, people across the nation recognized his vital leadership. Gandhi and his fellow satyagrahis called him *Sardar* for the first time, which in Gujarati and most Indian languages means *Chief* or *Leader*. It was after Bardoli that *Sardar Patel* became one of India's most important leaders.

# PARSI SATYAGRAHA AT BARDOLI

## Gujarat Anjumans Say an Emphatic no to the Cosmopolitan World Body

Who would have thought that the death knell of the infamous cosmopolitan world body would be sounded in a tiny hamlet of Gujarat, Bardoli. But then Bardoli is no stranger to fame. For it was from Bardoli that Mahatma Gandhi and Sardar Vallabhbhai Patel lead the satyagraha movement for peaceful resistance against the British, almost a hundred years ago. It seems to me that there is that something in Bardoli that inspires one to stand up for what one believes in.

How else can one explain the phenomenal success of the Community meeting organized single handedly by the Bardoli Jarthosti Anjuman, to awaken the community to the dangers of the cosmopolitan world body? This tiny Anjuman with a large heart hosted over one thousand four hundred (1400) Parsis and Iranis, on February 26th and 27th, and took upon themselves the task of creating awareness in the community about this vital matter. The silent majority of the community made their strong presence felt that day. Coming from the far corners of Gujarat they passed a Resolution (with one lone dissenter), against the Bombay Parsi Punchayet and the Federation of Parsi Zoroastrian Anjumans of India joining the cosmopolitan world body.

This was after well known scholar Khojeste Mistree had taken them through a Power Point Presentation, done in Gujarati especially for the occasion, in which he analysed and dissected the Constitution of the controversial world body. The Presentation highlighted, (1) the marginalization of the BPP and the Federation of India in the world body, (2) the absence in the Constitution of the all-important Parsi/Irani identity, 3) the cosmopolitan nature of the body, as shown by the various Clauses that would make it possible for converts to gain entry and the resultant adverse impact it would have on the community in India and elsewhere, and 4) the thus far unbroken link between the Parsi/Irani identity and the Zoroastrian religion, which they are seeking to break in this proposed world body.

Resolution after Resolution passed at various public meetings has rejected the very idea of this cosmopolitan body. At a Public Meeting organized by The Parsee Voice in Bombay, on Nov. 23rd 2003, 750 Parsis/Iranis present had passed a similar Resolution against joining the world body. At the meeting of the Federation of Parsi Zoroastrian Anjumans of India at Ahmedabad, 24 of the 29 anjuman representatives present, reiterated their opposition to it and forwarded their protest to the Chairman in writing. Since then, a remarkable fifty (50) of the 69 anjumans registered with the Federation have joined the opposition to the world body. If one considers that 13 of the 69 anjumans of FPZAI are defunct, in real term numbers this amounts to 50 out of 56 anjumans opposing the world body! If after all this, BPP spokesperson, Mr. Godrej Dotivala, says to the media, "they are in the minority", then it is obvious that Mr. Dotivala is deliberately misleading the media and through it, the community. Why doesn't Mr. Dotivala supply us with some proof of the "majority" he seems to think is for the cosmopolitan world body?

Coming back to Bardoli, what can I say? The tiny anjuman stole the show and our hearts. Their organizational skills were outstanding, their hospitality overwhelming and heartwarming, and the gaam nu bhonu, tastier than any lagan nu bhonu I've tasted this season. President of the anjuman Mr. Jamshed Mohta has wonderful ideas and big dreams for the community and has the confidence and ability to carry them through. MOHTA (meaning big) saheb's very name says it all; and his magnanimous actions match his name. Secretary of Bardoli Jarthosti Anjuman, Pervez Mehta is no less dynamic and he along with the other trustees and their families, all, opened up their homes and hearts to us.

Underlying all the hard work put in by the Bardoli team was their strong commitment and deep concern for the community and if our leaders and BPP trustees had been there with us, they would have seen for themselves that the good food and great hospitality, though greatly appreciated, were not the crowd pulling attractions they have been made out to be. The common cause at the Bardoli meeting was concern for the religion; and belittling those who had gathered at Bardoli, in a desperate attempt to dismiss the opposition to the world body, is not only in very bad taste, but also rather ludicrous. (Both the editor of Jame as well as BPP spokesperson Dotiwala have made snide remarks in the media, insinuating that 1200 community members had trooped to Bardoli solely for the food!!)

The support from Surat (Trustees and community members alike) was united and strong. Poona too was well represented and stands firmly behind tradition. The Trustees of Poona have in fact ratified the stand taken by them at the Federation meeting (opposing the cosmopolitan world body) by passing a Resolution emphasizing the same, at their AGM. These are leaders working with transparency and accountability, in consonance with the sentiments of their constituents; and one salutes them for that! Guest of honour, Vada Dastur Cyrus Dastur of Surat spoke passionately for preserving tradition and quoted extensively from the Scriptures to make his point. Chief Guest, illustrious industrialist Mr. Areez P. Khambatta captivated the audience with personal and professional tips on entrepreneurship; and having taken the lead in emphasizing the need for the community to form a Parsi/Irani world body to safeguard Parsi/Irani interests, he announced a personal donation of Rupees one crore towards a traditionally constituted Parsi/Irani world body that would uphold and preserve the tenets and traditions of our Religion and would function under the guidance of a Council of High Priests. WORLD ALLIANCE OF PARSI IRANI ZARTHOSTIS (WAPIZ) would be the voice of the Parsis/Iranis in the world.

18 year-old Zarvan Patvi provided a fitting finale when he requested the mike at the end of the Meet, to recite a few lines he had specially composed for the occasion. "I hope this message goes to the BPP and to all our other leaders" he said as he recited the couplets:

*Na jaane din, na jaane dharam,*
*Na khuda no dar, na aankh maa sharam.*
*Nathi je-lokonaa tan per sadro, nathi je-lokonaa tan per kusti,*
*Evaaone laiyne vadhaarvaa chaaliya vasti.*
*Pasti na moole vechai jase tamaari hasti, jo khuda ni saathe kari aavi harkat sasti.*
*Na bujhi chhe, na bujhse jyot maaraa Jarthosti Din ni.*
*Na bujhi chhe, na bujhse jyot maaraa Jarthosti Din ni; Jyaa sudhi hamaaraa dil maa chhe aatash parasti,*
*Chhaiye hame Jarthosti.*

The youth that came in large numbers to the meeting could teach many of us many a religious lesson. Gujarat has said an emphatic NO to the cosmopolitan world body. Bardoli Jarthosti Anjuman (the small anjuman with the large heart), and the Parsis/Iranis of Navsari, Surat, Ahmedabad, Mt. Abu and a host of other anjumans in and around Gujarat, have stood up for what they believe in. Are our leaders listening?

## CIVIL DISOBEDIENCE MOVEMENT

Sardar Patel became the President of the Indian National Congress in 1931, at the dawn of the Civil Disobedience Movement, or Salt Satyagraha. Patel organized Congress work before being arrested by police. He served his sentence with Gandhi in the Yeravda Jail till 1934. Gandhi and Patel grew very close, personally and spiritually in this time. Patel served Gandhi, affectionately looking after his personal needs, and Gandhi encouraged Patel to learn Sanskrit and read great Hindu epics. The two discussed many aspects of the freedom struggle, Indian history and national issues. Gandhi was especially proud of Patel's work in Gujarat, and of the inestimable help he was giving Gandhi in the work of revolution.

## POWER WITHIN THE CONGRESS

Sardar Patel was Gandhiji's right-hand man, and Congress Party chief. He commanded the wide loyalty and respect of the millions of Congressmen who had fought in the hot sun and been beaten, tortured and imprisoned for many years. He was Gujarat's chief, and no other Congress leader, not even Gandhiji could have overcome his strength in his home state. His great integrity, strict discipline and adherence to core principles of the struggle, complete disinterest in office and power as such, and fatherly care for his associates and fellow Congressmen made him the only man capable of standing up to Gandhiji. Thus even though he had been Congress President only once in 1931, he remained its second-most important leader after Gandhiji, exceeding the younger and charismatic Jawaharlal Nehru in authority and influence within the party and in government. It was acknowledged by many veteran freedom-fighters and his British opponents that only Sardar Patel could stand up to Gandhiji in a contest for the loyalty of most Congressmen and Indians. No one was a stronger ally of the Mahatma. Patel would break many other bonds of power, office, leadership, friendship and family before splitting from the Mahatma. Throughout his life, he viewed himself as a "soldier in Bapu's Army." He enjoyed a close spiritual bond with the Mahatma, and the Gandhi-Patel relationship has been described as one of older and younger brothers.

In Indian society, the older brother is a father-figure, with the younger brother bound with love, loyalty and respect to him.

Sardar Patel assumed a wide range of responsibilities by raising funds for the Party from businessmen and sympathizers, developing an election strategy and selecting candidates for the provincial and central elections of 1934 and 1937 under the Government of India Act 1935, and guiding the work of many Congress organizations dedicated to social upliftment and service. He was the guide and boss of the various Congress Ministries that took power in the provinces in the 1930s-never indulging in power and interfering in the work of public service, but holding an iron discipline over the ministers, preventing the British thus from dividing the leaders and ruling, and any corruption of power from hurting the purity of the overall cause for freedom.

In the eyes of some people, Patel gained infamy when he reprimanded P.F. Nariman, a Parsee Congress leader who coveted the premiership of Bombay, and Khare, another politician seeking the premiership of the Central Provinces. Both had tried to divide the party to unseat the preference of national party leaders, and to Patel, divide-and-rule was absolutely unacceptable. But his measures to oust both from were criticized as *authoritarian* and *dictatorial* by some in the press.

## NONCOOPERATION

Non-cooperation and peaceful resistance were Gandhi's "weapons" in the fight against injustice. In Punjab, the Jallianwala Bagh massacre of civilians by British troops caused deep trauma to the nation, leading to increased public anger and acts of violence. Gandhi criticized both the actions of the British Raj and the retaliatory violence of Indians. He authored the resolution offering condolences to British civilian victims and condemning the riots, which after initial opposition in the party, was accepted following Gandhi's emotional speech advocating his principle that all violence was evil and could not be justified. But it was after the massacre and subsequent violence that Gandhi's mind focused upon obtaining complete self-government and control of all Indian government institutions, maturing soon into Swaraj or complete individual, spiritual, political independence.

Sabarmati Ashram, Gandhi's home in Gujarat in December 1921, Gandhi was invested with executive authority on behalf of the Indian National Congress. Under his leadership, the Congress was reorganized with a new constitution, with the goal of Swaraj. Membership in the party was opened to anyone prepared to pay a token fee. A hierarchy of committees was set up to improve discipline, transforming the party from an elite organization to one of mass national appeal. Gandhi expanded his nonviolence platform to include the swadeshi policy – the boycott of foreign-made goods, especially British goods.

Linked to this was his advocacy that khadi (homespun cloth) be worn by all Indians instead of British-made textiles. Gandhi exhorted Indian men and women, rich or poor, to spend time each day spinning khadi in support of the independence movement. This was a strategy to inculcate discipline and dedication to weed out the unwilling and ambitious, and to include women in the movement at a time when many thought that such activities were not respectable activities for women. In addition to boycotting British products, Gandhi urged the people to boycott British educational institutions and law courts, to resign from government employment, and to forsake British titles and honours.

"Noncooperation" enjoyed wide-spread appeal and success, increasing excitement and participation from all strata of Indian society. Yet, just as the movement reached its apex, it ended abruptly as a result of a violent clash in the town of Chauri Chaura, Uttar Pradesh, in February 1922.

Fearing that the movement was about to take a turn towards violence, and convinced that this would be the undoing of all his work, Gandhi called off the campaign of mass civil disobedience. Gandhi was arrested on March 10, 1922, tried for sedition, and sentenced to six years imprisonment. Beginning on March 18, 1922, he only served about two years of the sentence, being released in February 1924 after an operation for appendicitis.

Without Gandhi's uniting personality, the Indian National Congress began to splinter during his years in prison, splitting into two factions, one led by Chitta Ranjan Das and Motilal Nehru favouring party participation in the legislatures, and the other led by Chakravarti Rajagopalacharya and Sardar Vallabhbhai Patel, opposing this move.

Furthermore, cooperation among Hindus and Muslims, which had been strong at the height of the nonviolence campaign, was breaking down. Gandhi attempted to bridge these differences through many means, including a three-week fast in the autumn of 1924, but with limited success. He was the Mahatma's no-nonsense lieutenant and his "executive arm."

Mahatma Gandhi gave the nation comprehensive inspirational leadership and the technique of "war without violence"—Satyagraha with Trimoola-Mantras, three Cardinal Foundational inviolable tenets—Satya (Truth), Tyaga (Sacrifice) and Seva (Service) as the watchwords. Tens of thousands, young and the not so young, all over the country joined India's Pilgrimage to Freedom.

They gave up their promising careers and cheerfully faced lathi blows, imprisonment and even the gallows. Sardar Vallabhbhai Patel is one of the most distinguished among them. He was the Mahatma's no-nonsense lieutenant and his "executive arm." He was a man of iron discipline and his forte was action. He subjugated all emotions and sentiments to the demands of reason and pragmatic idealism.

"Sardar was to Gandhiji what Lakshmana was to Sri Rama," averred Rajaji, the first among the astute of modern Indian leaders. According to Dr. Pattabhi Sitaramayya, the eminent historian of India's freedom movement and a former President of the Indian National Congress "If Gandhiji was the Christ, Sardar was John the Baptist" of Nationalist India.

## Prophetic Vision

The Sardar's prophetic vision is seen clearly in his perception of the Chinese threat from across the border when the cry throughout India was "Hindi-Chini Bhai-Bhai". In a letter to Pandit Jawaharlal Nehru, the then Prime Minister, the Sardar wrote on Nov.7, 1950.

"Throughout history we have seldom been worried about our North-East Frontier. The Himalayas have been regarded as an impenetrable barrier against any threat from the north. In our calculations we shall have to reckon with Communist China in the North and North-East, a Communist China which has definite ambitions and aims and which does not, in any way, seem friendly disposed towards us."

Jawaharlal Nehru wrote a note on China and Tibet that touched on some of the Sardar's points and sent a copy of Sardar.

He wrote: "I think it is extremely unlikely that we may have to face any real military invasion from the Chinese side. It is inconceivable that China should divert its forces and its strength across the inhospitable terrain of Tibet and undertake a wild adventure across the Himalayas. Thus I rule out any major attack on India by China." The attack on India by China that Sardar feared and Jawaharlal had ruled out took place twelve years thereafter.

## Simplicity of Sardar

The indomitable Sardar who decided the fate of hundreds of princes, many of them fabulously rich, and habituated to lavish living and giving, was so utterly unconcerned about accumulating any money for himself or his family. When he died, he left virtually nothing, not even a will. Like his Guru, the only "personal property" he left behind was a few pieces of clothes, one or two pairs of chappals and other minor personal effects.

## CHAMPARAN AND KHEDA SATYAGRAHA

The first Satyagraha revolutions inspired by Mahatma Gandhi in the Indian Independence Movement occurred in Kheda district of Gujarat and the Champaran district of Bihar between the years of 1918 and 1919.

### Champaran Bihar

In Champaran, a district in the then-province, now state of Bihar, tens of thousands of landless serfs, indentured labourers and poor farmers were forced to grow indigo and other cash crops instead of the food crops necessary for their survival. Suppressed by the ruthless militias of the landlords (mostly British), they were given measly compensation, leaving them mired in extreme poverty. The villages were kept extremely dirty and unhygienic, and alcoholism, untouchability and purdah were rampant. Now in the throes of a devastating famine, the British levied an oppressive tax which they insisted on increasing in rate. The situation was desperate.

### Kheda Gujarat

In Kheda, a district of villages and small towns in Gujarat, the peasants mostly owned their own lands, and were economically better-off than their compatriots in Bihar, although on the whole, the district was plagued by poverty, scant resources, the social evils of alcoholism and untouchability, and overall British indifference and hegemony. However, a terrible famine had struck the district and a large part of Gujarat, and virtually destroyed the agrarian economy. The poor peasants had barely enough to feed themselves, but the British government of the Bombay Presidency insisted that the farmers not only pay full taxes, but also pay the 23 percent increase slated to take effect that very year.

### Gandhi's Solution

While many civic groups sent petitions and published editorials, Gandhi proposed *satyagraha*-non-violent, mass civil disobedience. While it was strictly nonviolent, Gandhi was proposing real action, a real revolt that the oppressed peoples of India were dying to undertake.

Gandhi also insisted that neither the protestors in Bihar nor in Gujarat allude to or try to propagate the concept of *Swaraj*, or *Independence*. This was not about political freedom, but a revolt against abject tyranny amidst a terrible humanitarian disaster. While accepting participants and help from other parts of India, Gandhi insisted that no other district or province revolt against the Government, and that the Indian National Congress not get involved apart from issuing resolutions of support, to prevent the British from giving it cause to use extensive suppressive measures and brand the revolts as treason.

## In Champaran

Gandhi established an ashrama in Champaran, organizing scores of his veteran supporters and fresh volunteers from the region. He organized a detailed study and survey of the villages, accounting the atrocities and terrible episodes of suffering, including the general state of degenerate living. Building on the confidence of villagers, he began leading the clean-up of villages, building of schools and hospitals and encouraging the village leadership to undo purdah, untouchability and the suppression of women. He was joined by many young nationalists from the parts and all over India, including Dr. Rajendra Prasad and Jawaharlal Nehru.

But his main assault came as he was arrested by police on the charge of creating unrest and was ordered to leave the province. Hundreds of thousands of people protested and rallied outside the jail, police stations and courts demanding his release, which the court unwillingly did. Gandhi led organized protests and strike against the landlords, who with the guidance of the British government, signed an agreement granting more compensation and control over farming for the poor farmers of the region, and cancellation of revenue hikes and collection until the famine ended. It was during this agitation, that Gandhi was addressed by the people as *Bapu* (*Father*) and *Mahatma* (*Great Soul*).

## In Kheda

In Gujarat, Gandhi was only the spiritual head of the struggle. His chief lieutenant, Sardar Vallabhbhai Patel and a close coterie of devoted Gandhians, namely Narhari Parikh, Mohanlal Pandya and Ravi Shankar Vyas toured the countryside, organized the villagers and gave them political leadership and direction. Many aroused Gujaratis from the cities of Ahmedabad and Vadodara joined the organizers of the revolt, but Gandhi and Patel resisted the involvement of Indians from other provinces, seeking to keep it a purely Gujarati struggle. Patel and his colleauges organized a major tax revolt, and all the different ethnic and caste communities of Kheda rallied around it. The peasants of Kheda signed a petition calling for the tax for this year to be scrapped in wake of the famine. The government in Bombay rejected the charter. They warned that if the peasants did not pay, the lands and property would be confiscated and many arrested. And once confiscated, they would not be returned even if most complied. None of the villages flinched.

The tax withheld, the government's collectors and inspectors sent in Pathan thugs to seize property and cattle, while the police forfeited the lands and all agrarian property. The farmers did not resist arrest, nor retaliate to the force employed with violence. Instead, they used their cash and valuables to donate to the *Gujarat Sabha* which was officially organizing the protest. The revolt was astounding in terms of discipline and unity. Even when all their personal property, land and livelihood were seized, a vast majority of Kheda's farmers remained firmly united in the support of Patel. Gujaratis sympathetic to the revolt in other parts resisted the government machinery, and helped the shelter the relatives and property of the protesting peasants. Those Indians who sought to buy the confiscated lands were ostracized from society. Although nationalists like Sardul Singh Caveeshar called for sympathetic revolts in other parts, Gandhi and Patel firmly rejected the idea.

The Government finally sought to foster an honourable agreement for both parties. The tax for the year in question, and the next would be suspended, and the increase in rate reduced, while all confiscated property would be returned. Gujaratis also worked in cohesion to return the confiscated lands to their rightful owners. The ones who had bought the lands seized were influenced to return them, even though the British had officially said it would stand by the buyers.

## Success and Legacy

Gandhi's resulting fame spread like fire all over the nation. He had become a defining influence on Indian Nationalism. The proud peasantry of Gujarat still revere Gandhi and Sardar Patel, and their role in the freedom struggle. Gujarat is the most industrialized and progressive state in India today. In Bihar, poverty and social conflict pervades what was the founding of the Satyagraha movement. The Naxalite insurgency is centred around the same age-old problem of class struggle between poor farmers and rich landlords, now involving terrorism.

## DANDI MARCH

The march on foot undertaken by Gandhi and seventy-eight Congress volunteers was the most significant event in the history of the breach of salt law in our country. It was commenced in accordance with a fixed schedule to be carried on by them during the long journey ending at Dandi. Undoubtedly, it was a disciplined band of nonviolent satyagrahis who were to present a new model of satyagraha which later on converted into a bigger movement at all-India level.

On 12 March 1930 at 6-10 A.M. Gandhi came out of his room, calm and composed, accompanied by Prabhashankar Patani, Mahadev Desai and Pyarelal, his secretary. He offered prayers, looked at his watch and exactly at 6.30 A.M. commenced his march with seventy-eight volunteers.

With his usual gentle smile, betokening his unifying faith in the justice of the cause he was pursuing and in the success of the great campaign he had embarked upon, he headed the procession with quick and unfaltering steps.

'Like the historic march of Ram Chandra to Lanka, the march of Dandi would be memorable' exclaimed Motilal Nehru in a message. P.C. Ray called it the 'exodus of Israelites under Moses?

Jawaharlal Nehru called Gandhi, ' .... the pilgrim on his quest of truth, quiet, peaceful, determined and fearless who would continue that quiet pilgrimage regardless of consequences.'

The satyagrahis were to face a fatiguing journey through heat and dust of the Kheda villages. Thousands of men, women and children accompanied the marching column for a few miles and thousands lined the route and showered flowers, coins, currency notes and kum kum at the satyagrahis.

Following the commencement of his epic Dandi March, a tremendous wave of enthusiasm swept over the entire country. The historic day was celebrated all over India. Calcutta woke that morning amidst sounds of conch shells and shouts of 'Gandhiji ki Jai'. At a conference of the Congress leaders of Bengal a decision was taken to appoint immediately an ad hoc council to be called the Bengal Civil Disobedience Council, with the object of carrying out the programme outlined by Gandhiji. J. M. Sen Gupta appealed to all men and women of the province to enrol themselves as volunteers for the Civil Disobedience Movement. He said, 'Bengal is on trial. She had always been in the vanguard of the country's battle for freedom and cannot lag behind. Let us plunge head-long in the fight and regain the rights which are ours.'

In Bombay, a public meeting was held under the presidentship of K. F. Nariman. He exhorted the audience to get ready for the fight. The 'War Council' of the Bombay Provincial Congress Committee announced a it of 'iron-sides' to join the first detachment of volunteers from the town.

In Madras, at a public meeting at Tilak Ghat, prayers were offered for the success of Civil Disobedience campaign by the Madras District Congress Committee, Andhra Congress Committee, the Triplicate Congress Sabha and the political section of the Youth League. The meeting reiterated India's resolve to achieve Swaraj by nonviolent means under Gandhi's leadership by following his path.'

In Lahore, a band of Congress volunteers paraded the streets and raised shouts of 'Mahatma Gandhi Ki Jai'. In a mammoth meeting of the citizens of the town, held under the auspices of the City Congress Committee, Maulana Abdul Qadir, in opening the proceedings, said, 'The 12th of March would be a red letter day and it would figure in letters of gold in the future history of India'.

He hoped that the people of India, from that day onward would give practical demonstration of their determination to win freedom. He believed that as soon as the people of the Punjab would receive the news of Gandhi's arrest, they would suspend their business and work out the plan of the movement.

In Peshawar, the 'Satyagraha Day' was observed by taking out a procession and holding a public meeting. Resolutions reiterating the pledge of independence and wishing Godspeed to the soldiers of freedom and congratulating Vallabhbhai Patel on his imprisonment were unanimously passed. Besides, a large number of volunteers were enlisted for the satyagraha.

Civil Disobedience Day was celebrated in Delhi in a meeting attended by about 10,000 persons, including a large number of ladies. Devdas Gandhi gave the detailed history of the salt tax and called it the most 'barbarous' tax which effected the poor classes, and pleaded for its abolition immediately. He also exhorted the people to observe complete but peaceful hartal if Mahatma Gandhi was arrested.

Allahabad, the nerve centre of U. P. politics, witnessed scenes of enthusiasm in connection with the celebration of the commencement of the satyagraha campaign. Jawaharlal Nehru hoisted the national flag over the building occupied by the offices of the A.I.C.C., the City Congress Committee and the All-India Spinners' Association, U.P. branch. A large gathering participated in the ceremony. While addressing the audience, Nehru said that the pledge of satyagraha laid stress on nonviolence which was the very basis of the Civil Disobedience campaign. He warned that only those who were convinced of the efficacy of that method either as a creed or as a policy in the present circumstances of the country, should take the pledge. He opined that nonviolence was not a convenient shelter either for cowards or for those who wanted to prepare for violence. He asked the nonbelievers in nonviolence to withdraw from the movement to give others a chance. In Ahmedabad, a meeting of the Youth League was held in which a resolution was passed empowering the secretaries to enlist volunteers for Civil Disobedience Movement. About twenty-five names were enlisted on the spot including two secretaries and Miss Mridula Ambalal, daughter of a local mill-magnate.

The 'Dandi March Day' was observed in Nagpur by hoisting the national flag. A procession passed through the main bazaars of the town, and, thereafter, a public meeting was also held. Gandhi's letter to the Viceroy was read out and explained to the audience. An appeal for the enlistment of volunteers was also made. While exhorting the people to give the moment their whole-hearted support M. V. Abhyankar said, 'I shall perish in the struggle for Independence or live to enjoy freedom after its achievement?

Similar celebrations were held all over the country and considerable enthusiasm was aroused with people for participating in the Civil disobedience Movement. For the first time, a new spirit for Swaraj-full and complete-was found bubbling everywhere. The Viceroy informed the Secretary of State on 13 March 1930, 'Most of my thought at the moment is concentrated upon Gandhi. I wish I felt sure what the right way to deal with him is.'

The same day Gandhi and his satyagrahis reached a small village, Aslali, where they were received well by the villagers. Gandhi emphasised the importance of salt and criticised the salt tax levied by the government. He stated, 'The poor destitute villagers do not have the strength to get this tax repealed. We want to develop this strength... We should make a resolve that we shall prepare salt, eat it, sell if to the people and, while doing so, court imprisonment, if necessary. If, out of Gujarat's Population of 90 lakhs, we leave out women and children, and the remaining 30 lakhs et ready to violate the salt tax, the Government does not have enough accommodation in jails to house so many people.'

Next day, Gandhi, who was apprehensive of his arrest, informed Jawaharlal Nehru, 'The news given to me of my impending arrest was said to be absolutely authentic. But we have reached the second stage. We take the third tonight'

The second halt of the Dandi marchers was at Bareja, a village with a Population of 2,500. He emphasised the importance of khadi, its production and use by the villagers. 'Khadi is the foundation of our freedom struggle.... I request you to renounce luxuries and buy khadi from this heap before you.

'We have come forward to win our freedom from this tyrannical and oppressive Government. If we cannot put our own house in order in an organized manner, how shall we run the country's Government? I ask you, therefore, to learn order and organization.... This struggle against the Government on which we have embarked is not going to reach its conclusion with five, or twenty-five, or even millions of men getting killed. We have to look after other things also simultaneously.'

As Gandhi entered the Kheda district, memories-some sweet, some bitter-filled his mind. It was while working in this district that he became one with the lives of people. He had seen nearly all the villages of the district and had covered many of them on foot. He stated, 'I have come to Navagam in the middle of a battle... The Government found some pretext or other to arrest Vallabhbhai... Pressure was brought to hear on the Magistrate some how to serve a notice on Sardar and he was arrested. What could a poor Magistrate do where the entire atmosphere is vitiated?

When some headmen and matadars of Kheda district submitted their resignations as a protest against the oppressive policy of the government, Gandhi advised them, 'Remember that in the resignations, you have handed in I see God's hand. The Kheda District has made an auspicious beginning.'

At Vasana, where the villagers had gathered to accord reception to the marchers and listen to their leader, Gandhi explained that abolition of the salt-tax or remission of some taxes would not mean swaraj for them. Winning of swaraj was not going to be so easy as they might think. It was only a way to it and by following it they would reach the goal of freedom. He had a word of praise for the headmen of Navagam, Vavdi, Agam, Mahelaj and other villages who had tendered their resignations. 'Why should they stick to Headmanship for the mere five rupees a month that the government pays them? If the Collector summons a Headman, let him say, 'Give us back our Sardar. Grant us a remission in land revenue.'

At Nadiad, a town with a population of thirty-one thousand, Gandhi reminded the people, 'Bound by the chains of slavery, we are being crushed at present and we want to shake them off.' He wished all government servants to give up their jobs. A government job gave them the power to tyrannize over others. Finally, be asked them to enlist themselves as volunteers. And as soon as he got behind the bars or as soon as the All-India Congress Committee gave a call, they should come forward to offer themselves for being jailed. 'Then alone shall I believe that Nadiad has made its contribution to our struggle'.

In a letter to Jayaprakash Narayan which Gandhi wrote from Anand on 17 March, he explained, 'No where else have I observed such zeal for sacrifice as has been displayed by the Ashram women. At present the women are to a great extent managing the internal affairs of the Ashram. The chance of acquiring such experience will never be repeated. I would therefore advise you to send Prabhavati there. After my arrest the Ashram women too will court imprisonment. I think Prabhavati should join them. She is worthy in every respect.'

At Anand, an educational centre of Patidars, Gandhi demanded, 'In your hands lies the honour of the Patidars of Charotar. You are like salt in the sea of Patidars. If the salt loses its savour, wherewith shall it be salted? Salt is more sapid than either sugar or juggery. The latter may even cause jaundice, whereas a pinch of salt adds flavour to the meal. If Anand gives up its savour if courage and such other virtues which have been attributed to the Patidars are not displayed in Anand at this juncture, where else can one see them?.'

The students' services to the national cause were also applauded. They were advised to suspend their studies for as long as this struggle continued. Formerly, Gandhi had asked his students to leave schools and to set up national schools. But this time he asked them to leave schools and come out on the 'battlefield' and become 'mendicants' for the sake of the country. But he did not ask them to give up their studies for good, but only to give up book-learning so long as the struggle lasted.

At Borsad, the reception of Gandhi and his satyagrahis was celebrated with the immediate announcement of the resignations of headmen, matadars and ravanias of twenty villages of the taluka. Over one hundred village officers of twenty-five villages submitted their resignations.

The government sources commented, 'Gandhi's attention is directed on two points *i.e.* resignations of patels and enrolling volunteers. Under his instructions local workers are trying to get more resignations under the threat of social boycott.

They were warmly received by the village folk. They were keen to listen to Gandhi's discourse· He explained to them, 'Our patience has been severely tried. We must free ourselves from the yoke of this Government and we are prepared to undergo any hardships that we may have to suffer in order to secure swaraj, it is our duty as well as our right to secure swaraj.

'Today we are defying the salt law. Tomorrow we shall have to consign other laws to the wastepaper basket. Doing so we shall practise such severe noncooperation that finally it will not be possible for the administration to be carried on at all. Let the Government then, to carry on its rule, use guns against us, send us to prison, hang us. But how many can be given such punishment? Try and calculate how much time it will take a lakh of Britishers to hang thirty crores of persons.'

Gandhi once again exhorted the students to leave their institutions and join the struggle for independence. He desired that all students studying in the local high school and who were above the age of fifteen, and all teachers too, should enrol themselves. He pleaded that wherever revolutions had taken place, that is, in Japan, China, Egypt, Ireland and in England, students and teachers had played a prominent role. In Europe, war broke out on 4 August 1914, and when Gandhi reached England on the 6th of the same month, he found that students had left colleges and marched out with arms.

Gandhi further explained that his prostrating himself on the ground for the sake of removing the hardships of crores of people was of no avail. He had spared no efforts in drafting appeals.

He became a revolutionary when politeness and persuasion proved infructious. He indeed found peace in describing himself as a revolutionary and appealed that in a revolution of that nature which was calm, peaceful and truthful, people should get themselves enrolled regardless of the religious faith to which they belonged. He was confident that if they enlisted themselves with sincerity and if they could keep up their courage, the salt tax would have been abolished, this administration would have come to an end and all the hardships enumerated in the letter to the Viceroy as well as those which had not been enumerated would have to cease.

On 19 March, the party of satyagrahis reached Ras Taluka where Sardar Patel was arrested and sentenced to prison and in which he had carried on such a vigorous struggle in 1924 that the Government had finally to admit its 'error and mete out justice that should not have required a struggle. It is as if Sardar was sentenced to prison as a reward for having served you'.

During the short stay of Gandhi, some of the headmen and matadars had handed in their resignations. But Gandhi expressed unhappiness on the small number of resignations at Ras. In fact, the headman, talati and revania were the representatives of the government in the villages and it was through these persons that the latter carried on its administration. A village which was afraid of a handful of men and continued to act in a manner contrary to its own wishes, neither enhanced the prestige of the headman, the talati or the revania nor that of the villagers themselves. Sardar Patel had been making great effort to end this indignity.

Gandhi praised the services rendered by Sardar Patel. He also apprised the villagers of his mission. He explained 'Sardar neither made speeches nor came here to foment trouble. Neither the Magistrate nor you had acted any sort of trouble. The task for which Sardar had approached you was not a secret to anyone. A satyagrahi has no secrets ....... What secret can a satyagrahi like Sardar have?' He had come there to clear the way for Gandhi and he had not come there to convey the message regarding salt. Gandhi was at a loss to know about the offence committed by Sardar Patel and wondered that a man of his stature should have been awarded a sentence of three months' jail and labelled it a matter of shame to the Sardar and to the government. Gandhi wished that a person like Sardar Patel should be sentenced to a term of seven years' imprisonment or be exiled. 'It would not befit the Government to sentence me to three months' imprisonment. Exile for life or hanging would be a punishment fit for a person like me. I am guility of sedition. It is my dharma to commit sedition against the Government. I am teaching this dharma to the people. A regime under which tyranny is being perpetrated, under which the rich and the poor are made to pay the same amount of tax on an item like salt under which exorbitant sums are being spent on watchmen, the police and the army under which the highest executive receives a salary which is five thousand times the income of the cultivator, under which an annual revenue of 25 crores of rupees is derived from narcotics and liquor, under which foreign cloth of the value of Rs. 60 cores is imported every year, and under which crores of persons continue to remain unemployed, it is one's dharma to rise against and destroy such a regime, to pray that fire may consume its policies.

Meanwhile, the A.I.C.C. held a meeting on the banks of the Sabarmati on 20 March. Besides the president Jawaharlal Nehru, it was attended by other prominent leaders like Maulana Azad, Sarojini Naidu, P. D. Tandon, Abbas Tyabji, Darbar Gopaldas, J. B. Kripalani, N.C. Kalelkar, Kasturba Gandhi, Ansuyabehn and Mrs. Ambalal.

Many members excused themselves from attendance on the plea that they were busy with preparations for Civil Disobedience Movement, in their own areas.

The leaders met under a sense of 'heavy' responsibility and the result was foregone conclusion.

By its principal resolution, the A.I.C.C. confirmed the Working Committee's resolution authorising Gandhi to launch Civil Disobedience Movement. It laid down the conditions under which the various provinces should start satyagraha on a mass scale.

The Provincial Congress Committees were given wide discretion about the manner, the form and the place of Civil Disobedience. It was open to them, to prepare their provinces for any form of satyagraha, best suited to them. But it was clearly laid down that the salt satyagraha should be undertaken in every province when it was possible. Other forms of satyagraha might be prepared for, but should be reserved for the second stage of the campaign. In case Gandhi was arrested, the Provincial Congress Committees should immediately determine to start Civil Disobedience, and if he was not arrested, they should await instructions which he might issue on reaching his destination. He would give the necessary signal and the Provincial Congress Committees would be informed immediately through the A.I.C.C. Office.

The Government of India felt much concern over the resolution of Congress. The Home Member suggested, 'it is essential that we should able to give timely warning owing to local Governments'. He also suggested that the correspondence of the members of the Working Committee; the correspondence of the head office of the Congress and of all provincial Congress offices and provincial Congress Presidents and of any particular individual whose correspondence in local government concerned might regard as likely to yield 'specially important' information, should be censured.

It was barely ten days ago that Gandhi had begun his historic march and the actual campaign was yet to be started. The whole country was already in a state of forewent for a parallel to which one might recollect the 'hottest days' of the Noncooperation Movement of 1920-22.

People in the provinces were planning to start the movement, and in some cases preliminary steps had already been initiated. In Bengal, for instance, which had for the moment, lost both its outstanding leaders, a 'War Council' had been formed. In the United Provinces, the Provincial Congress Committee had started a satyagraha committee consisting of prominent leaders, including the President of the Congress himself. Judging from the signs, the whole country appeared in the throes of an agitation of unprecedented magnitude. The Civil Disobedience plans of Gandhi and the Congress leaders.

As the march proceeded, so the pressure of publicity and social boycott was built up and resignations began to occur in large numbers. By 22 March, approximate number of resignations were four from Ahmedabad district: twenty-seven from Kaita (of whom sixteen were from Borsad taluka) seventeen from Broach, and two from Surat. But Surat soon became the most affected district by 5 April. One hundred and forty headmen had resigned and ten clays later, the figure had risen to two hundred and twenty seven.

Gandhi warned them, 'It will be regarded as cowardice to hand in one's resignation and then to withdraw it. There is no compulsion to resign. It is advisable to give up the post of Headman, looking upon it as something base, dirty and filthy.'

The speech delivered by Gandhi at Broach on 26 March dealt with the communal question. He explained that he had never dreamt that he could win swaraj merely through his effort or assisted only by the Hindus. He sought the assistance of Muslims, Parsis, Christians, Sikhs, Jews and all other Indians. He needed the assistance even of Englishmen. 'But I know too that all this combined assistance is worthless if I have not one other assistance, that is, from God. All is vain without His help. And if he is With this struggle, no other' help is necessary.

In a letter to Jawaharlal Nehru on 31 March Gandhi expressed his optimism about he forthcoming movement. 'Things seem to be shaping very well indeed in Gujarat... I feel you are right in attention to the salt tax for the time being. What more we can or should do. Unless you hear from me to the contrary, please take 6th April as the date for simultaneous beginning.'

At Jambusar, Kamaladevi Chattopadhyaya arrived to see Gandhi to remove the general impression that had gone abroad that as he had not included women in his first batch of volunteers, they might not be taken up at all. Gandhiji told her, 'If impatient mothers will be a little patient they will find ample scope for their zeal and sacrifice in this national struggle for freedom'.

She asked Gandhi what women with children should do. He said that he neither desired nor expected women to neglect their children. They might have to wait and bide their time, and thus be of use in some ways. Those women, however, who could make some satisfactory arrangements to have the children well looked after, should join the struggle.

At Surat where Gandhi and the satyagrahis reached on I April, they received a big welcome. He called the salt tax as beastly, inhuman and a Satanic Law. 'I have not heard of such justice anywhere in the world where it prevails ... To bow to an empire which dispenses such justice is not dharma but adharma. A man who prays to God every morning at dawn cannot, must not, pray for the good of such an empire. On the contrary while praying or saying the namaaz he should ask God to encompass the destruction of such a Satanic empire, such an inhuman government. To do so is dharma.'

In a message to the nation in the issue of Young India dated 3 April 1930, Gandhi exhorted the people 'Remember 5th April', and scart mass Civil Disobedience regarding the salt laws. He advised them to observe nonviolence in the fullest sense of the term. This was to be the spontaneous action. The workers were required to merely guide the masses in initial stages. Later, the masses would regulate the movement themselves.

The congress volunteers would render aid wherever needed. They, however, would be expected to be in the forefront. They were advised not to take sides in any communal quarrel. Wherever, there was a violent eruption, volunteers were expected to die in the attempt to quell violence. Those who were to be engaged in Civil Disobedience were occupy themselves and induce others to be engaged in some national service, such as khadi work, liquor and opium picketing, foreign-cloth shops, village sanitation, assisting the families of civil resistance prisoners in a variety of ways.

Gandhi also expected that if there was a real response about civil resistance regarding the salt tax, people should by proper organisation secure boycott of foreign cloth through khadi and secure total prohibition. This would mean a saving of 91 crores per year, and supplementary work for the millions of unemployed. 'If we secure these things, we cannot be far from independence. And not one of these things is beyond our capacity. Thus at each village, where the party stopped, Gandhi spoke briefly, telling the villagers that a great ordeal was at hand. He filled his political appeal with exhortation relevant to village life, such as khadi, cow-protection, cleanliness and untouchability. His appeal was not for money but for change of attitudes: he called on village officials to resign their posts which buttressed the exploitive regime. As he journeyed, he continued to give press interviews and to write to Navajivan and Young India, spreading his massage of swaraj and giving instructions for the conduct of the campaign during the days ahead.

Out of twenty-five days, which the journey took, the party of satyagrahis had walked for twenty-two days, excluding three days of Gandhi's silence. On his way, Gandhi passed by forty villages and towns and everywhere he addressed the audience. The whole countryside was awake to the call of the Mahatma.

At least fifty thousand persons heard his stirring message to the nation: his speeches were generally impassioned and always brave and there was a tone of pathos which had gone home to the hearts of the listeners. Despite all the fatigue and other hardships of the journey, he never allowed himself any comfort that was denied to the last man of his 'army'.

The satyagrahis reached Dandi on 5 April. Sarojini Naidu had already arrived there to welcome them. When interviewed by special correspondent of The Bombay Chronicle, Gandhi said, ' Government, perhaps, deserves congratulations for their policy of non-interference which is not exactly in keeping with their proved capacity for provoking popular sentiment.'

Next day he was to break the salt tax law. If the Civil Disobedience Movement become widespread in the country and the government tolerated it, the salt law, Gandhi declared, might be taken as abolished. He indeed had no doubt in his mind that the salt tax stood abolished the very moment that the decision to break that salt laws was reached.

'If they arrest me or my companions tomorrow, I shall not be surprised. I shall certainly not be pained. It would be absurd to be pained if we get something that we have invited on ourselves.'

Gandhi advised the people to make salt freely in every home, as our ancestors used to, and sell it from place to place, and they should continue doing so wherever possible till the government yielded, so much so that the salt in government stocks would become superfluous. 'If the awakening of the people in the country is true and real, the salt law is as good as abolished'.

Gandhi highlighted the importance of Dandi and praised the efforts of the people of the taluka. He explained,' Dandi was chosen not by a man but by God. How otherwise could we have chosen for the battlefield of satyagraha such an out-of-the-way place-a place where no food grains are to be had, where there is scarcity of water, where thousands can assemble only with difficulty, walking ten miles from the railway station, and where if you are travelling on foot, you have to negotiate creeks full of slush and mud? The truth is that in this struggle we have to put up with suffering. You have made the road from Navsari to Dandi famous throughout the world by arranging for free drinking-water at frequent intervals all along it... Dandi should be a sacred ground for us, where we should utter no untruth, commit so sin. Everyone coming here should come with this devout feeling in his heart.'

'If you have not yet gone out to remove salt, let the whole village get together and go. Hold the salt in your fist and think that you are carrying in your hand salt worth Rs. 6 Crores. Every year the Government has been taking away from us Rs. 6 Crores through its monopoly of salt.'

Gandhi and his volunteers broke the salt laws at 8-30 A.M. on 6 April 1930 by taking a lump of natural salt which was deposited in a small pit. Hundreds of persons witnessed this scene. Sarojini Naidu stood by Gandhiji's side, and, as the symbolic gesture was made, she cried, 'Hail Deliverer'.

Gandhi, while picking up a lump of salt in his hand, said, 'With this, I am shaking the foundation of the British Empire.' Not a single policeman or excise officer was present there. While talking to the representative of the free press, Gandhi said, 'Now that the technical or ceremonial breach of the Salt Law has been committed it is open to any one who would take the risk of prosecution' under the Salt Law to manufacture salt wherever he wishes and wherever it is convenient. My advice is that the workers should everywhere manufacture salt to make use of it and to instruct the villagers to do so.'

'Thus the war against the salt tax should be continued during the national week. Those who are not engaged in this sacred work should devote themselves to a vigorous propaganda for the boycott of foreign cloth and the use of Khadar. They should also endeavour to manufacture as much Khadar as possible.'

After Gandhi had addressed the meeting on 6 April about two tolas of salt which was taken by him in the morning and also cleaned by him, was auctioned for Rs. 525/-to Seth Ranchhod Shodhan, a mill-owner of Ahmedabad.

Gandhi's march on foot, form village to village through Gujarat which was his home and where his influence was greatest, aroused considerable interest and excitement. It has in fact appealed to the imagination of multitudes of people who were emotionally swayed by the dramatic turn of events. Throughout the march, Gandhiji went on preaching his cult of truth and nonviolence to the multitudes that gathered from far and near and he did not hesitate to impose the strictest discipline on the satyagrahis that flocked to his banner. The salt became the symbol of India's will to freedom. The same day the salt laws were broken throughout India at least by five million people at over 5,000 meetings. The entire countryside became acutely conscious of the struggle for Swaraj which was intensifying. The Dandi march received world-wide publicity. Soon the Civil Disobedience Movement spread simultaneously in western, northern, central, eastern and southern regions of India.

## PATEL AND QUIT INDIA MOVEMENT

The Quit India Movement *(Bharat Chhodo Andolan* or the *August Movement*) was a civil disobedience movement launched in India in August 1942 in response to Mohandas Gandhi's call for immediate independence. Gandhi hoped to bring the British government to the negotiating table. Almost the entire Congress leadership, and not merely at the national level, was put into confinement less than twenty-four hours after Gandhi's speech, and the greater number of the Congress leaders were to spend the rest of the war in jail.

## PROCESSION WIEW AT BANGALORE

### World War II and Indian involvement

By 1942, Indians were divided over World War II, as the British had unilaterally and without consultation entered India into the war. Some wanted to support the British during the Battle of Britain, hoping for eventual independence through this support. Others were enraged by the British disregard for Indian intelligence and civil rights, and were unsympathetic to the travails of Britons in the United Kingdom, which they saw as revenge for the subjugation of Indians.

### Opinions on the War

At the outbreak of war, the Congress Party had during the Wardha meeting of the working-committee in September 1939, passed a resolution conditionally supporting the fight against fascism, but were rebuffed when they asked for independence in return.

Gandhi had not supported this initiative, as he could not reconcile an endorsement for war (he was a committed believer in nonviolent resistance to tyranny, used in the Indian Independence Movement and proposed even against Hitler, Mussolini, and Tojo). However, at the height of the Battle of Britain, Gandhi had stated his support for the fight against fascism and of the British War effort, stating he did not seek to raise a free India from the ashes of Britain. However, opinions remained divided.

After the onset of the war, only a group led by Netaji Subhas Chandra Bose took any decisive action. Bose organized the Indian National Army with the help of the Japanese, and, soliciting help from the Axis Powers. The INA fought hard in the forests of Assam, Bengal and Burma, but ultimately failed owing to disrupted logistic, poor arms and supplies from the Japanese, and lack of support and training. Bose's audacious actions and radical initiative energized a new generation of Indians. The Quit India Movement tapped into this energy, channelling it into a united, cohesive action.

## Cripps' Mission

In March 1942, faced with an increasingly dissatisfied subcontinent only reluctantly participating in the war, and deteriorations in the war situation in Europe and South East Asia, and with growing dissatisfactions among Indian troops-especially in Europe-and among the civilian population in the subcontinent, the British government sent a delegation to India under Stafford Cripps, in what came to be known as the Cripps' Mission. The purpose of the mission was to negotiate with the Indian National Congress a deal to obtain total cooperation during the war, in return of progressive devolution and distribution of power from the crown and the Viceroy to elected Indian legislature. However, the talks failed, having failed to address the key demand of a timeframe towards self-government, and of definition of the powers to be relinquished, essentially portraying an offer of limited dominion-status that was wholly unacceptable to the Indian movement.

## Resolution for Immediate Independence

On July 14, 1942, the Indian National Congress passed a resolution demanding complete independence from Britain. The draft proposed that if the British did not accede to the demands, massive civil disobedience would be launched.

However, it proved to be controversial within the party. A prominent Congress national leader Chakravarti Rajgopalachari quit the Congress over this decision, and so did some local and regional level organizers. Jawaharlal Nehru and Maulana Azad were apprehensive and critical of the call, but backed it and stuck with Gandhi's leadership till the end. Sardar Vallabhbhai Patel and Dr. Rajendra Prasad were openly and enthusiastically in favour of such a disobedience movement, as were many veteran Gandhians and socialists like Asoka Mehta and Jaya Prakash Narayan.

The Congress had lesser success in rallying other political forces under a single flag and mast. Smaller parties like the Communist Party of India and the Hindu Mahasabha opposed the call. Muhammad Ali Jinnah's opposition to the call led to large numbers of Muslims cooperating with the British, and the Muslim League obtaining power in the Imperial provincial governments. On August 8, 1942 the Quit India Resolution was passed at the Bombay session of the All India Congress Committee (AICC). At Gowalia Tank, Bombay, Gandhi told Indians to follow nonviolent civil disobedience. He told the masses to act as an independent nation. His call found support among a large number of Indians.

# 5

# Princely State and Patel

## INTEGRATION OF STATES

Sardar Patel's integration over 560 princely states was really a great triumph for the sense of realism and responsibility. In respect of this great task, he has often been compared with Chancellor Bismarck who unified Germany in the late 19th century. But Patel's achievement is far more remarkable than that of Bismarck.

The latter had only to deal with about a dozen states; Patel had to handle 561. While Bismarck resorted to the policy of 'blood and iron', Patel brought about a bloodless revolution. He showed an amazing capacity to size up men and moments and strike when the iron was hot. Without splattering any blood, he caused about 800,000 sq km of land to be added to the Indian Union, besides a population of 86 million.

Both Gandhi and Lord Mountbatten warmly recognised Patel's great contribution. Gandhi observed: "The task of dealing with the princes was truly formidable, but I am convinced that the Sardar was the only person who could have coped with it." Lord Mountbatten, in his letter of June 19, 1948, to Patel, wrote: "There is no doubt that by far the most important achievement of the present Government is unification of the States into the Dominion of India. Had you failed in this, the results would have been disastrous. But since you succeeded, no one can see the disastrous consequences that you avoided. Nothing has added to the prestige of the present Government more than the brilliant policy you have followed with the States."

Patel first formulated a great design for a well-knit India and then proceeded to materialise it on the ground. He aroused the patriotic sentiments of the princes and reminded them: "We are at a momentous stage in the history of India. By a common endeavour, we can raise the country to a new greatness, while lack of unity will expose us to fresh calamities."

At the same time, Patel took care not to allow any grass to grow underneath his feet. He scotched Nawab of Bhopal's idea of grouping a few States and securing a separate dominion status. And when compulsive denigrators of India, like Winston Churchill, tried to complicate the Hyderabad problem by propping up the divisive game of the Nizam, "an old and faithful ally of the Empire", Patel responded clearly and firmly: "It is only in goodwill spirit and not on the malice and venom of Mr Churchill's tongue that an enduring relationship can be built between India and Britain and other members of the Commonwealth." The message went home and the browbeating of India stopped.

Patel's approach to the highly complex issues of integration of a wide variety of princely states was marked by an inspired vision, tact, magnanimity, inflexible will and 'resolute practicability'. When Nikita Khrushchev visited India in 1956, he significantly observed: "You Indians are a remarkable people. You have liquidated the princely states without liquidating the princes." It was, by implications, a great tribute to the remarkable work of Patel.

## PATEL AND KASHMIR

If Patel had handled Jammu & Kashmir, the subsequent confusion and contradictions would have been avoided and we would not have found ourselves in the bloody and brutal mess of the present day. Patel had correctly sized up Sheikh Abdullah and sensed his proclivity to bully. His practical sense forbade him to believe that all Indian eggs could be safely placed in the Sheikh's basket. He bemoaned India's reference of the Kashmir case to the United Nations. He tried his best to secure deletion of the words, "plebiscite under the UN auspices", from Jawaharlal Nehru's radio broadcast on October 28, 1947.

In his private conversation, he sometimes satirically referred to the 'expertise' of the two votaries of the UN in the Government of India—Lord Mountbatten and Nehru. Patel was also against Gopalaswamy Ayyangar being sent as leader of the Indian delegation to the UN and Sheikh Abdullah as member. He preferred Sir Girja Shankar to the former; about the latter, he feared that the "Sheikh's flamboyant personality might easily swamp the boat".

It was unwise to agree to many of Sheikh Abdullah's unreasonable demands and bolster his ego to such an extent that he started nursing illusions of carving out a virtual 'Sheikhdom' for himself and his coterie. Had Patel remained on the scene, he would have halted the appeasement in time. To the extent Patel was able to influence the course of events in Jammu &

Kashmir, his contribution was fruitful. When the raiders were on the outskirts of Srinagar and Lt Col Ranjit Rai and Major Som Nath Sharma of the Indian Army had been killed, being heavily outnumbered, Patel, accompanied by Defence Minister Baldev Singh flew to the State capital, assessed the situation on the ground and on return to New Delhi ordered stoppage of all airline services and diversion of all planes for flying troops to Srinagar.

The timely arrival of reinforcements enabled Brigadier Sen to lure the raiders in the net of Indian forces, near Shaltang, and attack them on November 5 from three sides. The raiders were routed. Three hundred of them were killed. The battle of Shaltang (November 7) proved decisive. Three days afterwards, advancing Indian troops recaptured Baramullah.

If Patel had his way, he would not have allowed Maharaja Hari Singh to be humiliated. Left to himself, he would have struck a proper balance between the requirements of the Union and the State and also harmonised, within a sound and truly secular and democratic framework, the aspirations of Sheikh Abdullah, Maharaja Hari Singh and those of the people of three main regions—Jammu, Kashmir and Ladakh.

## Reorganisation of Civil Services

During the freedom struggle, the Indian Civil Service was on the other side of the fence and incurred the wrath of the Congress leaders. Nehru berated it as "neither Indian nor civil nor service". As the freedom movement gained momentum and the spectacle of Partition loomed larger over the Indian horizon, the members of the Indian Civil Service became uneasy about their future. Thanks to the constructive genius of Patel, the tangle was satisfactorily resolved.

Patel's approach was that of a statesman. He did not allow the past rancour of the Congress against the ICS to blur his vision. He firmly believed that the All-India Services had a vital role to play in building a strong and united India. He advocated the retention of ICS and IP and proposed the constitution of two new All-India Services—the Indian Administrative Service and the Indian Police Service. Patel explained his reasons for favouring the continuance of the institution of the ICS during the debate in the Constituent Assembly. A few members criticised his proposals. Saxena reminded the Assembly: "It was the steel frame of the ICS that had enslaved us." Ayyangar said: "It means that they were the rulers under the old regime and that they will continue to be so in this regime." But Patel defended the ICS vigorously.

In a speech, which must be reckoned as historic in the arena of public administration in India, Patel said: "In point of patriotism, in point of sincerity and in point of ability, you cannot have a substitute... As a man of experience, I tell you, do not quarrel with the instruments with which you want to work. It is a bad workman who quarrels with his instruments."

Patel's acknowledgement of the role of the Indian Civil Service boosted the morale of the officers and gave them a new sense of confidence and purpose. They saw in him a "great guardian of their legitimate interests". He, with the enthusiastic support of the officers, not only completed the integration of the states and steered the country through a critical phase, but also put the Indian administration on a secure foundation.

## Developing a New Model of Civic Governance

Though little known, Patel's work in the field of civic administration was no less remarkable. In 1948, the Bombay Corporation held a civic reception in honour of Patel. On the occasion, he was asked what he considered to be the 'finest hour' of his illustrious career. Nobody expected him to say what he said. Inviting attention to his work first as chairman of the Sanitary Committee (1917-22) and then as president of the Municipal Board (1924-28). Patel reflected: "To cleanse the dirt of the city is quite different from cleansing the dirt of politics. From the former you get a good night's rest, while the latter keeps you worried and you lose your sleep."

Patel's approach was direct and dynamic. He often combined his morning walks with the inspection tour of the city. In the company of GV Mavalankar and civic officers, he moved into the narrow streets, ascertained the problems from the people and took prompt remedial measures. We constructed a model which solved many of the acute problems of sanitation, health, water supply, waste disposal and traffic. Sometimes Patel appeared on the streets, himself leading the sanitary team. This created a new fervour not only among his staff, but also the youth who joined his campaign.

Taking cue from Patel's selfless work in the streets of Ahmedabad, Gandhi advised the municipal councillors all over the country "not to seek honours or indulge in mutual rivalries, but to have real spirit of service and covert themselves into unpaid sweepers and road-makers and, above all, take pride in doing so."

## Protector of True Interests of Minorities

Patel has been accused of being anti-Muslim. Unfortunately, in the present-day India, this accusation has to be faced by all those who are the real benefactors of Muslims, but have the courage and commitment of calling a spade a spade, and making a distinction between appeasement and fairness, between whetting the appetite of a trouble-maker and telling him to behave. Patel, it is often forgotten, was the chairman of the Minorities Sub-Committee of the Constituent Assembly. The liberal provisions which our Constitution contains for the protection of linguistic and cultural rights of the minorities speak volumes about his catholicity.

Gandhi's unflinching faith in Patel's secularism comes out clearly in a letter of October 24, 1924, written to him by Mahadev Desai, during Gandhi's famous 21-day fast for Hindu-Muslim unity. Mahadev said: "Whatever may happen on Hindu-Muslim front in Gujarat, as long as you are there, Bapu is at peace. If a storm occurs despite your presence, Bapu will assume that it was not possible to prevent it."

## Sizing-up of China

Patel was a realist to the core. He was the first to see through Chinese aggressive designs. In a letter of November 7, 1950, to Nehru, he had observed: "The final action of the Chinese is little short of perfidy. The tragedy of it is that the Tibetan put faith in us, and we have been unable to get them out the meshes of Chinese malevolence. Chinese irredentism and Communist imperialism are different from the expansionism or imperialism of the Western Powers. The former has a cloak of ideology which makes it 10-times more dangerous." Patel's warning proved prophetic. We all know what a humiliation India suffered at the hands of Chinese in 1962.

## Standard of Probity

Patel was an embodiment of probity in public life. The only property he left comprised a few *dhotis* and *kurtas* and a suitcase. He did not tolerate malfeasance anywhere. Even a minor impropriety by his partymen was sternly dealt with. Today, when things in India are falling apart and the Union is tottering, the national leadership ought to take a leaf from Patel's book and show the same constructive vision and iron will which he showed at a critical juncture of our history.

Aside from the matter of official language was the dilemma of "linguistic provinces." This was a question of political administration debated long before independence; the solution would in fact replicate the decision the Indian National Congress had taken to facilitate its anti-colonial struggle. Under Gandhi's leadership, the Congress had long championed Hindi-Hindustani as the emblematic all-India language, in both Devanagari and Persian script forms. But the Congress as well recognized that in terms of organization and political expediency, it could better function through a regional-language architecture. After Independence, the Constituent Assembly appointed the Linguistic Provinces Committee to study the issue. No easy compromise could be found; to be sure, the committee recognized that there was considerable demand for the redrawing of provincial boundaries, and that administering education, public life, and legislatures would be expedited if they could be organized into more homogenous linguistic units. But they were concerned above all about whether the formation of new boundaries along linguistic lines would bring new sub nationalisms into existence, and further what the impact might be in terms of creating new relations of majority-minority dynamics.

For example, should a new Kannada-speaking state be carved out of Madras and Mysore states, a significant minority of Marathi-speakers would find themselves in a new subordinate position. Within the south, in what was then-Madras state, agitations emerged for a separate state of Telugu speakers as well as a partitioning of Marathi and Kannada speakers. Gujarati speakers in Bombay State argued for a separate Gujarati-speaking state; Marathi-speakers wanted a Maharashtra. Punjabi-speakers sought to rescue themselves from a minority status in a Punjab that had suddenly become primarily Hindi speaking as a result of Partition and the exodus of millions of Punjabi-speaking Muslims to Pakistan. The question of linguistic provinces became a serious matter of public debate, with the biggest names in Indian political life issuing reports either recommending a linguistic provinces reorganization (Ambedkar, for example) or against— it for example Patel, Sitaramayya, and Nehru.

The argument against however raised the specter of imminent Balkanization, invoking the recent trauma of Partition and the necessity for the Indian Union to foster great unity rather than further divisions, exemplified by this sentence from the Patel, Sitaramayya, and Nehru report: "The context demands, above everything, the consolidation of India and her freedom...the promotion of unity in India. It demands further stem discouragement of communalism, provincialism, and all other separatist and disruptive tendencies.

Despite this, a massive reorganization of state boundaries did indeed take place, in shifts, absolutely along linguistic lines, and through a process of combining princely states and carving up the huge British-organized "presidencies." First, the 1953 Andhra State Act carved a Telugu-speaking state of Andhra out of Madras. Chandemagore was folded into West Bengal in 1954. Then the 1956 states reorganization produced the "new" states of Andhra Pradesh (by adding more territory to Andhra), Kerala, Madhya Pradesh, and Tamil Nadu; it also redesigned the borders of Himachal Pradesh,

West Bengal, Assam, Bihar, and the various Union territories. The 1959 Rajasthan and Madhya Pradesh Transfer of Territories Act reapportioned land to each; the 1960 Bombay Reorganisation Act created Gujarat and Maharashtra; the 1962 Nagaland Act created Nagaland; the 1966 Punjab Reorganisation Act forged a new Hindi-speaking Haryana and created majority Punjabi-speaking Punjab. The 1968 Andhra Pradesh and Mysore Transfer of Territory act created Kannada-speaking Karnataka, and finally the 1971 North-eastem States Reorganisation Act threw up Meghalaya, Mizoram, Tripura, Manipur, and Arunachal Pradesh. The 1990 language conflict in Bangalore for example, has involved anti-Tamil demonstrations, and protests against attempts in 1994 to broadcast Urdu-language news on local (state-operated) television Bangalore, resulting in protests.

Nearly fifty years after the major states reorganization of 1956, most contemporary observers judge the administrative organization to have been a policy success, for language conflict is now relatively rare (again, Assam the salient exception) and language riots practically non-existent.so Did the creation of more homogenous administrative territories produce new sub nationalisms? From the perspective of the centre, the answer appears to be broadly no. Yet if we ask this same question from another vantage point, that of speakers of a minority language within the linguistically demarcated states, we do find that the majoritarian language hegemony Patel, Sitaramaya, and Nehru worried about has come to pass. Two points should be noted in this regard. First, for minority language speakers within states-using Dua's example of Dakkani speakers in Mysore-the required language repertoire can be as high as five languages (Dakkani, high Urdu, Kannada, Hindi, English). This is a dramatic load compared to a Hindi belter's ability to get by with studying only Hindi and English.

Yet this appears not to be a significant source of conflict, and in any event high levels of multilingualism have long characterized the South Asian region. But the second point, perhaps more apposite, lies in the way that new relationships of linguistic categories have indeed created new minorities and new majorities with unequal relations of power. After the major states reorganization in 1956, individual states in India passed their own state-level laws to promote and develop various official languages of state. The composite Hindustani effort would end, to be replaced by separate Hindi and Urdu broadcasts. Regional nodes of AIR (renamed Akashvani, or "voice from the sky" in official Hindi), would create programming in regional languages, following the pattern of the linguistic provinces. Doordmshan, India's state television, follows a similar structure: national programs are created in Hindi and English, relayed throughout the country, with additional programs created at the state level in the various regional languages. India's unique literary heritage was considered so critical for national development that a government resolution in 1954 created the Sahitya Akademi (India's National Academy of Letters). It began operation in 1956. The Sahitya Akademi exists entirely to serve as a sort of national bureau of literary recognition, with programs to translate work from one Indian language into another, as well as into English, not to mention the annual bestowing of awards for literary merit in each of the languages recognized in the Constitution. This is a self conscious effort to establish a national sensibility of unity-in-diversity through literature. Of course, the project is not without its conceptual dilemmas. As Sheldon Pollock argues, a paradox inheres in the fact that this Akademi had to be created in order to forge awareness of the national literature it assumes to already exist.

Jyotirindra Das Gupta in turn notes, the "Hindi literati" played a significant role in the creation of modem standard Hindi-picking up from where the Hindi language movement left off in the late 19th century—coining an extensive array of new terms for modern life from Sanskrit, and promoting a brand new form of the language that aimed to create a veneer of a different kind of linguistic geneology, *i.e.*, the modem inheritor of the great Sanskrit tradition.

The post Independence efforts to make a national language in the singular fell on the sword of its own diversity, producing a multilingual national policy that effectively mirrors the sort of multilingual existence deep-rooted in the region. In this sense practices with much longer precedents rode roughshod over the bureaucratic imagined idea of a national language. The ideological "content" carried by the national language project and its proponents, namely organizations seeking to fuse the national language and thereby the nation with an Aryan overlay, was the most important feature of the conflict with India's southern states, particularly Tamil Nadu.

The Dravidian anti-Brahmin populism which characterized the state's politics of the 50s and 60s could hardly have welcomed the introduction of a language explicitly presented as some high-water mark of Aryan cultural achievement. This demonstrates how the social-ideological context trumped the program for forging national linguistic unanimity. Secondly, the case of India shows how and why literature and its histories matter. Long senses of literary traditions inscribe the history of regions with cultural exemplars, a narrative biography of a language's past. These ideas are difficult to undo. But because of its size, the decision to administer a federal system with states drawn along lines of language communities, and considerable efforts to incorporate the work of the many language associations as effective arms of language policy, perhaps India cannot offer the most appropriate comparison for the language policy decisions taken by Pakistan. The Pakistani nation-state sought to present Urdu as the natural and exclusive emblem of the Muslim nation of the Indian subcontinent, investing the idea of the language with a peculiar religious sacredness, this claim would pragmatically dissociate the literary traditions central to Pakistan's regional languages from the realm of faith. Partition ushered in the era of the nation-form along with its essentialist presumptions of large-scale uniformity, including in the realm of language. This pursuit, in India as well as in Pakistan, drew upon teleological narratives of the past and of religious community that had their roots in a nineteenth-century language controversy in northern India. Specifically, the presumption that Urdu was the obvious national language of the region's Muslims was the outcome of two intertwined phenomena: the geographical base of the Muslim League's primary support, and the pre-history of what became known as the "Hindi-Urdu controversy." Up until 1946 the primary support for the Muslim League's Pakistan demand was located in the North-West Provinces, termed the "Muslim minority" provinces. This was the very same territory of the contentious Hindi-Urdu controversy that took place in the second half of the nineteenth century. This meant that a salient political issue for Muslims in the region was the "protection" of Urdu, even though Muslims in the vast expanse of British India and the various princely states obviously spoke a wide variety of other languages; but with the political core centred on the North-West Provinces, ideas about who and what constituted Islamic India collapsed the cultural imagination onto the great historical and cultural traditions of that particular land to the exclusion of everywhere else.

Indeed, the historical record here underscores the contention of linguistic controversy, which paved the way for a growing consensus that linked language and religion into the slogans "Hindi-Hindu-Hindustan" in opposition to "Urdu-Muslim Pakistan"." The social and literary histories of Hindi, Urdu, and their schismogenesis are now becoming voluminous. Given the factual conundrum that neither Hindi nor Urdu, at least in the forms they would assume by the twentieth century, had any particular role in sacred religious texts, their opposition appears all the more perplexing in retrospect. In effect, these two languages would become the bearers of religion first, then nation by proxy. In fact what is calld Urdu today could-at any point from perhaps the late sixteenth through nineteenth centuries-have been called, variously, HindvI, Hindi, Dihlavi, Gujri, Dakani, Rekhtah, "Moors" (a British coinage), Hindoostanic, Hindoostanee, and so on.

The former usage of "Moors" apparently was synonymous with "the black language," at least for officers of the Royal army.

The name "Urdu" is itself a short fonn of "Zaban-e-Urdu-e-Mu'alla," or "Language of the Exalted (Military) Camp"-attesting to the belief that the language's origins lie in the interaction of Turkish and Persian-speaking military troops with indigenous Indian soldiers in the Mughal employ. This is the standard narrative of Urdu's birth, though even that is under revision.

Shamsur Rahman Faruqi argued that the name ''Urdu'' did not come into existence until the end of the eighteenth century, the very tail end of the historical period which supposedly produced the language. And that the belief that the name "Urdu" referenced the military camp is incorrect, and that it refers to Shahjahanabad instead, and that the actual birth of Urdu as a literary language stemmed from the production of works by Sufis in the Deccan and in Gujarat.

And like our above case study suggested, As the nineteenth century continued, advocacy for Hindi in the Nagari script continued to gain force, and the demands became political. Hindi advocates petitioned the colonial authorities for the equal privilege to use Nagari-script Hindi in the courts, and as well for the right to a Hindi-language primary education. Pamphleteering for Hindi's right to participate in the official spheres of public life allied the language with the masses-the Hindu masses-and forged a discourse at once about religion and the spread democracy, through language. Urdu was figured as a foreign imposition, an alien script with alien words that came from alien invaders. As Hindi became a more potent sociopolitical force, Urdu speakers felt themselves under attack. Urdu then became a language in need of "defending," a language represented by its partisan proponents as a core aspect of Muslim life itself. The Hindi-Urdu Controversy in north India, in conjunction with movements for religious reformation within Hinduism and Islam slightly predating and continuing during the same period, participated in community schismogenesis, a process which at its end points, would result in the complete association of Urdu with Islam and Hindi with Hinduism. And while it is generally recognisde to have been an important concern for residents of the North-West Provinces, it rose to a similar level of primacy in the territories which would eventually form Pakistan. In fact by the time of Pakistan's birth, the elision of Urdu-Muslim-Pakistan was complete, and yet highly controversial. There was a disjuncture between the territorial imagination of the Urdu Muslim synecdoche and the actual practical situation of the territory that was Muslimmajority and which would become Pakistan.

## PRINCELY STATES IN BRITISH INDIA

The early history of British expansion in India was characterised by the co-existence of two approaches towards the existing princely states. The first was a policy of annexation, where the British sought to forcibly absorb the Indian princely states into the provinces which constituted their Empire in India.

The second was a policy of indirect rule, where the British assumed suzerainty and paramountcy over princely states, but conceded some degree of sovereignty to them. During the early part of the nineteenth century, the policy of the British tended towards annexation, but the Indian Rebellion of 1857 forced a change in this approach, by demonstrating both the difficulty of absorbing and subduing annexed states, and the usefulness of princely states as a source of support.

In 1858, the policy of annexation was formally renounced, and British relations with the princely states thereafter were based on indirect rule, whereby the British exercised paramountcy over all princely states with the British crown as ultimate suzerain, but at the same time respected and protected them as allies. The exact relations between the British and each princely state were regulated by individual treaties, and varied widely, with some states having significant autonomy, some being subject to significant control in internal affairs, and some being in effect the owners of a few acres of land with little autonomy.

During the 20th century, the British made several attempts to integrate the princely states more closely with British India, creating the Chamber of Princes in 1921 as a consultative and advisory body, transferring the responsibility for supervision of smaller states from the provinces to the centre in 1936, and creating direct relations between the Government of India and the larger princely states superseding political agents. The most ambitious was a scheme of federation in the Government of India Act, 1935, which envisaged the princely states and British India being united under a federal government. This scheme came close to success, but was abandoned in 1939 as a result of the outbreak of the Second World War. As a result, in the 1940s, the relationship between the princely states and the crown remained regulated by the principle of paramountcy and the various treaties between the British crown and the states.

Neither paramountcy nor these arrangements could continue after Indian independence. The British took the view that because they had been established directly between the British crown and the princely states, they could not be transferred to independent India. At the same time, they imposed obligations on Britain that it was not prepared to continue to carry out, such as the obligation to maintain troops in India for the defence of the princely states. The British government therefore decided that paramountcy, together with all treaties between them and the princely states, would come to an end upon the transfer of power.

## Reasons for Integration

The Saurashtra and Kathiawar regions of Gujarat were home to over two hundred princely states, many with non-contiguous territories, as this map of Baroda shows.

The termination of paramountcy would have in principle have meant that all rights that flowed from the states' relationship with the British crown would return to them, leaving them free to negotiate relationships with the new states of India and Pakistan "on a basis of complete freedom." Early British plans for the transfer of power, such as the offer produced by the Cripps Mission, recognised the possibility that some princely states might choose to stand out of independent India. This was unacceptable to the Congress, which regarded the independence of princely states as a denial of the course of Indian history, and consequently regarded this scheme as a "Balkanisation" of India. The Congress had traditionally been less active in the princely states because of their limited resources which restricted their ability to organise there and their focus on the goal of independence from the British, and because Congress leaders, in particular Gandhi, were sympathetic to the more progressive princes as examples of the capacity of Indians to rule themselves. This changed in the 1930s as a result of the federation scheme contained in the Government of India Act, 1935 and the rise of socialist Congress leaders such as Jayaprakash Narayan, and the Congress began to actively engage with popular political and labour activity in the princely states. By 1939, the Congress' official stance was that the states must enter independent India, on the same terms and with the same autonomy as the provinces of British India, and with their people granted responsible government. As a result, it insisted on the incorporation of the princely states into India in its negotiations with Mountbatten.

A few British leaders, particularly Lord Mountbatten, the last British viceroy in India, were also uncomfortable with breaking links between independent India and the princely states. The development of trade, commerce and communications during the 19th and 20th centuries had bound the princely states to British India through a complex network of interests. Agreements relating to railways, customs, irrigation, the use of ports, and other similar agreements would disappear, posing a serious threat to the economic life of the subcontinent. Mountbatten was also persuaded by the argument of Indian leaders such as V.P. Menon that the integration of the princely states into independent India would to some extent assuage the wounds of partition. The result was that Mountbatten personally favoured and worked towards the accession of princely states to India following the transfer of power, as proposed by the Congress.

## RAJPUTANA UNDER BRITISH PARAMOUNTCY

***The Failure of Indirect Rule :*** When India became independent in 1947, nineteen princely states and three chiefships of Rajputana were amalgamated into a single political unit, Rajasthan, that became a state within the Indian union. The special form of indirect rule, paramountcy, which Britain exercised in the princely states had not prepared Rajputana for independence. Princely rule and legitimacy, based on birth, was abruptly replaced by parliamentary government and the authority of democracy. Institutional changes which had taken place in British India over more than one hundred years were brought into being in Rajasthan in less than five. This work was accomplished not by those who stood at the head of the old regime but by those who had opposed it from within and by the new men of the central government in Delhi.

Rajasthan succeeded states which, after the making of treaties with Britain in 1818, had lived under that ambiguous conception of sovereignty which deprived the princes of their foreign powers and left their domestic powers subject to certain supervision. The gentle breezes of change and British political influence modified Rajput monarchial and feudal institutions but did not replace or even fundamentally transform them. The princes and their administrators learned what makes a respectable modern state and began, often with British guidance to construct new institutions. Sometimes these were effective and meaningful; more often they had the insubstantiality of stage setting. The political community expanded very little, but newly aware groups did take shape and hover near its boundaries waiting to assert their claims. The gradual extension of the rule of law and a growing appreciation for modern administration began but did not complete the separation of the state and its public offices and finances from the private estate, retainers, and income of the prince. These changes contributed to a consciousness of political rights and liberties but failed to make them constitutional. Until the crises and traumas of 1947 revealed their hollowness and fragility, the traditional ideas and practices of legitimacy and rulership, which paramountcy was designed to protect from external and internal dangers, continued intact.

Vagueness concerning the limits of power is likely to be helpful to those who exercise it. The British Government studiously avoided precision in defining paramountcy, the exercise of power over princely states. Its meaning derived from a wide variety of treaties concluded with different princes and a system of case law and precedent whose interpretation lay with the paramount power. The Butler Commission concisely summarized the deliberate ambiguity of paramountcy in 1928 when, in response to a request from the princes to define the concept, it merely stated: "Paramountcy must remain paramount." Paramountcy implied that the governor-general of India would exercise power in the field of foreign affairs, defense, communications, and coinage on behalf of the princely states. It left the states internally autonomous while guaranteeing the rulers protection against enemies foreign and domestic. The guarantee against domestic enemies brought with it unsystematic intervention in domestic affairs to insure that there would not be too many of them. An agent or a resident drawn from the special administrative cadre known as the political service represented the governor-general in the state and exercised these powers.

The influence of the British on the states depended on the overall policy espoused by the governor-general and the respective qualities of the political agents and the princes. A hands-off policy toward the princely states followed the rebellion of 1857, which frightened the British government away from strong interventionism. This policy ended at the turn of the twentieth century when Lord Curzon began to impress the princes with their responsibilities. The example of Maharaja Ganga Singh of Bikaner, who in 1899 sharply protested against the political agent's desire to review the dismissal of two petty state officials, was not exceptional in the Curzon era. "Nothing is further from my mind [the agent wrote] than interference with your orders, and I trust there will never be any greater need than there is now for contemplating such interference. It is, however, the duty of every political agent to satisfy himself that the state with which he is, is well and justly governed, or how it is governed, and he can only do this by occasionally asking for reports on selected petitions." Lord Minto's easy-going policy eased the pressures for reform and intervention that Curzon had applied, but Lord Linlithgow's viceroyalty in the 1930's once again brought an emphasis on administrative modernization and reform, and hence greater intervention.

The British exercised influence through numerous channels even in areas beyond the ordinary concerns of paramountcy. The crown drew to itself the right to recognize the successor to the *gaddi* (throne) of any state, and thus became involved in settling succession disputes. Since legitimate successors were often minors, and since during succession disputes unprotected minors sometimes expired prematurely, the crown took some responsibility for the minority administration. It appointed the regent, often making its selection within the state, sometimes sending in a member of the political service to conduct the administration. Minority rule provided the occasion for strong, often creative, intervention and laid the basis for subsequent influence. At the end of a twenty-year minority administration exercised on behalf of Maharaja Umed Singh of Kotah by the political agent to that state, he offered the following "advice" to the newly invested ruler: "Your Highness will in all important matters consult the political agent, be guided by his advice, and obtain his concurrence before introducing any important change in the measures carried out during your minority." Similar "advice" was given at Bikaner at the same time, although in later years the maharaja of that state became notoriously independent.

The channels of British influence were both direct and indirect. The political agent advised in the matter of the prince's education. In the twentieth century especially, English tutors were often employed, unless the prince attended one of the princes' and nobles' schools established with Government of India blessings to transmit the more superficial trappings of English public school education. Less superficial traits, like the dutiful asceticism of ruling classes trained at Eton, Harrow, and Winchester were more difficult to transmit to heirs who arrived with retinues of ten servants. In the twenty years before independence, the larger states often appointed Englishmen from the political department as *dewans* (chief ministers) and ministers. In the latter years of the British *Raj*, when Indian members of the Indian civil service began to control provincial administration under the direction of Indian ministers in British India, a senior member of the political service observed: "The administration in so-called Indian India was sometimes more under the control of British officers than it was in British India."

The emergence of nationalism in British India had a curious effect on both the British attitude toward the princes and on the princes themselves. To the extent that the princes were a bulwark of British power, particularly when it began to be challenged in British India, the Government of India was inclined to treat them generously. To the princes, generosity meant being left alone. Yet the need for internal improvements became more apparent as nationalism and reformist sentiment grew. Improvement meant interference.

The chamber of princes was established on a permanent basis in 1921, the year after Gandhi turned the nationalist movement in British India in a popular direction. The chamber provided a forum in which princes could protest against efforts by the government to intervene and hurry them along and a context in which they became more conscious of one another and of the requirements that accompanied being a "modern ruler". The chancellor of the chamber of princes in 1927 circulated a memorandum summing up some of the most significant reforms on which he hoped they might all agree; suggested reforms included limitation of the privy purse to 10 per cent of state revenues, an independent judiciary, security of tenure for state civil servants, a promulgated code of law, and the maintenance of an efficient and honest police force. The chamber began to create an environment in which good government became more fashionable. Princes vied with one another to secure the services of one of the four or five men who had built all-India reputations as able chief ministers in princely states. Paramountcy did, then, affect the structure and quality of government in the princely states. But the channels of British influence were too irregular and undefined to exploit consistently the available opportunities. Imperial policy, which varied with the outlook of the viceroy, his agents, and the developments in British India, never achieved the direction or firmness necessary to make it otherwise.

Caste, clan, land, and chivalric reputation had legitimized rulership in the old princely states ruled by Rajputs, members of the warrior-ruler caste (Kshatriyas). After conclusion of the subsidiary alliances in 1818, British recognition and support were required as well. The addition did little, however, to change explicitly the way most Rajastbanis understood the legitimacy of their maharajas or nobles; ascriptive factors justified the exercise of power in 1947 as they had done in 1818.

Yet the old ideas about what made government legitimate were subtly undermined during the period of paramountcy by a tentative new concern with effectiveness and consent. The example of events in British India and British pressures suggested that a prince justify his rule by performance. As Lord Curzon, who was wont to lecture the princes on this subject, put it: A ruler's "*gaddi* (throne) is not intended to be a divan of indulgence, but the stern seat of duty", and "by this test will he, in the long run, as a political institution, perish or survive." Princes were pressed to convert their courts into more "public" institutions and to orient their rule towards public rather than personal and familial benefits. The differentiation of the princes' privy purse from the public revenue, incomplete as it was in many states, and reports on administration that provided a rudimentary accounting of how government had discharged its task were the chief manifestations of this shift. The same influences affected the bureaucracy, which was urged to consider itself a public and professional service, not a body of private retainers.

The idea that greater public service would not only add luster to the name of the maharaja—that idea had already existed in pre-British days—but also become a condition of legitimate rule was by no means universally understood. Only a few, some of the new-style court bureaucrats and members of a tiny educated class, saw its relevance and import. But a good many maharajas, affected by their English tutors or schools, pressure from the political department, the communications spill-over from British India or far-seeing ministers, began to believe that they should serve as well as rule. Their consciousness of themselves as public men was affected by this idea even though they failed often to act on it. At the time of independence, the maharajas' feeble resistance to the challenge of democratic authority and leadership arose in part from an awareness of their failure to meet the new standards.

Traditional ideas of legitimacy were modified in another and more subtle respect. Ordinarily the maharaja sought not to offend and listened to the grievances and advice of the limited political community of the twice-born castes, the Brahmans, Kshatriyas and Vaishyas who could help or hinder him spiritually, militarily, and financially. Most Rajasthanis were politically irrelevant and thought that they should be. Before 1935, only a tiny circle of intellectuals and modern nationalists without status and power thought otherwise. After 1935, the potential political community, those seeking to share power in the state and to influence government, expanded. A handful of schoolmasters, lawyers, and journalists began to awaken the urban and rural common people by telling them that their interests and aspirations were relevant for government and that its authority should rest on their will. They made little progress; only after independence during the first general election of 1952 did Rajasthanis begin to perceive a connection between popular sovereignty and legitimacy.

If some maharajas accepted the notion that their right to rule depended in a measure upon performance and service, none conceded that it depended upon the support of organized public opinion. Some used means to consult public opinion, such as great annual *durbars* (royal public audiences), to inform themselves and their governments of public grievances and aspirations, but none entertained the notion of reigning rather than ruling by transforming the state into a democratic constitutional monarchy. Only toward the end of World War II, when the signs of the times pointed to the loss of British support and a more democratic future, did some princely states introduce elections based on limited franchise for legislatures to be dominated by an official or appointive majority.

The presence of the idea of democratic authority, though it lacked a large social base and effectively organized political support, weakened older beliefs and paved the way for its own ultimate realization. The strongest safeguard for any concept of legitimacy is for it to appear as natural; without rivals, its self-evidence stands unquestioned. The innocence of alternatives, which was traditional legitimacy's most powerful safeguard, was shattered by knowledge of the growing influence of organized public opinion in British India and its nascent expression within Rajasthan.

Prior to the British arrival, power in the Rajput states was shared by a territorial nobility and a maharaja, who was often their clan chief. The initial effect of British paramountcy in the nineteenth century not only sustained this diffusion of power but also undermined the attempts of some rulers to centralize power at the expense of their nobility. Sir Alfred Lyall in the late nineteenth century saw the nobles as a countervailing power of the kind that had created feudal liberties in the West. This belief persisted into the twentieth century when it was challenged but not replaced by a British policy of centralization designed to create financial viability and orderly and efficient administration. In the small states, the new policy was resisted by the maharajas since it involved partial if not total surrender of sovereignty, but in the larger states modest advances were achieved.

The pattern of decentralization in the nineteenth century had not been uniform. In Kotah, Dewan Zaiim Singh virtually replaced the maharaja and reduced the independent territorial power of the nobility by making them dependent on the crown. In Dholpur and Bharatpur, two eastern states of Rajasthan ruled by Jats rather than Rajputs, territorial nobility on the Rajput pattern never existed. Formally classified as a peasant caste, the Jats had a recent history of military prowess and local rulership. Their states were centralized in the negative sense that they lacked strongly articulated local power, but not in the positive one that they possessed a vigorous central government. The Rajput states confronted a dual task: to reduce the power of the nobility and to strengthen state government.

Maharaja Sawai Man Singh's efforts in Jaipur throughout the 1930's to strengthen his hand against his feudality illustrates one of the more successful attempts to reduce feudal power. It did not produce striking results. His effort to diminish the extensive financial, civil, police, and judicial powers of the state's great nobles in Shekhawati began in 1932 with his appointment of C.V. Wills, a British Indian official, to investigate the historical and legal relations between the maharaja and his nobles. The proceeding itself, utilizing Western legal concepts, departed from traditional methods. Wills' findings, perhaps not surprisingly, established that the nobles' claims to a separate and quasi-autonomous status had no legal or historical justification. Not until 1939, seven years after Wills began his labours, did the Jaipur *durbar* venture to assert the powers which his investigations had persuaded it that it could claim: to vary the assessments of the *thikanas* (nobles' estates) which, by remaining fixed, had rendered the state revenue inelastic; to treat the state as a single economic and commercial unit by extending its customs cordon to include the *thikanas*; to abolish residuary civil and criminal powers reserved by some *thikanedars*. Only in 1939, then, did Jaipur clearly claim the minimum fiscal and legal powers characteristic of a modern state. Having done so, the *durbar* announced that in practice it would insist on only some of them. The *durbar* was "graciously pleased," it announced, for example, "to order that the *muamla* (assessments) be declared to be permanently fixed at the existing figure in all cases," foregoing, thereby, that enhancement of revenues so vital for substantial expansion of state functions.

The paramount power's responsibility for external security rendered the military forces of the states less significant, but they too reflected the diffusion of power. State forces were maintained to keep law and order and for ceremonial purposes and, from the 1890's, as imperial service troops to aid the Government of India in foreign wars. The *thikanas* kept armed retainers to satisfy their obligations to the maharaja and for their own purposes. Only in 1925 was the end of feudal military relations in Jaipur formally recognized. At that time the *thikanedar's* obligation to provide mounted and foot soldiers to the Jaipur *durbar* was commuted to cash. After this change some, nevertheless, continued to maintain military units. In 1937, the Jaipur *durbar* confronted the last gasp of feudal military power when its forces faced ten thousand armed retainers in Sikar, the state's largest *thikana*. Bikaner, more forward in this respect, faced its last significant challenge in 1905.

It is possible that, but for British intervention, effective centralization might have gone further in such vigorous and forward-looking states as Bikaner and Jaipur. The political department tried, on the one hand, to encourage modernization and on the other, to prevent an efficient autocrat such as Bikaner or a gentler one such as Jaipur from running roughshod over his nobility. The two aims were incompatible. Effective centralization could not proceed without reducing or transforming the civil and judicial power of the nobles, as well as the immense economic power they exercised over their estates, which covered over half the territory of most Rajput states. Crucial to control of the *jagir* (nobles' grants) areas were settlement operations that would establish occupancy rights and revenue payments, and state intervention to enforce these and other relationships between peasants and nobles. But vigorous efforts to restrict and control the landed nobility, such as in Bikaner in the first decade of the century, Jaipur in the 1930's, and Jodhpur in the 1940's, invariably generated resistance and raised the possibility of the paramount power having to fulfil its pledge to protect rulers from internal rebellion.

The political department considered risking such difficulties. In 1942 it prepared to press for fair rent, occupancy rights, and records of rights in Rajasthan, especially in Jaipur. But the advice of officers familiar with the area persuaded the department that the proposal was too risky. The political department's desire to avoid the difficulties that economic or social or administrative changes entailed, especially when the Congress in British India was prepared to use such difficulties for its own purposes, was buttressed by a solicitude for the property rights of the nobility. The result was a policy of marginal and limited changes in land relations. On the other hand, without British supervision most Rajput princes would not have pressed for radical change. Efforts to amalgamate police, judicial, and certain administrative functions of some of the smaller Rajasthan principalities, for example, ran into resolute opposition from princes concerned to preserve their dynastic and territorial sovereignty and individuality. The political department considered centralization and greater administrative efficiency desirable but was not prepared to risk much on their behalf by forcing the princes or coercing the nobles.

Most states sought to rationalize government in such a way that central power could reach further as it became stronger. The establishment of specialized government departments with defined responsibilities and jurisdictions strengthened executive control. A letter by the twenty-one-year old Maharaja Ganga Singh of Bikaner illustrates the early efforts of an able Rajput ruler:

There is nothing laid down as to the limits of power which each Member [of Council] or the Dewan [chief minister] can exercise over the departments under their control. The result is that sometimes important things are decided and settled by officers above mentioned, whereas some trifling things are sometimes referred to the full Council or to me. In fact, owing to there being no rules everything is done in a haphazard way. There is also a general tendency to shirk responsibility as much as possible, and for everybody to try to have a finger in the pie whenever they have a good opportunity. The result is unsatisfactory and injurious to the interests of the state while much extra work is thrown on my shoulders. Ganga Singh eventually became the ablest Rajput ruler in the twentieth century, but he too opposed the development of regular procedures where they interfered with his personal rule. He saw that bureaucratization itself, even without responsible government, involves a restraint on power. For years he resisted appointing a permanent and responsible chief minister to direct the government even though he was often out of the country. Ganga Singh also resisted the establishment of competitive civil service recruitment. On the other hand, Bikaner state was divided into districts and subdistricts for purposes of revenue administration as early as 1872, strengthening crown control. Not until 1945, and then only for the crown lands, did Jaipur establish district officers responsible for revenue, law, and order and give them powers approximating those of British Indian officers.

The competence of the bureaucracy in many states increased during the era of paramountcy. Academic qualifications, reflecting the growth of educational opportunities in the twentieth century, were added to those of caste and heredity, but since they were no guarantee of competence, the state administrative cadres remained something less than merit services. The qualifications, however, did represent a concession to recruitment by achievement rather than by ascription. The increasing emphasis on educational qualifications can be seen from a comparison of princely state officials recruited in the 1920's, 1930's and in 1940-47. Among 143 *tahsildars,* chief administrative officers for *tahsils* (subdivisions of a district), selected from princely state services for positions in the administration of post-independence Rajasthan, 10 per cent of those recruited in the 1920's, 56 per cent of those recruited in the 1930's, and 94 per cent of those recruited in the 1940's had B.A. degrees.

Apparently no state recruited through competitive examinations before 1940, and none established security of tenure. In 1941 Udaipur established a formal civil service, recruited competitively; Jodhpur began competitive recruitment in 1942, Jaipur in 1943 (judicial) and 1944 (civil), but Bikaner never did. Thus, while professional competence was more highly valued, the states did not, until World War II, give bureaucrats the job security nor insist on the merit which might have strengthened them against accepting irregular subventions from below or currying favour above. Taken as a whole, the princely state civil servants selected for the post-independence services of Rajasthan showed the marks of patrimonial service and court relations in their manners and style.

These years also saw the growth of new ideas of financial and administrative accountability. Their realization, however limited, played a significant part in the conversion of princely rule from private and familial estate management to rule directed toward public concerns and benefits. The demand that princes give some public account of their administration first came from the paramount power toward the end of the nineteenth century.

In response, the states began to issue annual reports on public administration which gave abbreviated statements of the fiscal situation of the state and of programmes and policies. They provided even less enlightenment than the dullest British Indian provincial reports. But the need to publish a rudimentary budget encouraged the modern-minded maharajas to differentiate their privy purses from public funds. This led in turn to a sense that purses should have a known and regular relationship to state revenue. In time, 10 per cent came to be considered the correct proportion. This limit was not always observed.

Thus Kotah, in 1935-36, allocated 16 per cent of state revenues to palace expenses, and Bikaner allocated about 17 per cent in 1935-36. States often conveyed the impression in annual reports that they observed the 10 per cent limit when they did not, hiding major palace construction in the figures for the public works department. In 1937-38 Jaipur reported a Rs. 1,428,255 palace expenditure but did not choose to report how much of the Rs. 1,586,649 public works department figure had gone to the splendid Jaipur House then being built in Delhi, or the George V Solarium, also under construction. (One wonders to what extent princes protected themselves against criticism from the political agent by naming some extravaganza "Prince of Wales Hall.") The reports did not circulate widely but did provide the basis for some public scrutiny. Spokesmen for the sporadic democratic movements in the states liked to point out that the maharaja of a million people ought not, perhaps (as in Bikaner), receive a privy purse of approximately $450,000 when his state spent only about $50,000 for education.

Princes gave such accountings as they did because they were anxious to win approval of the political department. A "red tick" put opposite their names by the political agent was thought to be most undesirable. The remarks by the viceroy, Lord Irwin, addressed to the maharaja of Jaipur at the maharaja's formal assumption of office in 1932 indicate the steps taken by the Government of India to insure a ruler's concern with administrative performance, and also illustrate the benignly paternal atmosphere from which that concern took its meaning.

For the last six months you have been receiving administrative training in your own State under the personal supervision of Mr. Glancy. In that time, short though it is, you have had an opportunity of studying the working of all principal State departments, have regularly attended the meetings of the Council and have made several tours of inspection in more distant portions of the State. It is a great pleasure to have received from Mr. Glancy such favourable reports of quick understanding displayed by your Highness of State affairs and of your appreciation of duties of your high position.

The more educated princes were also eager to win respect in the world of modern-minded maharajas. Enough of the twentieth-century rulers had been abroad or had received a cosmopolitan education to know what was expected of a modern state and to develop some aspirations to build one. Democratic movements, made up of individuals whom the princes considered inferior or *declasse*, were probably least influential among those to whom the maharajas felt accountable.

All of these reforms, from the known and limited privy purse to departmental reorganization, while they did introduce elements of rationalization and reduce the scope of personal government, were more formal than substantive. If an annual report bore witness that the appurtenances of contemporary administrative practice had been achieved, they also contained more aspirations than accomplishments. The larger states did more than the smaller, and of the larger, Bikaner, Jaipur, and possibly Jodhpur progressed farther than traditional-minded Udaipur. The quaint accounts of visiting political agents and the quainter language of the administrative reports sometimes give a more reliable impression than the administrative reports' facts. In Udaipur, for example, according to Sir Arthur Lothian who had occasion to know it well as resident, the attempt to maintain personal rule in the literal sense continued to recent times. His account of the maharana of Udaipur, who died in 1930, illustrates how thin a veneer reforms could be:

I have never seen a finer or more dignified countenance than that of the old Maharana. Kindliness and nobility were written all over it. He was the quintessence of courtesy, and an excellent Ruler, according to his lights. He, old-fashioned however, attempted to control the administration of his big state in every detail himself, which under modern conditions was beyond the capacity of any human being. Although, therefore, he wore himself out with his constant labours, the arrears became so great that the administration got hopelessly clogged.... One instance of the arrears into which things had fallen came to my personal knowledge. The return of prisoners in the State Jail happened to be shown to me one day, and I noticed that two men had been confined in jail under sentence of death for twelve years. On enquiry into what had happened, it transpired that the death sentences, which required the Ruler's confirmation, had been sent to the late Maharaja twelve years before for this purpose, but had got mislaid somewhere amid the masses of papers awaiting his attention, and the prisoners were, therefore, kept on indefinitely as if they had been under trial. In the outcome this redounded to their advantage as they were sentenced to twenty years rigorous imprisonment in lieu of the death penalty and the years they had already served in jail were deducted from this.

Changes in the relationships between princes and noblemen, the degree of public accountability, and administrative and financial reforms were paralleled by movements to expand the political community, to make government popularly accountable, and to secure the rights of subjects through settled legal and administrative procedures. The Rajputana states had insulated themselves with remarkable success from the social and intellectual ferment that affected British India in the mid-nineteenth century. What is sometimes (and curiously) referred to as the Indian "renaissance," that mixture of English liberal and Indian nationalist ideas which captured the consciousness of the burgeoning professional and business middle classes, affected Rajasthan hardly at all.

Nor did changes in the economy, communications, and education touch it substantially. Control of the press and bad communications conspired to prevent the excellent British Indian papers from circulating regularly in Rajasthan. Jai Narayan Vyas, later chief minister in post-independence Rajasthan, had to print nationalist literature in Ajmer, a British Indian enclave set in the midst of the Rajasthan states, and to smuggle it out. Some of the princely states insisted that not merely presses but even typewriters be registered. Education lagged, and so did the emergence of a modern economy and modern middle classes. Urbanization was insignificant. Political associations were few and usually ephemeral and severely restricted.

The feebleness of modern associational life until the mid-1930's was in part due to the lack of interest or the timidity of subjects. Also responsible was the Indian National Congress decision, taken in 1920 when it laid plans for the mass organization of nationalism, not to include the princely states. In its Nagpur Constitution of 1920, Congress assigned responsibility for particular princely states to established provincial Congress committees. Political activists from the princely states could belong to the nearby provincial committees, but Congress failed to take the same interest in their activities as it did in those of British India. Both practical and ideological considerations shaped this policy of self-restraint. Many members feared, Patabhi Sitaramayya wrote, "Congress [would] be embroiling itself with the local vagaries and idiosyncracies of a variety of states, 562 in number, a task obviously beyond the pale of the practical politics of Congress." Gandhi went further: "That part of India which is described as British has no more power to shape the policy of the states than it has (say) that of Afghanistan or Ceylon,"His views were representative of the conservative wing of Congress. To its adherents foreign autocracy was more reprehensible, apparently, than was indigenous autocracy. The Congress Left, including Nehru, opposed "this hush-hush policy [of non-interference] . . . adhered to by [Gandhi] in spite of the most extraordinary and painful occurrences in the States." Nehru pictured Gandhi's views as most welcome to the rulers.

Gandhi's attitude toward Indian princes, under whom his father and grand-father had served as chief ministers, was indeed positive. Their benign autocracy did not disturb him, although specific abuses might. If (for certain purposes and in certain contexts) he supported democracy, he never fully committed himself to the principles of popular or representative government over those of responsive autocracy. In line with important aspects of Indian traditional thought, which looks to inner virtue rather than institutional restraints as the guarantor of public morality, Gandhi was more concerned in the 1920s with the personal debauchery of princes, where it existed, than with their failure to grant political liberty:

My ideal of Indian states is that of *Rama Rajya* [the rule of the epic hero Rama] ... By abandoning his kingdom and living in the forest for the sake of truth Rama gave to all kings of the world an object lesson in noble conduct. By his strict monogamy he showed that life of perfect self-restraint could be led by a royal householder. He lent splendour to his throne by his popular administration and proved that *Rama Rajya* was the acme of *swaraj* [self-rule]. Rama did not need the very imperfect modern instrument of ascertaining public opinion by counting votes. He had captivated the hearts of the people. He knew public opinion by intuition, as it were. . . Such *Rama Rajya* is possible even today.

Although the All-India States Peoples Conference was formed by prominent Congressmen in 1927, and thereafter acted as a kind of sister organization to Congress, it was hardly militant in its early years. Some of its leaders, moderates in Indian politics like C.Y. Chintamani and Ram Chandra Rao, former chief minister of Mysore, were not involved with the more radical nationalist movement and steered the conference conservatively. Only in the later 1930's under the leadership ofPattabhi Sitaramayya and eventually Nehru, did the States Peoples Conference take a more militant turn. At the same time, both Gandhi and Congress shifted to a more active interventionism. They did so partly because pressure by popular movements in some non-Rajput princely states, notably Mysore, forced them to. As Sardar Patel, the Congress's great organizing talent, put it: "The policy of non-intervention by the Congress was, in my opinion, a perfect piece of statesmanship when the people of the States were not awakened. That policy would be cowardice when there is all-round awakening among the people of the States." Congress also changed its policy following the passage of the Government of India Act of 1935 because the prospect of a federal government under it, including representatives from the princely states, spurred Congress on. So long as government in the princely states was autocratic, the princely states' delegations could be counted upon to be nominees of the princes, who in turn could be expected to support conservative and anti-nationalist policies in the federal legislature.

Faced with a coalition of princely state representatives and other non-Congress elements. Congress could expect to be a minority. By devoting more attention to the movement for freedom in the princely states. Congress hoped to soften or neutralize if not capture their representatives. In the event, the princely states could not make up their minds to join the federation, and a federal legislature never met. Before this result became apparent, however, the prospect of it so doing affected associational life and political consciousness in the princely states.

The policy of the Congress began to shift in 1936, and the Haripura session in 1938 sanctioned the organization of Congress committees in princely states provided they undertook neither parliamentary activity nor direct action in Congress's name. By 1939, Gandhi personally backed the States Peoples Freedom Movement, as it became known, to the extent of reviewing and guiding all the activities of the Jaipur Praja Mandal (Jaipur People's Society), the popular movement's organization in that state. He was drawn into its activities by his close friend and disciple, a wealthy Rajasthan businessman, long-time Congressman, and treasurer of the Indian National Congress, Jamnalal Bajaj. Bajaj, as president of the Jaipur Praja Mandal, was refused entry to the state, and the Mandal was forbidden to bold public meetings and proceedings. Bajaj and his followers offered civil resistance and were sent to jail. One brief letter exchange illustrates Gandhi's close but conservative interest in Jaipur affairs. Bajaj wrote to Gandhi on January 29, 1940: "I showed you the letter I received from the Home Minister of Jaipur. I enclose a draft of the reply I propose to send him. You will kindly return it to me with the necessary corrections." Gandhi replied: "Your draft is not properly worded. Your complaint is directed against the Maharaja. I don't consider it advisable to bring him in."

Most of the larger princely states had active movements toward the end of the 1930's, though some had them much earlier. The movements were led mostly, though not exclusively, by Brahman and Kayasth (caste of scribes) schoolmasters, such as Hiralal Shastri in Jaipur, Haribhau Upadhyaya in Ajmer, Bhogilal Pandya in Dungarpur, Manikyalal Verma in Udaipur, and Master Bhola Nath in Alwar, and by the new profession of lawyers, generally also Brahman or Kayasth, and were supported by some members of the merchant castes.

That the literate castes should have been leaders in the movement is not surprising, since their literacy made available to them currents of thought other than those generally accepted in Rajasthan. On the other hand, it is not self-evident that their leadership should have been directed toward social and political change. One of the most fascinating features of Indian political and social development has been the role of the Brahmans, guardians per excellence of tradition and the sacred order, as the bearers of the new political and social ideas. The vicarious authority which Brahmans and members of the other twice-born castes lent to innovation may help explain the relative ease with which India has taken to social and political change over the past 150 years.

Most of the prominent members of the literate castes in Rajasthan were attached to the bureaucracies of the princely states, or dependent on the court for trade and other patronage.. But those who led the freedom movement had, almost without exception, some independent occupational base: as school-masters and lawyers they were not directly dependent on court patronage. If they were dependent, like Shastri (office superintendent under Finance Member Atal in Jaipur State) they left their posts before becoming active in the Praja Mandal. For the most part they were city men; the peasant castes and rural people were scarcely represented.

Members of the merchant castes were active in the freedom movement, especially in Jodhpur. Jamnalal Bajaj, one of Gandhi's most important financial supporters, was an important figure in Jaipur State as well as on the national scene. Gandhi's efforts to organize and encourage non-political social service organizations and through them his campaigns to prevent the sale or consumption of alcoholic drinks and even to aid untouchables appealed to the merchant castes, already attached by religion and custom to teetotalism and nonviolence. In the mid-1930's members of merchant castes were particularly prominent as officers of the Harijan Sevak Sangh (Service Society for Untouchables). Formally apolitical, it had strong reformist over-tones and was explicitly connected to Gandhi's programme.

Some of those who joined the freedom movement did so because of their mobile sensibilities, their capacity to imagine themselves and others under circumstances other than those which the traditional society prescribed; some joined because they had fallen from favour; some because a rebellious disposition made them unable and unwilling to "succeed" under the conditions of courtierly behaviour required in a princely state. Even Rajasthanis who did not join the nationalist movement speak with bitterness of remembered humiliation, of being made to "feel small" in the presence of ministers, of not being offered a seat by those in authority, or of being required to express themselves in ways they foqnd degrading. Some joined because they were idealists prepared to take risks. The Gandhian appeal made sense to these men because it did not demand the martial style which was incompatible with their non-Kshatriya aversion to violence. Instead, it proposed self-suffering of a kind long familiar to Brahmans, whose ancestors had fasted or immolated themselves in response to unjust exactions. It appealed to the instincts for pedagogy of the traditionally literate castes now in the roles of schoolmasters or lawyers, who were asked to carry their Gandhian and nationalist teachings to rural people, bringing the message of moral and material conditions as they were elsewhere and might be here too. Still others, having been educated in British India, found the political climate in Rajputana incompatible with what they had learned.

The earliest activities of the freedom movement are difficult to isolate and identify. A variety of local issues just after World War I and, subsequently, during Gandhi's first civil disobedience campaign, took on added meaning from national events and concerns. In 1918, Manikyalal Verma and Vijay Singh Pathik organized a peasant *satyagraha* (nonviolent resistance campaign) against forced labour at Bijolia, Udaipur. Verma's arrests in 1918 and 1922 vaguely united the political consciousness arising out of protests over local grievances with that of the larger nationalist movement. The Marwar Hitkarni Sabha (Marwar Improvement Society) formed in the early 1920's in Jodhpur State by Jai Narayan Vyas and other Jodhpuri political activists, aimed at freeing the state from the rule of "aliens": a chief minister and other non-Jodhpuri officials both Indian and English. Its motto was "Marwar [Jodhpur] for the Marwaris" and its design to protect local interests from the effects of administrative reform. The maharaja, happy to free himself from the implicit restraints which outsiders represented, gave the Sabha his blessing, while Vyas saw his role in it as his first contribution to the freedom movement. Such political ambiguity was not unique to Jodhpur.

In the "Sikar rebellion" of 1937, the backward looking Rao Raja of the largest estate in Jaipur asserted the claims of feudal liberty against those of centralizing absolutism in resisting the maharaja's British-officered armed forces. In this struggle between prince and feudal aristocrat, the middle-class Jaipur Praja Mandal to a degree backed the claims of Sikar in an effort to advance the fortunes of representative government and public liberties. At the same time, the maharaja was inclined to be more sympathetic to the Praja Mandal under the Jaipuri leadership of Bajaj than was his government under the direction of a British chief minister. Freedom movements affected by local patriotism and susceptible to palace influence were sometimes useful in dealing with pressures for administrative reform from the political department and a maharaja's own government.

Freedom organizations of a clearly anti-princely cast, however, faced grave obstacles. Jai Narayan Vyas, whose first organization, the Hitkarni Sabha, was banned in 1924, became adept at shaping new ones as those he created were outlawed. He formed in quick succession the Jodhpur Praja Mandal, the Youth League, and the Marwar Lok Parishad. Whenever Vyas had trouble in his home state of Jodhpur, or was ordered out of other states in the areas, he guided his movements from Ajmer, the British enclave in the middle of Rajasthan, or from Bombay. Ajmer played an important role throughout the nationalist years since British administration made it a haven for agitators expelled from the princely states. In 1921 and again in 1930-32, the civil disobedience movement of British India found its counterparts there.

The less political Rajasthan Sevak Sangh, a Gandhian non-political service organization, fared better, although its leaders sometimes engaged in political activities. It began at Ajmer in the late 1920's and even employed paid workers in some states. Early activities in Bikaner, Kotah, and other states coincided with the civil disobedience movement of 1931-32 in British India. In Kotah, the Haravati Praja Mandal imitated the British-Indian agitation by picketing liquor and foreign-cloth shops in 1931 and 1932. But even these associations tended to lead precarious lives since most states disapproved of any association which, in the words of the Bikaner Public Safety Act of 1932, was "likely to create disaffection against the Maharaja or his government." Assembly, publication, and speech were more restricted than in British India. But the pattern of restriction varied: Kotah reports meetings of up to three hundred persons in 1937-38, not insignificant for a small (population 700,000) state, and successive meetings through at least 1941 favouring responsible government, federation of princely and British India, compulsory education, and temperance. In Bharatpur, the Praja Mandal sought "to secure responsible government under the aegis of His Highness the Maharaja." When it attempted to organize a campaign to withhold payment of land revenue from the state, the Mandal was declared unlawful in April 1937. Four hundred and seventy-three individuals were detained in connection with the campaign and 212 were arrested-again, not a small agitation in a state containing only 500,000 people. Jaipur and Jodhpur alternately forbade and permitted Praja Mandals and Lok Parishads to function. In Jodhpur in 1937, the Civil Liberties Union and the Praja Mandal were declared unlawful and their president, A.P. Sharma, arrested. Since Seth Jamnalal Bajaj, the Jaipur leader, was a man of national stature and treasurer of the Indian National Congress, the Jaipur *durbar* was in constant embarrassment regarding methods of dealing with him, but eventually admitted both him and the Praja Mandal to public activity. In Bikaner, the Public Safety Act of 1932 acted as a strong deterrent. Udaipur banned the Praja Mandal in 1938, as soon as it was founded, and expelled its founder. Sirohi and Alwar also had active movements, while Dungarpur and Banswara had developed a tiny but impressive service organization working in a Gandhian spirit among the Bhil tribes.

The life of the "old nationalists" was not always easy, Manikyalal Verma came out of the nonviolent resistance movement at Bijolia badly beaten, as did Gokulbhai Bhatt out of a Sirohi meeting in 1939. Mrs. Verma was imprisoned for two years in 1934. Narottamlal Joshi, later speaker of the Rajasthan legislature, was beaten twice on the same day by Rajput landholders of small estates for the effrontery of campaigning for political freedom and tenant rights in Jaipur's first election in 1945. He was attacked near a police station, the occupants of which remained inactive throughout the assault, and believes he escaped death only because his assailants stuck at Brahman killing. Unable to walk, he was tied to a camel and abandoned in a forest.

The attempt to win responsible government did not succeed. In 1913 Maharaja Ganga Singh established what he liked to call the "Bikaner Representative Assembly." The organization had the power to pass bills. In reality, however, it provided no forum for criticism, much less for the exercise of power by representatives independent of the crown, since the assembly was dominated by a majority nominated by the maharaja, and the climate of the institution was courtierly and placating. "I have nothing special to mention in connection with the budget," a representative said in speaking in the budget debate, "except that this year's budget is an occasion of great delight for us as it contains a provision for the estimated expenditure of the celebration of His Highness Sri Maharaj Kumarji Sahib's auspicious marriage, which auspicious marriage celebration has come after many years, and it would be an occasion of great delight for every loyal subject of the state."

The budget had been delivered to members on the day previous to the debate, and it passed in a few hours. The assembly met for three days in the year. Similar bodies were introduced in Jaipur and Jodhpur in the 1940's, but until after the war their powers were insignificant. The Jaipur assembly saw a budget for the first time in 1946. After the war, as independence rushed ominously closer and democracy began to loom as a real possibility, most of the states moved swiftly toward popular governments, which were soon superseded by the amalgamation of Rajasthan's twenty-two princely states into one.

In British India, the political associations and representative institutions of the nationalist era served as an important recruiting ground for post-independence political leadership. In Rajasthan this function was indifferently performed. The experience which British Indian Congressmen developed in the Swarajist days of the 1920's when they joined legislatures, or in the short-lived provincial governments of the 1930's, or in district boards and municipalities was missing altogether in Rajasthan, where there were no meaningful representative institutions, unless a few municipalities deserve the title. And the Praja Mandals too were inadequate training grounds for later state politics. The small movements required devotion and idealism, but they did not develop new organizational and administrative skills on the part of their leaders. Because they were personal, comradely organizations, each coinciding with a princely state, they resembled the small state governments in that no high professional competence was required to manage them.

The British Indian political movements, because they covered large linguistic areas, developed in their leaders a capacity to build rational and effective political structures, to coordinate diverse political interests, and to formulate and communicate policies. The Rajasthan political organizations, because they were very small operations, developed few qualities that would equip their alumni in later years to take over the large-scale unified government of the twenty-two states of Rajasthan. In fact, this early political experience may even have disqualified them for their later tasks.

They carried the narrow horizons of parochial princely states into the politics of the larger state, failing to shift easily to the more abstract general perspectives required in the new circumstances. Many remained small-town politicians when faced with the responsibility of governing fifteen million people in new Rajasthan. Yet, when independence came and the old order was superseded, they were the only ones available for the new politics.

Apart from the freedom associations, Rajasthanis did not form voluntary organizations of the kind that grew in British India and structured its emerging middle classes' turn to politics. The Rajasthan middle classes, such as they were, developed few modern institutional channels for action. The universities, the chambers of commerce, the bar, and a host of social, literary, cultural, and political associations had given focus to the organized interests of British Indians in the days before a mass movement gave new strength to nationalism. Higher education in the princely states was feeble and dependent on the maharaja. The bar was weakly developed since much legal practice rested with the traditionally trained *vakils* (pleaders), and a modern legal profession had still to emerge. The merchantry was organized in caste associations, but not into any association cutting across caste on the basis of economic or civil interests. Such associations as existed were mostly natural groups congruent with the old society and polity and felt no special reason to upset them. Thus, in 1912, at the silver jubilee of the maharaja of Bikaner, addresses were offered by the following groups: officials of the government, Maheshwari Sahukars (a merchant caste), Oswals (a merchant caste), Brahmans, Pushkarna Brahmans, Jain Swetamber Yatis (Jain holy men), Mohammedans, Sikhs, the Nagri Society, two secondary educational institutions, and the bar association. They made no political demands, restricting themselves to requesting traditional favours, such as the maharaja's intervention in a serious caste dispute among the merchants or support for some new building or educational enterprise.

Neither the old corporate groups nor the new political associations explicitly demanded expansion of the political community, although that was sometimes a long-range objective. The cry for responsible government amounted rather to a demand for institutions that would make effective the influence of those who already had some claim to be *de facto,* though not *de jure,* part of the political community-the literate, the twice-born. For the most part, the Brahmans and Vaishyas (merchant castes) and Kayasths in the Congress appealed to others like themselves. But there were exceptions. In a few areas, for example in Jodhpur and Jaipur in the early 1940's, members of the peasant caste ofJats began to develop political consciousness, and elsewhere Congressmen who took seriously Gandhi's guidance went to the rural areas to preach social reform if not political participation.

The 1930's, however, brought one additional sign that the times were changing and that new groups were emerging at the edge of the political community. Census reports as far back as 1891, and other official records of much earlier vintage, record that in the British Indian provinces certain lower and middle castes were beginning to organize themselves to press courts, temples, and administrative bodies for recognition of rights, privileges, and higher status than tradition assigned them. These efforts foreshadowed attacks on the traditional order of castes. The censuses of Rajasthan in the twentieth century, on the other hand, reported very few developments of this sort before 1930. In 1911, a Kayasth group tried to list itself as Brahman, as did the Bhargavas (another caste). Some individual members of castes made up of illegitimate descendants of Rajputs tried to have themselves listed as Rajputs. But the efforts were sporadic and apparently involved very few people.

The main agricultural caste in Rajasthan is the Jats: they comprise the largest single caste in the state (9 per cent), and were, in the 1930's and even earlier, the most self-conscious and prosperous among the peasant castes. In

1935 their claims to certain privileges led to a series of clashes between them and the Rajputs, who resisted their attempts to revise accepted signs of status. The clash of 1935 is reminiscent of similar ones in other areas between lower castes on the rise and higher established castes.

The Jat demonstrations broke out in Sikar, the largest *thikana* in Jaipur State, and involved both economic and social issues. The Jats in the area had formed two associations, the Sikarwati Jat Panchayat and the Jat Kisan Sabha, and had received some help and encouragement from the British Indian province of Uttar Pradesh. Some of these "outsiders" were organizers for the socialist-oriented Kisan Sabha which attempted to mobilize the peasantry in the 1930's in response to radical pressures in the Congress.

The initial demonstration in Khuri village on March 27, 1935, was occasioned by a social issue, whether a Jat bridegroom should be allowed to ride to his bride's house on a horse, a ceremonial act asserting higher station than Rajputs were prepared to concede. The Rajputs objected, the Jats insisted, fighting broke out, and an old Jat was killed. The incident led to further clashes, and the *thikana* police, the Sikar Lancers, under command of the English chief of the Sikar police, charged the Jat crowds with *lathis* (quarter-staffs), injuring many. This incident was followed by others as Jats in the area protested against the revenue collections and resisted and attacked Sikar revenue officials on April 22 at Bhaironpura and at Kudan village on April 25. The Sikar police killed four Jats while putting down this last demonstration and arrested 104 persons. The anti-rent agitation eventually involved some twenty-one villages, and local headmen were as active as any outsiders. A school where, according to the Jaipur *durbar*, unlawful doctrines were being preached by a Jat teacher from outside the state, was knocked down. The agitation had some effects. The Rao Raja of Sikar remitted all arrears of revenue previous to 1934 and promised to open schools, provide loans where needed, and embark on a permanent land settlement that would introduce some certainty into the vagaries of the *thikana's* revenue demand.

There was some evidence that the more advanced peasantry were beginning to insist on some regulation of their land rights. Beginning as early as 1872 in Alwar, most states undertook survey and settlement operations in *khalsa* (crown lands), that is, they prepared records of rights and established regular revenue demands. In the judgment of an inquiry committee of high civil servants from British Irdia that reported on tenant rights at the time of independence, "the tenant (of *khalsa*) has his rights defined and secured, and there is, on the whole, little cause for him to complain." But in the *jagir* (nobles' estates) lands, which made up a substantial part of most states (about half), records were rarely kept, collection procedures remained arbitrary, and peasants had no protection. Only 32 per cent of the 16,7 80 *jagir* villages in all of Rajasthan had been settled (their revenue obligations officially specified and limited) by 1947. A number of *durbars* tried to press settlement, but their efforts were strongly resisted by the *jagirdars*. No one doubted that tenants had customary rights, including in many cases rights of inheritance, mortgage, and fixed rents. But so long as these rights were not established by enforcible laws and administrative procedures, they were subject to the*jagirdars* discretion; the nobles rightly regarded settlement as a diminution of his own powers. But it was a limitation that would in turn have conferred upon tenants rights most fundamental in a peasant society-rights in land.

Most *durbars* did not undertake *jagir* settlement before the 1930's and 1940's. Such operations as were undertaken in *jagir* lands proved dangerous, especially in small holdings where the landlord and tenant were not very far apart economically. In 1937, the Jaipur *durbar* pressed settlement in Udaipurwati, an area adjoining Sikar, where the Jat agitation had taken place, only to see its revenue officials chased out by irate small *jagirdars*. In 1947, the Jaipur *durbar* passed enabling legislation for laying down rules concerning rights in land and for establishing procedures and principles fixing land rent in *jagir* areas, a clear indication that the 1937 effort had not advanced far.

Legal procedures were regulated, at least as far as the maharaja's hand reached, by taking over British Indian legal codes with only minor alterations and by establishing courts at various levels to administer that law. A graduated court system with defined jurisdiction existed at Jhalawar and Jaipur in the 1870's, and written codes were taken over, at least formally,. in most states by 1910-20.

These changes marked an advance toward promulgated law which could be anticipated. It is difficult to say just how meaningful the adoption of the codes and the creation of courts was. Most states were reluctant to have defendants bring in lawyers from British India to argue before these tribunals, a policy which may have been due to a feeling that the local system would not stand scrutiny, or to provincial fears that the local judiciary might be made to look foolish by "slick" Bombay barristers, or both. In any case, the new law impinged less than in British India on the local, pluralistic caste and customary law, a circumstance that may have been congenial to Rajasthanis but that illustrates the restricted development of the legal power of the state.

The new conceptions of government were compelling enough to teach some maharajas how a respectable ruler conducts himself. Responsibility to the public welfare and effective performance were added to birth in judging the legitimacy of rule. Public reports of government action implied that princely expenditure amounted to a public budget, not merely a private household account, and thus favoured the differentiation of the public and private roles of the prince. They also implied that the prince in his public capacity was accountable to someone other than himself.

Associations developed enough to introduce, at least in the minds of the literate, ideas of representation and consent and to undermine the self-evident quality of princely rule. Advances in administration, particularly fixing of the revenue demand, introduced the principle that government action ought to follow certain rules. The prince often consulted his fellow princes, or the political department, or his now more modern conscience. But his new sense of public responsibility, of effective performance, and regular procedures fell short of establishing a modern state or constitutional rule in Rajasthan.

The emergence of a modern state, the revision of traditional notions of legitimacy, and the growth of popular politics progressed too slowly under paramountey to be of any real help to Rajasthan when it became part of India. The attempts to centralize authority and regularize administration did not carry very far and were often more formal than substantive. Compared to British India, the development of associational life in Rajputana was slight. No real concessions were made to political participation and institutional restraints on autocratic power. Important changes did occur, but, without roots in society and consciousness, they lacked substance

***Ahmedabad:*** Piping hot bhajiyas with tea! Who can resist them? Not even the iron-willed Sardar. Patel's passion for this delicacy has found a mention in the Ahmedabad Municipal Corporation's booklet ' Amdavad ni Krantiyatra'.

So much so, that during his early days as a lawyer, Patel was an active member of a 'Bhajiya Club' in the city. In 1913, when Sardar began his practice as a barrister in Ahmedabad, it was a ritual to meet friends over a cup of tea and bhajiyas. This gathering came to be known as the 'Bhajiya Club'. The sessions provided food for thought too.

Narayan Desai, in his book 'Agnikund Man Khilelu Gulab' on his father and Gandhiji's secretary Mahadev Desai, has quoted an incident referring to this club. The book quotes a letter by Mahadevbhai to Pyarelal, a senior Congress leader, which mentions Sardar's love for bhajiya.

He wrote, "When Vallabhbhai came to Ahmedabad after the successful Bardoli Satyagraha, he received a grand welcome in the city. And surprisingly, he forgot all his fatigue when he mingled with his own bhajiatmak club.

We should thank Jugatram for the word bhajiatmak." This letter clearly spoke of Sardar's affiliation towards 'Bhajiya Club'. Initially, the club members gathered at Krushnalal Desai or Dr. Kanunga's house. Later, it shifted to Dr. Kanunga's dispensary on Gandhi Road where bhajiyas and tea were ordered from a nearby hotel. Dr. Kanunga, Chimanlal Thakor, Maganbhai Patel, Krushnalal Desai, Jivanlal Barrister, Dr. Chandubhai and Dr. Hariprasad Desai were the members of this club.

Many government officers and professionals were a part of this gathering. Everything except politics was discussed here. Adarsh Prakashan on Gandhi Road today is where Dr. Kanunga's dispensary used to be.

After Sardar become a national leader in 1935, this club rarely gathered. Leaders like Mahadev Desai, Pyarelal and Jugatram knew of Sardar's love for the bhajiya

## SAURASTRA (INCLUDING JUNAGADH)

Since the smaller states of West Gujarat, which were virtually ebbing out, but had a good organization for rousing the political consciousness of the people in so far as the Congress was concerned they attracted the attention of Sardar Patel in his very first attempt towards their integration. The West Gujarat known as Saurastra constituted a number of small states which did not have much potential from the point of view of economic and political independence. In all, 327 such States existed in Gujarat. These States were attached to some of the adjoining bigger States in April, 1943, as per the attachment scheme. But the attachment scheme terminated with the lapse of paramountcy on August 14th, 1947. The Home Department prepared a revised Instrument of Accession for these states. In the new Instrument of Accession, the States were to be freed from the attaching states and to be administered by the Government as in the pre-attachment period. The states would vest all residuary powers and jurisdiction in the Central Government. The modus operandi was very simple, as those states did not have any capability of declaring independence with the lapse of paramountcy. There was also no possibility for those states to accede to Pakistan due to political and geographical conditions. Sardar succeeded in bringing the small states together and it was a very important step towards national solidarity.

It was reported that the Jam Saheb of Nawanagar was strengthening his armed forces with a desire to be the overlord of Kathiawad. Sardar had a very good contact with the people of Kathiawad states as he was associated with some of State's Peoples' Union. Sri U.N. Dhebar was Sardar's disciple and was the leader of the people of the Kathiawad States. It was reported that the rulers of Kathiawad, on the advice of the political agent, met under the leadership of the Jamsaheb to form a union of Kathiawad, covering the whole of the peninsula and decided to declare sovereign independence subject to the right of Junagadh to declare separate independence or to join Pakistan. The Jamsaheb would be the president of the Union comprising seven states viz. Jamnagar, Bhavnagar, Gondal, Probandar, Morvi, Dhrangadhra and Junagadh. They were helped by the political agent with the intention of Balkanizing the country. Sardar, on receipt of such information and with the help of his comrades like Dhebar and other leaders of the people's conference of the states, tactfully dealt with the situation and ultimately persuaded the princes to join the Indian Union. Sardar wrote to

B.L. Mitter on 28th June, 1947. "The question of smaller states will now engage my attention as a Member in charge of the new states' department. Along with these will come the question of ports? I have no doubt, I shall find your note of assistance in this respect"....

Sardar, then fully concentrated on the states of Kathiawad and with his efforts and support from the people of the states, he could bring the rulers to agree to the accession.

Junagadh created a big problem for the solidarity of the country. It was one of the strongest States in Saurastra at that time and was ruled by a Muslim ruler but the inhabitants were mostly Hindus. Geographically, it was close to India, though it had direct access to the sea through its port of Veraval. In the beginning, Junagadh assured that it would accede to India. Such impression was created by the *Dewan,* A.K.M. Husen and his brother Nabi Baksh, the Constitutional Adviser. But Husen had to go abroad for treatment and in his absence his place was taken over by Shah Nawaz Bhutto. The *Nawab* was not at all serious about the administration and welfare of the people. The change of *Dewan* occurred on 10th August, 1947 and the *Nawab* was virtually a prisoner in the hands of his new Dewan. Junagadh was so much connected with other States that a part of its territory fell into the area of the States which had acceded to India. There were two other small States called Babariwad and Mangrol headed by Muslim rulers under the control of the Junagadh State, that had acceded to India, but the *Nawab* argued that Mangrol had no authority to negotiate any instrument of accession without the permission of Junagadh. Till 14th August, 1947, Junagadh did not accede either to India or to Pakistan. However, on 15th August, 1947, the people of the state were shocked on hearing that the state had acceded to Pakistan and that the accession had been accepted by the other party.

The people resented such an undemocratic action Sardar agreed that the armed forces on surrounding Junagadh would be kept in readiness so that they could be deployed in no time. V.P. Menon was sent to meet *Nawab* and explain about his wrong decision. The Government of India press Communiqué dated 25th September, 1947, strongly denounced such action of *Nawab* and asserted firmness in dealing with the situation. Under the leadership of Shamaldas Gandhi, who had taken consent of Sardar Patel, Kathiawad People's Front was formed and supplies to Junagadh were stopped. Bhutto appealed to Pakistan for help but in vain. Violence started in the State and encouraged by the Kathiawad people's Front, the subjects of the State started a demonstration against the *Nawab*, who fled to Karachi with his family.

On October 27th, Bhutto admitted that the people did not accept the *Nawab*'s accession to Pakistan. Bhutto fled to Pakistan after requesting the Union Government to take over the administration. The people's verdict and ultimately found support and Junagadh came under India, due to the tactful handling by the States' Department headed by Sardar Patel. Sardar, in his speech on November 13, 1947 at Junagadh, explained at length the strategy adopted by the Government of India. He explained that the Government had tried its best through negotiations to come to a peaceful settlement in the interest of the country. Though the things were moving in the proper direction, the Government of India had to take drastic steps due to a sudden change in the *Nawab*'s policy, to bring the state under its control, which he thought as the correct step. Finally Junagadh merged was merged in Kathiawad States, which became a part of the Gujarat state. U.N. Dhebar, a dedicated Congressman and Sardar's follower, became the first Chief Minister of Kathiawad states. The way Junagadh was made to accede to India was very clear from legal and democratic point of view.

Junagadh's accession to Pakistan raised lot of Public controversy; but from the point of the guideline of the British Government's partition programme, Junagadh had to accede t India on geographical and economical grounds, though the state was ruled by a Muslim ruler. Taking the population into consideration the state having a majority of Hindus should be a part of India. On similar consideration, Bahawalpur, a state adjacent to India and Pakistan was allowed to accede to Pakistan.

Sardar, thus acted in a finest way in his handling of the Junagadh situation without keeping any loopholes open for any controversy in future.

Hyderabad: Sardar's greatest role in the integration of states was his able handling of the Hyderabad crisis. Most of the states acceded to India, Hyderabad, the largest of the native states with a Muslim ruler and 86% Hindu population created a threat to the solidarity of the country. Hyderabad was surrounded by the Indian Territory on all sides and did not have nay access to the sea; but the ruler, the Nizam, had high aspirations and wanted to proclaim sovereignty after the paramountcy was withdrawn. In order to negotiate with the Nizam, Lord Mountbatten was chosen and Sardar agreed to this, knowing fully well its pros and cons. Sardar knew that, if the problem was handled by Mountbatten, it would be good for India since international and communal repercussions could be avoided. Moreover, as Walter Monckton, the adviser of the Nizam, was a friend of Mountbatten, negotiations would be easier. However, the decision on any point of controversy beyond the agreed formula was vested in the Congress High command only. Thus, Sardar was sure that, it would not be dangerous for India even if the negotiations were carried on by Lord Mountbatten. On the contrary, Sardar would formulate the policy without coming into direct confrontation with the Nizam.

The negotiations with the representatives of the Nizam started in July, 1947 but an accord could not be reached. Sardar, in his letter dated 24th August, 1947 to Lord Mountbatten, clearly indicated that Nizam should accede to the Dominion of India in line with the instrument of Accession prepared for the other states. Sardar stated that the Nizam should follow the same path as the other states and in case he did not agree to the same, he should agree to allow the people of the state to decide the issue of accession. But, in spite of the best efforts of Mountbatten, the negotiations failed. Ultimately with great reluctance an extension of two months was granted to Hyderabad to decide about the accession. Sir Walter Monckton, in his note dated 15th September, 1947, stated:

"I know that Mr. Patel was and is against any extension of time to Hyderabad and that the Viceroy prevailed over the cabinet of the Dominion to allow him personally two months time to see whether I, could find a compromise satisfactory to both sides".... Sardar could foresee the difficult situation which the country was facing and in his letter dated 19th September, 1947 to Mountbatten, Sardar explained the situation in Hyderabad and stated about the steps that would be necessary in future due to the wrong policy of the Nizam as he had created his own *Frnakentstein-Ittehadul-Mussalmeen.*

After some more discussions with a number of delegates from Hyderabad, some concessions were granted by Sardar to the Nizam and the Standstill Agreement for one year and the collateral letters were signed on 29th November, 1947. The same day Sardar made a statement in the Constituent Assembly and explained that the period of one year granted to the Nizam would be helpful for final accession. Thus, he agreed with the settlement reached by the government on the ground that accession of Hyderabad would be peaceful.

It is said that Razvi, a member of the Ittehad-ul-Mussalmeen, and controlling the policy of the Nizam, met Sardar Patel in Delhi to try for additional concessions from him; but Sardar quickly disposed him and firmly indicated that there was no possibility of accepting Hyderabd as being independent. When Razvi indicated that Sardar should realize their difficulties, and that in case Sardar did not concede his request, Hyderabad would fight tooth and nail, Sardar remained unmoved and replied:

"How Can I stop you from committing suicide if you want to"? This proves that Sardar was confident that in the course of time he would be able to merge Hyderabad with India.

As per the new agreement, K.M. Munshi a trusted man of Sardar was sent to Hyderabad as Agent General of India and detailed reports about the political conditions were received through him. Sardar also kept in touch with the members of the Hyderabad Congress and formulated his policy on the basis of the information he received from time to time. Sardar was not at all hopeful about the settlement in Hyderabad in line with the Stand still Agreement for one year…

Inspite of Standstill Agreement for one year, the Nizam did not give up his hope of attaining complete independence with the help of foreign powers. His doubtful actions, were reported to Sardar by K.M. Munshi, other trusted people and the reports of the news-papers regarding the reign of terror and the oppression of the Hindu Community. The Razakars started arson and looting in the neighbouring States. The Nizam wanted to represent his case to the Security Council to internationalize the issue. People, in India became impatient but Sardar was preparing for the final assault and counting the days. In his letter to Nehru, Sardar stated: "I have already decided to issue instructions to Hyderabad and Bhopal States regarding the composition of their armed forces. We are telling them that we are bound to take it into account in making allotments of arms and equipments and that the composition of these forces should be readjusted in order to create more confidence among the non-Muslim majority"…

When the situation was becoming alarming, Sardar intimated Nehru that the time came to tell Hyderabad that the Nizam should accede unconditionally. Sardar wanted that the situation should be tackled firmly so that it did not go out of hands. In his letter dated 21st June, 1948 to N.V. Gadgil, Sardar cautioned that the decision about Hyderabad's accession should be similar to that of the other States and the situation could be brought under control. He advised the Indian Military to be alert as he apprehended that the trouble, any time, might demand immediate military action.

Sardar sought information from defense ministry and was informed that in case of nay military action, it would not take more than three weeks. In spite of his illness, Sardar kept in close touch with the day to day events on Hyderabad. Though Nehru was hesitant due to the international reaction, Sardar was firm in his stand. It was decided that military would march into Hyderabad, on 13th September, 1948 and Sardar did not agree to postpone the operation. At the instance of Sardar, C. Rajagopalachari, the then Governor-general called a meeting of the cabinet to regularize the action. Sardar's assessment was correct and Hyderabad was captured practically without any bloodshed within a week's time. It was a great achievement. Sardar's conviction regarding the action taken against Hyderabad was very clear. He was very confident that actions taken by him were without flaw and would sand against any criticism. On October 30th, 1948 he boldly said:

"We shall do what the interests of the people of Hyderabad demand and what they themselves desire. It would be for them to take a decision and no outside interference can succeed in keeping the Nizam on the throne if people wish otherwise"....

There were suggestions regarding the dividing Hyderabad into three linguistic parts but Sardar indicated that this would be done at an appropriate time, if necessary. With the merger of the State with India, the next step for financial and social integration started automatically and ultimately it gave birth to a new linguistic state called Andhra Pradesh which contributed to a greater consolidation in removing all doubts of any disintegration at a later date. A bold step taken at, an appropriate time has strengthened the process of Nation-building in India. Kashmir: Kashmir was also a problem. The state was ruled by a Hindu ruler, whereas the population was Muslim. It occupied a strategic position. Till August 15th, 1947 Kashmir did not accede to India. Sardar knew the importance of Kashmir from its geographical position and wanted to tackle the problem himself as the Minister of the States, but, Nehru was willing to deal with Kashmir, and Sardar did not object to it. But Sardar too did not fail to give his best advice in this regard. As observed by Allen Campbell Johnson in his book 'Mission with Mountbatten': "Indeed the states Ministry under Patel's direction, went out of its way to take no action which could be interpreted as forcing Kashmir's hand and to give assurances that accession to Pakistan would not be taken amiss by India"....

When the Maharaja of Kashmir agreed to accede to India, in similar lines as the other states, the question of sending the army to Kashmir to help the Maharaja rebuff an armed attack by the intruders was discussed at a meeting. Everybody including army generals, Nehru and Mountbatten could not find a solution but Sardar got up and said that Kashmir should be defended at all costs. The committee decided to send an agent to Kashmir and Kunwar Sir Daleep Singh was posted as Agent in Jammu.

At the instance of Mountbatten, the Kashmir dispute was referred to the United Nations on 1st January, 1948, but Sardar was not present in Delhi at that time. Sardar, however was skeptical about the reference to the United Nations. Had Sardar's advice on Kashmir been heeded by Nehru, the problem we are facing now would not have risen at all. At K.M. Munshi said: "But for Jawaharlal Nehru, who, under the influence of Sheikh Abdullah, took away the portfolio of Kashmir from Sardar's States Ministry, Kashmir would never have become the problem that it has been"...

Kashmir still poses a problem for the country; but the steps taken by the Indian leaders in sending the army to Kashmir at the request of the Maharaja was in the Cabinet Mission Plan. The action regarding Kashmir was defended by the Prime Minister when he informed the Prime Minister of the U.K. that: "Helping Kashmir is an obligation of national interest to India...I should like to make it clear that the question of aiding Kashmir in this emergency is not designed in any way to influence the States to accede to India"... Sardar also played his role by holding a secret meeting with Ramchandra Kak, the Prime Minister of Kashmir.

The position of Kashmir, as it stands today, is much better for India from the strategic point of view, and such a political situation created in Kashmir is a kind of an interim solution and has helped the country to stand against any onslaught from the external powers. The solidarity of the country has been strengthened with the accession of Kashmir to India. Other States: Regarding the accession of the other states, Sardar acted like a magic-stick. In no time, he could merge the States of Orissa, Chhatishgarh, Rajasthan, Punjab and so on. He realized that the people of states were supreme and by organizing the States', people for establishment of popular government, he could achieve success. He had, with him, able workers and supporters who had worked untiringly to bring such a merger in record time.

The *Maharaja* of Mysore was not inclined to join the Union of India after withdrawal of British power. His Dewan M. Sankar Lingegowda had a series of correspondence with Sardar through which he expressed that after the lapse of paramountcy, the Maharaja of Mysore should get back the territory ceded in 1799 and sovereignty should return to the King, Sardar, clearly explained to him, in his reply, that even in England the sovereignty rested with the people with the King as the head of the State. Similarly, in a democratic country, the authority of the people is supreme. He also warned that Maharaja should carefully note that after June, 1948, paramountcy would evaporate in air and he would have a hard time; hence to maintain his honourable position even after the lapse of paramountcy, the Maharaja should take the Mysore

Congress into confidence. Sardar's advice had sobering effect on the King and ultimately he joined the Constituent Assembly and sent seven representatives there out of which few were elected representatives of the people of the state. Sardar's handing of the situation was not in the normal way but he gave a human touch while he pointed out the future of the King after departure of the British power. He acted on the basis of information he used to get from various sources through reliable party cadres.

Indore was also a trouble spot. At the beginning Maharaja Holkar of Indore in collaboration with *Nawab* of Bhopal wanted to attract some more states like Jodhpur to form a group against accession to Indian Union. But in Indore the State's People Conference was very active. Maharaja was given an ultimatum that by May 25, 1947 popular government had to be established, which was not acceded by the King. On the other hand without the consent of Praja Mandal, the King appointed one Mr. Horton, a Britisher as his Prime Minister.

Praja Mandal launched a statewide agitation and invited Sardar Patel to intervene. Maharaja did not succeeded in his negotiations for remaining independent but his accepted Instrument of Accession was not received by the States' Department before 15th August, 1947. To create pressure on the King, it was indicated to him that since the Instrument of Accession was not received in time the terms and conditions would be revised. Sardar met Maharaja of Indore on 19th August, 1947 and the King signed the revised Instrument of Accession and acceded to India, Sardar's careful handling of the Indore affairs and timely action could pave the way for integration of Indore. It is interesting that afterwards the King became friendly with Sardar.

Bhopal was a State ruled by a Muslim ruler; but geographically it had no connection with Pakistan. The *Nawab* of Bhopal was very powerful and he was the chairman of the negotiating committee of the Chamber of Princes. The *Nawab* had no intention to accede to Indian Union, rather he was keen in maintaining his sovereignty or joining hands with Pakistan. The *Nawab* and King of Indore had a joint interview with Mountbatten, the viceroy on 4th August, 1947 when Viceroy intimated that he did not have any authority to alter the terms and conditions of accession and final decision rested with Sardar Patel. He, however, assured that Sardar Patel would not be unkind to them. After a considerable time *Nawab* did not find any alternative, so he acceded to India. In spite of his earlier anti-Indian attitude, Sardar realized that the *Nawab* was a changed man when he admitted his fault and apologized to him. Sardar took him as his friend and exchanged his cordial relation in the coming years. *Nawab* in later years was very helpful in tackling the refugee problem. Sardar thus gave a humanitarian touch to politics of integration of States.

There are innumerable instances where Sardar could bring down the rulers of the States to terms and agree them to accession to India as per the terms and conditions stipulated by the Government of India. Sardar had to deal with diversified Kings having different attitude with caution and applying varied, human, social, political and psychological approach.

Sardar will always be remembered as the man who laid the foundation stone for a United India. The complex process of integration of the Princely State, which ended with success, has paved the way for the stability and prosperity of the country. In the face of partition, it was not sure whether the departure of the British power from India would create a vacuum and leave behind the possibility of creating a third force contributing towards the balkanization of the country. Even the initiators of partition were not fully convinced regarding the establishment of peace and harmony in the post-partition period. The Congress leaders, baffled by the thrust created through disturbance and communal riots by the Muslim League. Had to look for a solution to such a calamity and had to reconcile to the idea of partition, without looking deeply into the problems that might come ahead, while Sardar was prepared to face the consequences. His conviction was crystal clear, when he brought an analogy between a riot-stricken country and a mutilated leg of a person which needed amputation to save the rest of the body. Even on the eve of partition Sardar was fully aware that the post-partition period would be full of immense problems and the first and foremost task would be to integrate all the Princely States into the Union of India a positive step directed towards the unity of the country as the prerequisite for nation-building. His actions, aimed at establishing a sovereign democratic country in divided India, were too commensurate with the need of the time. The immediate requirement after partition was the unification of the country by merging the princely states in the Indian Union and Sardar could decide upon the speed with which the action was to be undertaken.

The integration of the princely states in India was handled in a well-organised manner by Sardar. The pattern of integration was also not identical in case of all the states. Sardar could visualize the socio-political environment in the various states based on which, his action-plan was formulated to suit the requirement. It is interesting to find that his approach to the problem had a broad base and diversified modalities wee adopted. It is unimaginable what a spade work he did to obtain the political information of the various states to formulate his action plan. His association with the State's people was very close. By virtue of his ingenuity, he followed the path of persuasion with friendly states, threats with smaller states and even confrontation with the states which were found to be unmanageable through normal channels of action programme. In all such cases, Sardar followed a well-organised path of action, keeping in view peace and harmony and preparing the country for a better future and promising its citizens overall prosperity as a nation of the world.

The after effect of the integration process is also interesting from the point of the contribution it had made in the nation-building activity. Though at the time of merging the states into the dominion of India, certain complexities like misunderstanding and enmity developed between the ruling Congress party and the rulers of the States, the same did not persist for a long time but ended in a happy note of mutual adjustment. As Sardar could generate confidence in the minds of the people of the various states, his task in bringing back normalcy and healthy administrative set up in the integrated states became easier. The mechanics of integration of the states turned out to be so simple that the total number of five hundred and odd states could be integrated in a short span of time without even a single drop of blood being shed. Sardar's overall management of the integration system has proved to be far superior to any other integration process in the world surpassing the ingenuity of Bismark, the great unifier of Germany. His multipronged attack with definite objective of homogenization of the country, his stage play in the integration drama with the help of his Lieutenant like V.P. Menon, U.N. Dhebar, K.M. Munshi, J.N. Chaudhari, V. Shankar and others has proved to be a great success as we can see from the results which have followed in the successive years.

The efforts of Sardar have led the country towards democratization and prosperity through the economic steps which were taken in the post-integration period.

The absence of a third force has resulted in the solidarity of the country and we are now poised for great promises in the coming years as one of the recognized nations of the world. Sardar's role in the dynamics of nation-building through the process of integration has paved the way for a glittering future of the country.

"If this integration of princely states" writers Geoffrey Tyson in 'Nehru' "had not been carried out with a skilled and sure had by the late Sardar Patel the sub continent might easily have suffered division into a third major segment in which the smaller princely states would have grouped themselves round the more powerful rulers in independent blocks, with resultant balkanization of a large part of the land".

The integration of the princely states thus acted as a synchronizing phenomenon and established a State of balance between chaos and segmentation and solidarity of the newly born Indian Union.

## IMPERIALISM UNABLE TO RULE IN THE OLD WAY

We have noted Commander-in-Chief Claude Auchinleck's appreciation, of 24 November 1945, of the Indian situation, with which Viceroy Wavell generally agreed. On 19 February 1946, Wavell recorded in his diary that he had seen Porter, Secretary, Home Department, who was all for capitulation to the I.N.A; that he had discussed with Bewoor, Secretary, Posts and Air Department, about a postal strike; that he had talks with Carr, A.O.C-in-C, about R.I.A.F mutiny; with Griffin, Chief Commissioner of Railways and Conran Smith, Secretary, War Transport Department, about a railway strike; and "finally the C-in-C, most gloomy of all, about R.I.N. mutiny in Bombay and the I.N.A trials; What a cheerful day – prospect or reality of three mutinies and two strikes", commented Wavell.

After referring to the "serious rioting in Bombay", "a mutiny in the R.I.N., much indiscipline in the R.I.A.F., some unrest in the Indian Army" and "threatened strikes on the Railways, and in the Post and Telegraphs", Wavell wrote to King George VI on 22 March 1946: "Perhaps the best way to look at it is that India is in the birth-pangs of a new order..."

When in late March 1946, the Cabinet Mission with Secretary of State Pethick-Lawrence, Stafford Cripps and A.V. Alexander came to India to negotiate, mainly with Congress and League leaders, a settlement of the constitutional issues and met the Viceroy's Executive Council, Edward Benthall said on behalf of it that " *the Council was unanimous that a change of Government at the Centre was imperative*... It [ the Council's lack of confidence] is due to the uncertainty of Indian troops and police to whom they must look for defence and support in the future."

### Champaran, Kheda, Khilafat and Amritsar

Mahatma Gandhi had shown in South Africa and in 1918 in Champaran, Bihar and Kheda, Gujarat that the only way to earn the respect and attention of British officials was to actively resist government activities through civil disobedience.

Now in Champaran and Kheda in 1918 he led impoverished farmers, mired in social evils like unhygienic conditions, domestic violence, discrimination, oppression of women and untouchability. On top of their miseries, these people were forced to grow cash crops like indigo, tobacco and cotton, instead of food, and virtually not compensated. In addition, they would have to pay taxes despite a famine.

The Governments of the affected regions signed agreements suspending taxation in face of the famine, allowing the farmers to grow their own crops, releasing all political prisoners and returning all property and lands seized. It was the biggest victory against the British Empire since the American Revolution.

Mahatma Gandhi was assisted by a new generation of Indian revolutionaries like Rajendra Prasad and Jawaharlal Nehru. In Kheda, the entire revolt had been led by Sardar Vallabhbhai Patel, who was to become Gandhi's lieutenant.

Millions of India's Muslims were also antagonized by the Government's support of Mustafa Kemal of Turkey, who had overthrown the Sultan of Turkey, considered the Caliph of Islam. Muslim leaders formed the Khilafat committee to protest the actions and find a way to effectively stop the British authorities from neglecting their concerns.

A public meeting of unarmed civilians at Jallianwala Bagh in Amritsar was fired upon by troops under the command of Reginald Dyer. Hundreds of people died and perhaps thousands were injured. Women, children and the elderly were not spared. The outcry in Punjab led to thousands of arrests, beatings and more deaths at the hands of police and some violent protesters. The Amritsar Massacre became the most infamous event of British rule in India. To Gandhi and many others, it became clear that a reckoning with the British was not far off.

## Satyagraha

Gandhi's idea was a nationwide protest against the Rowlatt Acts. All offices and factories would be closed. Indians would be encouraged to withdraw from Raj-sponsored schools, police services, the military and the civil services, and lawyers to leave the Raj's courts. Public transportation, English-manufactured goods, especially clothes would be boycotted.

Veterans like Bal Gangadhar Tilak, Bipin Chandra Pal, Mohammed Ali Jinnah, Annie Besant opposed the idea outright. The All India Muslim League also criticized the ideas. But the younger generation of Indian nationalists were thrilled and backed Gandhi. The Congress Party adopted his plans, and he received extensive support from Muslim leaders like Maulana Azad, Mukhtar Ahmed Ansari, Hakim Ajmal Khan, Abbas Tyabji, Maulana Mohammed Ali and Maulana Shaukat Ali. Gandhi was elected President of the Indian National Congress in 1919 and 1920, as well as the All India Home

Rule League-the latter erstwhile dominated by Gandhi's critics like Jinnah, Besant and Tilak.

## Success and Suspension

The success of the revolt launched was a total shock to British authorities and a massive encouragement to millions of Indians.

Then on February 4, 1922, in the Chauri Chaura, after violent clashed between the local police and the protestors in which three protestors were killed due the insuing police firing, Gandhi felt that the revolt was veering off-course. He did not want the movement to degenerate into an orgy of violence where police and angry mobs attacked each other back and forth, victimizing civilians in between.

Gandhi went on a fast lasting 3 days, appealing to the Indian public for all resistance to end, and called off the mass civil disobedience movement.

## Aftermath

Non-co-operation movement was withdrawn because of the Chauri-Chaura incident. Despite stopping a national revolt single-handedly, on March 10, 1922, Gandhi was arrested, and on March 18, 1922, he was imprisoned for two years for publishing seditious materials. The British judge who passed the sentence was shaking with emotion of admiration, and said he would himself be the happiest if the government released Gandhi.

Although most Congress leaders remained firmly behind Gandhi, the disillusioned broke away.

The Ali brothers would soon become fierce critics, and Motilal Nehru and Chittaranjan Das formed the Swaraj Party, rejecting Gandhi's leadership. Many nationalists had felt that the Non-Cooperation Movement should not have been stopped due to isolated incidents of violence, and most nationalists, while retaining confidence in Gandhi, were depressed. Contemporary historians and critics suggest that the movement was successful enough to break the back of British rule, and possibly even result in the independence most Indians strove for till 1947.

But many historians and Indian leaders of the time also defend Gandhi's judgment. If he had not stopped the revolts, India would probably have descended into an anarchy-style rebellion which would alienate common Indians and impress only violent revolutionaries.

# 6

# Patel with Gandhi

## PATEL ACCORDING TO GANDHI

Gandhiji said: "It was a great privilege for me to have been with Sardar Vallabhbhai. I was well aware of his bravery and his burning love for the country, but I never lived with him as I have had the good fortune during the six months. The affection with which he covered me recalls to me that of my own dear mother. I never knew him to possess motherly qualities. If the slightest thing happened to me he would be out of his bed. He superintended every single little detail in connection with my comforts. He and my other associates had conspired me to do nothing, and I hope that the Government will believe me when I say he always showed a remarkable comprehension of the difficulties of the Government whenever we discussed any political problem. His solicitude for the farmers of Bardoli and Kaira I can never forget."

With these touching words Gandhiji invited the Government to take him back to Yeravda to join his companion.

Patel is a simple hermit at heart, full of the life of simple pleasures. He forgets the storms of life by smoking a cigarette, concealing his head in a quiet corner. This is his only luxury, which he sparingly uses.

He is loyal to the cause and country. The change in the political kaleidoscope has not shaken his loyalty o his early idea or early colleagues. He was the President of the Congress Parliamentary Board. He conducted the Baroli Satyagraha .The task was very onerous but he accomplished it with rare tact and ability.

He is strong alike in his friendship and hatred. He remembered his foes with rancor and his friends with gratitude. He galls his enemies with taunts and lashes them with his invective. To enter into a controversy with him is to court disaster, as recent events have proved. He has an eye for the able man. He has marshaled a picked band of workers to assist him He never makes swans of geese. He loves victory but organization better. He is a rhetorician. He keeps the weapon of oratory sharp and polished and uses it not for display but for propaganda. The language is free from artifice and frills but direct and penetrating. He has a capacity for prophetic wrath against wrong.

His success in politics is not merely that of a courageous adventurer but that of a shrewd and high-principled man. The Indian political leader Vallabhbhai Patel (1875-1950) helped to organize the Indian nationalist movement and after independence in 1947 succeeded in integrating several hundred princely states into the Republic of India.

Vallabhbhai Patel was born on Oct. 31, 1875, in Gujarat, western India, into the traditionally agriculturalist Lewa Patidar caste. Both Patel and his older brother Vithalbhai learned English, travelled to Britain, and were called to the bar. On returning to India, Patel developed a lucrative practice in Ahmedabad and began to participate in civic and political affairs. In 1917 Patel came under the influence of Mohandas Gandhi and was an important organizer of several *Satyagraha,* or militant nonviolent campaigns, to secure justice for the peasants of Gujarat. These included the Kheda Satyagraha of 1917-1918 and the famous Bardoli Satyagraha of 1927-1928, during which he received the title of Sardar, or leader. Between 1917 and 1928 he also served in the Ahmedabad municipality.

With the fame he gained in the Bardoli Satyagraha and in the Ahmedabad municipality, Patel emerged as an important figure among the Gandhian leadership of the Indian National Congress at the end of the 1920s. He served for many years on the working committee of the Congress, was Congress president in 1931, helped organize noncooperation efforts, and was a member of the parliamentary board of the Congress. The British-run government of India imprisoned Patel numerous times during the 1930s and World War II.

From 1945 Patel was virtual co-leader of the Congress with Jawaharlal Nehru. They accepted plans for the partition of India even over the objections of Gandhi. Patel was a minister of the interim government and, following independence and the partitioning of the subcontinent into India and Pakistan, became deputy prime minister in 1947. He was also minister for states and, with the assistance of V. P. Menon, carried through the extraordinary feat of persuading several hundred semi-independent princely states to join the Indian union. This effort was crucial to the national integration of India and was the most important accomplishment of Patel's career. Throughout his political career, Patel concentrated on party organization, often displaying strength and decisiveness. By background and inclination he was a staunch Hindu and tended to be a conservative in politics. He identified with the Indian business community and generally opposed Nehru's socialism. Patel was distrustful of the Indian Moslems but was pressed to a moderate position on communal affairs by Nehru. Patel had a severe heart attack in 1948, some months after Gandhi's assassination. Although he continued his work for 2 years, he never fully recovered.

## Equal Partners

India got freedom on 15th August 1947. Almost 200 years of British colonial rule in India came to an end. The independence proclamation known as 'Lord Mount Batten proclamation' or 'proclamation of June 3rd' was signed by the viceroy Lord Mount Batten and Pandit Jawaharlal Nehru ,Sardar Vallabhbhai Patel, Acharya kriplani etc the representatives of the Indian National Congress. Muhammad Ali Jinnah, Liyakhat Ali Khan, Abdulrub Nishdar signed the document for Muslim league and representative of the Sikh Sardar Baldevaiso signed in it. Both Indian national congress and All India Muslim league approved this proclamation and the country got independence. Two nations were formed.

It was not Mount Batten who first took initiative to form an agreement between the various communities of this country. The efforts were started from the beginning of 20th century itself. In 1919-20, British parliament approved the 'Montegu-Chemsford Law reformataions'. There was continuous efforts to achieve unity among the most powerful communities-Hindus and Muslims. Two round table conferences were held in London. As a result the 'Indian federation law' of 1935 was framed. Even though many efforts were on to achieve a pact between the majority community and minority community all the attempts failed.

Just before the end of Second World War British government sent 'Crips Mission' to India to discuss the Indian independence. The mission did not succeed. Then three cabinet ministers of British ministry came to India and held discussions and prepared the 'Cabinet Mission Plan'. They clarified all the doubts. At one stage, both Indian national congress and All India Muslim league almost approved the plan. But a few leaders gave new interpretations to the plan and in the end it was discarded.

It was only after all these developments Mount Batten was sent to India. He held consultations with all communities and proclaimed the decision to divide India. This was recognized by both the two powerful political organizations—Indian National Congress and Muslim League. That is how

India became an independent country as we see it today. But the blame of dividing India was put on the shoulders Muslims.

So many formulas were put forward for the approval for an undivided India. But all of them were rejected by the congress. Muslim minority only asked for some rights to protect and preserve their religion and culture. They demanded reserved seats in the parliament as per their population ratio and contended for the same in the government jobs. But the humble and just requests of the minority community were totally rejected by the congress. If senior leaders of Indian national congress had farsightedness the partition could have been avoided.

In Every country there are minorities. Minorities due to language, religion, class, cultural differences etc. They have every right to preserve their culture, religion, language etc. It is good to remember the example of Egypt here. Egypt like India was a colony of Britain. When Egyptians struggled for independence the British government tried to dismiss it by applying the old policy—divide and rule.

In Egypt there was 95% of Muslims who speak Arabic and 5% of 'Coptic' Christians who also speaks Arabic. Exploiting this situation the British tried to continue their rule arguing for the protection of minorities. But the powerful political organization 'Wafd Party" and its leader Shri. Nahas Pasha organized all Christians and gave them a signed unwritten paper asking them to write whatever they wanted in it. This action was called 'Blank Checque" by the media at that time. The old tactic of divide and rule could not stand before this action and British had to leave from there.

Indian Muslims did not ask for a 'Blank checque' like this. They only asked for some rights to preserve their religion and culture. The denial of their just demands led ultimately to the division of the country.

Vallabhbhai Jhaverbhai Patel occupies a prominent place among those heroic personalities who worked for India's freedom and helped not only to win it but also to consolidate it. During thirty three years of his work for the cause of the nation he dominated the politics of the nation during the crucial period from 1920 to 1950 along with Gandhiji, Jawaharlal Nehru and other great leaders. Apart from being a leader of masses he was a statesman with broad vision of what future of India should be and an able administrator who handled the complex problems of the new government with consummate mastery and finesse. In the words of Jawaharlal Nehru:" History will record many things about him in its pages and call him the builder and consolidator of new India." The following is a list of important events of Sardar's life in chronological order:

1) 1875-Born on October 31, at Nadiad town of Kheda district. Native Karamsad village, Fourth son of Father Jhaverbhai and Mother Ladbai. Primary schooling up to English. Standard III at his home village Karamsad.
2) 1893-Married to Zaverba at Gana village near Karamsad.
3) 1897-Passed the Matriculation Examination from English School, Nadiad.
4) 1900-Passed the District Pleaders' Examination, started legal practice at Godhra, the headquarter of Panchmahals district.
5) 1902-Shifted legal practice to Borsad from Godhra. Won Laurels as an accomplished criminal lawyer.
6) 1903-Birth of daughter Manibehn in April.
7) 1905-Birth of son Dahyabhai in November.
8) 1909-Death of wife Zaverba in Bombay on January 11.
9) 1910-Went to England for qualifying at the Bar At Law in August and got admission to the famous Middle Temple Law College.
10) 1912-Passed the Final Bar At Law Examination with first class. Awarded a prize of 50 pounds. Left for India.
11) 1913-Started practice as criminal lawyer at Ahmedabad in February.
12) 1914-Death of his father Jhaverbhai at Karamsad.
13) 1915-Started his public career by becoming a member of Gujarat Sabha at Ahmedabad.
14) 1916-Met first time with Gandhiji. Patriotic feelings for freedom of the nation became strong. Participated in the Lucknow session of Congress as a representative of Gujarat Sabha.
15) 1917-Became a member of Ahmedabad Municipality for the first time. Got elected as the Chairman of the Sanitary Committee. Succeeded in cancelling the appointment of an English officer as the Municipal Commissioner. Presided over the first meet of the Gujarat Regional Executive Committee at Godhra. Started agitation against bonded labour.
16) 1918-The Gujarat Sabha was given financial assistance at his instance for fighting the menace of influenza and constructed a temporary hospital. Successfully led "No-Tax" agitation against Land Revenue recovered by the Government from farmers of the drought-hit Kheda district.
17) 1919-Chaired the Managing Committee of the Ahmedabad Municipality. Fought against the Rowlatt Bill imposed by the government to curb

Freedom Movement. Started publishing "Satyagraha Patrika" in Gujarati from April 7.

18) 1920-Won all the seats during the elections of Ahmedabad Municipality for Congress. Adopted Khadi and boycotted western clothes. Passed the resolution in support of Civil Disobedience Movement. Collected a fund of Rs.10 lakh and made 3 lakh Congress members from Gujarat for the Tilak Swaraj Fund in pursuance of the Nagpur Congress Resolution. Decided to establish Gujarat Vidyapith with Gandhiji.

19) 1921-Became the first Chairman of the Gujarat Regional Congress Committee. Chairman of the Reception Committee of the XXXVIth Congress Session held at Ahmedabad in December.

20) 1922-Collected a fund of Rs.10 lakh from Rangoon (Burma) for the establishment of Gandhiji's dream Gujarat Vidyapeeth.

21) 1923-Masterminded the National Flag Satyagraha at Nagpur against the British Government. Got cancelled the punitive "Haidiya Tax" imposed by the government on the people of Borsad Taluka in December. Became the 'Suba' of Borsad.

22) 1924-Got elected as the President of Revived Ahmedabad Municipality.

23) 1927-Obtained a huge Flood-relief Fund amounting to Rs. 1 crore from the government for Gujarat which faced an unprecedented flood calamity.

24) 1928-Resigned as the President of Ahmedabad Municipality. Started Bardoli Satyagraha against an arbitrary increase in revenue on the farmers. Received the title of "SARDAR" for the freedom movement at the Calcutta Congress Session. Made a special place in the hearts of farmers as SARDAR-the leader of farmers.

25) 1929-Presided over the Maharashtra Political Conference held at Poona and the Kathiyawad Political Conference held at Morbi.

26) 1930-Arrested on March 7, from the public meeting at Ras village while canvassing for the Salt Satyagraha and jailed. Freed on June 26. Elected as Congress President on June 30. Arrested again on August 1 and sent to Yeravada Jail.

27) 1931-Released from the jail in March on Gandhi-Irwin Pact. Presided over XLVI Congress Session held at Karachi.

28) 1932-Enjoyed the company of Gandhiji for 16 months in the Yeravada Central Prison. Both had been jailed for taking leadership of agitations against the Govt. Mother Ladbai expired at Karamsad in November.

29) 1933-Transferred to Nasik jail. Death of elder brother Vitthalbhai in Switzerland on October 22.

30) 1938-Leadership of the Regional Congress to obey the discipline of the Central Congress Party. Presided over the Kathiyawad Provincial Conference.

31) 1940-Sent to Sabarmati Jail on November 18 for taking the leadership of the Freedom Movement led by Gandhiji. Later on shifted to Yeravada jail at Poona.

32) 1941-Released from the jail following an ailment of intestines.

33) 1942-Passed the "QUIT INDIA" resolution in the All India Congress Committee Meet at Bombay on August 8. Arrested on August 9 and sent to Ahmadnagar Fort in Maharashtra along with other members of the Committee. Imprisoned there till 1944.

34) 1945-Shifted to Yeravada prison near Poona. Released on June 15.

35) 1946-Participated for the first time in the session of the Indian Constitution.

36) 1947-Inaugurated the Vitthalbhai Patel Mahavidyalaya at Vallabh Vidyanagar on April 4. Constitution of a "New Riyasati" Department in Centre under his chairmanship on July 5 to solve the problems of Princely States. Persuaded the Princely States to work unitedly in the interest of country's freedom and integrity. He was sworn in as the first Deputy Prime Minister and Home Minister of Independent India on August 15. Visited the Somnath Patan on November 13 in Gujarat and decided to renovate the Somnath Mahadev Temple.

37) 1948-Constitution of Saurashtra Rajya Sangh at Bhavnagar on February 15. Inauguration of the Rajasthan Sangh on April 7 constituted with the States of Jaipur, Jodhpur, Bikaner, Jaisalmer, Udaipur, Bharatpur. Signed the agreement to constitute the Sangh of the United Gwalior, Indore and 23 Princely States of Central India on April 22. Awarded the "Doctor of Law" degree by the Nagpur, Banaras and Allahabad Universities on November 3, 25 and 27 respectively.

38) 1949-Awarded the "Doctor of Law" degree by Osmania University on February 26. Worked as the Acting Prime Minister of India between October 7 to November 15 during the visit of the Prime Minister Jawaharlal Nehru to USA, Canada and Britain.

39) 1950-Attended the Congress Session held at Nasik from September 20 to 22. Died in Bombay on December 15 after a short illness.

Sardar Vallabhbhai Patel was conferred "BHARAT RATNA" posthumously on July 12 1991 by the then President Shri R. Venkata Raman at Delhi. The award was received by his grand-son Shri Vipinbhai Patel. Vallabhbhai Patel was an Indian freedom fighter and senior leader of the

Indian Independence Movement and of the Indian National Congress. For his determined leadership, wisdom and integrity, he is lovingly and reverently referred to as Sardar Patel (*Sardar* stands for *Chief* or *Leader*), and often as the Iron Man of India.

Patel led freedom fighters in the Satyagrahas in Kheda, Bardoli and was regarded as the right-hand man and lieutenant of Mahatma Gandhi. Patel was considered by Indians and British alike, as the second-most powerful man in the Congress Party, widely respected for his integrity, character and determined leadership. Following Independence on August 15th, 1947, he became the Deputy Prime Minister of India and Union Minister for Home Affairs and the States. He is regarded as personally responsible for the Political Integration of India, integrating 565 princely states to weld a united nation.

Vallabhbhai Jhaverbhai Patel was born on October 31, 1875, in Nadiad, Gujarat, India. Vallabhbhai himself stated that *I have to bluff* when people asked him how old he was, for his actual date of birth was never officially recorded. Patel entered October 31st as his date of birth on his matriculation examination papers. He was the fourth son of Jhaverbhai Patel and Ladba, and lived in the village of Karamsad, in the Kheda district. Somabhai, Narsibhai and Vithalbhai Patel were his elder brothers; the latter was also a major figure in the struggle for Independence, although at odds with Gandhiji's leadership. He had a younger brother, Kashibhai, and a sister, Dahiba (she died at a young age).

Young Vallabh was the middle child and had to struggle more than his other siblings. He entered school late, and received virtually no interest or support for his education from his family. He travelled from Nadiad to Petlad and Borsad to complete his schooling, living on his own with other boys like him, and taking his matriculation at the age of 22. At this point, he was seen as an unambitious, average young man with no perceivable future save as a householder.

But Vallabhbhai assiduously worked to a ambitious yet sober plan: he would pass the Pleader's examination and earn as a simple lawyer. Saving enough money, he would journey to England to become a barrister.

During the many years it took him to save money, Vallabhbhai the pleader earned a reputation of fierceness, ruthlessness as a lawyer. His name was revered by his peers. He had built a character of stoicism and discipline, lancing a painful boil without hesitation on his own, and living for years away from his parents and brothers to make his own way in life.

Vallabhbhai also cared for a personal friend when the plague swept the state, and even briefly, yet terribly suffered from the killer disease. When he learned that he had caught the disease, he immediately sent away his young family to safety and left his home for a temple, where he mercifully recovered.

During these years, Vallabhbhai fetched his wife Jhaverba (they had been married when children), and set up his household. His wife bore him two children-Mani, a girl in 1904, and Dahya, a boy in 1906. Not much is known about his wife since she died tragically at the young age of 29 in 1909 in Bombay, and Vallabhbhai was an extremely reserved man.

In addition to his personal reserve that enabled him to bottle up the grief of his wife's death and raise 2 nascent children on his own, Vallabhbhai never flouted the tradition of reverence for his parents and elder brothers.

Assiduously taking on the burdens of his homestead even while saving for England and supporting a young family, Vallabhbhai also made way for his brother Vithal to travel to England in place of him, on his own saved money and opportunity. The famous episode occurred as the tickets and pass arrived in the name of "V.J. Patel", and arrived at his brother's home, who bore the same initials. Vallabhbhai did not hesitate to make way for his elder brother's ambition before his own, and funded his trip as well.

At the age of 36, he journeyed to England and enrolled at the Middle Temple Inn in London. Finishing a 36 month course in 30 months, Vallabhbhai topped his class (which is remarkable for a non-Englishman of no college or city education experience, despite his professional credentials). He returned to the city of Ahmedabad, and became one of the city's most sought-after and prominent barristers.

Before becoming Sardar Patel of national fame, he was also Ahmedabad's sanitation commissioner and municipal president in the 1920s, improving life for the common people while increasing his experience in public administration and politics. During his terms, Ahmedabad was extended a major supply of electricity, a massively improved drainage and sanitation system and major education reforms. He even took on sensitive Hindu-Muslim issues with an iron hand, with the overall objective of looking after the wider population of the city.

## GANDHIJI AND PATEL AT GUJARAT

Such simple food made Gandhiji a experience mental purity and really became a real aspirant after 'moksha'. This increasing religious attitude and spirit of renunciation created a bitter disharmony In Gandhiji's domestic and family life. The ideal of the Ashrama at Phoenix and on the Tolstoy Farm was of community life and as such Gandhiji looked more after the need of others than of Kasturba and his sons. This led to a deep sense of dissatisfaction in them. Gandhiji was opposed to the-then prevalent system of education So, he had not sent his sons to any school and he himself could not find time to teach them because he was always busy with public affairs. This distressed the sons and in May 1911 his eldest son, Harilal left his father's house. Gandhiji tried hard to win him back and even permitted him to stay in Ahmedabad and prosecute his studies at an. English school. But with the passage of time the gap between the father and the son increased and Hairball's life was proved to be a sort of painful atonement for Gandhiji and he bare it without blaming Harilal, Gandhiji had a life of spiritual disciple at the Phoenix Ashram and on the Tolstoy Farm bore fruit in 1913, In 1910 the four colonies of South Africa had amalgamated themselves into an Union of South Africa, The Union Government did nothing to remove the Indian's complaints, So, in September 1913 Gandhiji resumed his movement, The movement was against two new grievances.

In addition to the two old grievances relating to the law of registration certificates and the law based on racial prejudice and Indian from entering South Africa. Court had given a decision declaring illegal all those marriages not performed according to Christian rites and registered in the country. This decision of the Supreme Court made illegal all the marriages performed according to Hindu and Muslim rites' and reduced Hindu and Muslim wives to the position of concubine. This was an insult to the Indian women. Gandhiji inspired the women residing in the Phoenix Ashram to oppose this decision. Kasturba became the leader of these women. The second issue was about the 'indentured labourers. According to the agreements these labourers were to return to India after five years. A tax ok three pounds on each adult of those labourer's families who did not do so had been imposed since 1893. Then in 1902 a law was passed requiring indentured ,Indian sons above the age of 16 and daughters, above the age of 13 were also made liable to pay the same tax of 3 pounds if they refused to return to India. Gopal Krishna Gokhale had visited South Africa in 1912. At that time South Africa's Ministers had promised him that this tax would be withdrawn. But they did not keep their promise. So, during this last movement the women residents of the Tolstoy Farm, acting with Gandhiji's consent, inspired the indentured labourers to go on strike.

Thousands of labourersmen and women joined the strike. Gandhiji collected all of them together and marched from Natal towards the Transversal. After Gandhiji had been arrested the police and the army let loose a reign of terror on the workers When the news about this reached India, the whole country was agitated. The Viceroy, Lord Harding, made a speech sympathizing with the Indians in South Africa. As a consequence, the South African

Government was compelled to arrive at a settlement with Gandhiji. The Government released Gandhiji and appointed an Inquiry Commission to inquire into the grievances of the Indians and recommend measures to remove them. The commission made recommendations which removed all the grievances of the Indians and the Union Parliament in June 1914 passed a law to implement these recommendations After the successful conclusion of the struggle, Gandhiji left for India after meeting Gokhale in London. Before his departure, different classes of Indians presented him addresses. The Indentured Indians had also arranged one such meeting.

Gandhiji was impressed by these labourers' sacrifice during the struggle and after his release from the jail he had adopted their mode of dress. In reply to their address of honour, too Gandhiji took them a pledge to dedicate his whole life in the service of the afflicted and the oppressed. He said, "your indenture is for five years with one man. I will be an indenture with you for the whole of my life" After returning to India, he kept that pledge both in letter and spirit. When Gandhiji reached London to meet Gokhale, the first world war had already started and in London he inspired the Indian students there to offer their services in the cause of the injured soldiers.

But in London Gandhiji became afflicted with pleurisy and he could not stay there longer. He launched at the port of Bombay on January 9, 1915, overflowing with joy and dreaming to give himself to the service of the motherland. Thus started a new stage of service in his life. When Gokhale had visited South Africa in 1912 he had made Gandhiji a promise that he would not express opinion about any issue in public for one year after his return to India. So, Gandhiji passed his first year in India in travelling in the different parts of the country and in understanding the situation. But before doing so, in May 1915, he established the Satyagraha Ashram at Ahmedabad with the object of bringing about a total regeneration of the country He introduced strict vows to be observed by the inmates in the Ashram. These vows included, the traditional five vows of truth, nonviolence 'Brahmacharya' 'non-stealing' and 'non-possession' Together with these, keeping in mind the then prevailing conditions in the country, he had added removal of untouchability, equal respect for all religions, swadeshi and manual labour and some others. A few months after the Ashram had been established Gandhiji admitted an untouchable family to the Ashram, and so invited the opposition of the orthodox in the city.

Thus began his career in India as a reformer. When the year of silence on public affairs was over Gandhiji seized the first opportunity to express his views. Banaras Hindu University was inaugurated in February, 1916. Gandhiji was invited to speak on that occasion. He used the opportunity to make a moving speech describing the sad state of the country. He strongly castigated the region of fear prevalent in India. This led to an uproar in the audience. All the princes as well as Annie Besant had been sitting on the dais left it before Gandhiji had ended his speech. This speech of Gandhiji raised a country wide controversy. This was the first occasion in the public life of the country when anyone had voiced such views fearlessly at a function at which the Viceroy was the chief guest and in the presence of the ruling Princes, After one year Gandhiji got an opportunity of practicing fearlessness in public and with that started his active public life in India. In the Champaran district of Bihar the white landlords compelled their tenant-peasants to cultivate indigo one some portion of their and the peasants were oppressed in the process. 'Gandhiji went to Champaran to study the peasant grievances at the request of a farmer named Raj kumar Shukla. The collector of Champaran asked him to leave Champaran but Gandhiji disobeyed the order. In defending his action, Gandhiji said in the court that he was ready to accept the punishment for disobeying the Collector's order.

The Government withdrew the order and allowed Gandhiji to make his inquiries, This incident had a miraculous effect in the whole district and crowds of peasants started visiting Gandhiji fearlessly to give statements of their grievances. Kaiendrababu who was practicing in Patna and other educated persons joined Gandhiji in this work, While Gandhiji's inquiry was proceeding, the Bihar Government appointed a commission for solving the problem and nominated Gandhiji as one of its members. The commendations of this Commission removed most of the grievances of the peasants, Thus, Gandhiji gave his first lesson in India of nonviolent Satyagraha. Gandhiji derived another great benefit in the course of inquiry, and that was that he saw the poverty of Indian villages and started thinking how to remove it. This sowed seed of the Khadi programmes which he later presented to the people. He also started in the villages of Champaran district the constructive programmes of cleanliness and primary education. This programme did not succeed fully but he followed in India, the policy he had done in South Africa that resistance against injustice should be accompanied with the purification of people's life. From this programme developed in the course of time the multifarious constructive activities that he inspired later on. After the work of the inquiry was over, Gandhiji presented his original views on two important question in his presidential addresses to two conferences in Gujarat.

The first of these was the Second Gujarat Educational Conference held at Bharuch on 20th October, 1917 and the second was the first ever Gujarat Political Conference held at Godhra on 3rd November of the same year. He laid stress on the use of the mother-tongue as the medium of education at the Bharuch conference and gave a picture of the educational system, which was later to be adopted by national 'Vidyapeeths': In the political conference, he presented his policy, according to the principles of Satyagrahee bringing about a change of heart among Englishmen through nonviolence and explained the need for a comprehensive programme of public service in that connection. Soon after the work in Champaran was over, Gandhiji took up, at the suggestion of the request of Ansuyaben Sarabhai, the problem of the textile workers of Ahmedabad. He undertook a fast for three days in this connection and got mill-owners to appoint an arbitrator to inquire into the demands of the mill workers. With this he also continued his efforts to purify the internal life of these workers. Thus he gave an example of the policy of arbitration and mutual cooperation in place of class-war in regard to the issues between industrialists and workers. Inspired by this experiment of Gandhiji, many provinces and the centre later passed laws to solve the issues between the employers and employees. Such laws· were also enacted and implemented in the field of education. No sooner had the problem of Ahmedabad workers ended, the issue of the farmers of the Kheda district arose.

The crops had been less than the normal owing to excessive rains in the previous year. So, the farmers had requested the Government for remission of revenue or postponement of its collection. The Government had rejected this demand. So at the request of Vallabhbhai Patel, Gandhiji took up the issue, made an on-the-spot study and advised the farmers not to pay the revenue and bear the consequences. This was the first experiment of direct resistance to Government's injustice. It was not totally successful but it created some sense of confidence in the farmers of the Kheda district that, if necessary, they could resist the Government. Thus during the year 1917-1918, Gandhiji put before the public his concept of Satyagraha in three different contexts. This experience made him one of the front-rank leaders of the country. After that within a year he became the centre of its political stage.

In August 1918 he had an attack of dysentery which had resulted in piles. In January, 1919 he underwent an operation to get the piles removed and on Kasturba's insistence he compromised with his vow of not taking milk and started taking goat's milk. But before he could regain his strength after the operation, a very serious problem cropped up for the country. Sporadic terrorist activities were being indulged in certain parts of the country and particularly in Bengal and the Punjab. These activities were not such that they could not be controlled by ordinary laws in force in India. But in February, 1 91 9 Government introduced two Bills in the Central Legislature giving extraordinary powers to police and civil officials to suppers these activities.

Indian members of the Legislature strongly opposed these Bills but the Government ignored their opposition, Gandhiji felt that the people would be much humiliated and a rule of terror would prevail in the country if these bills were allowed to be passed. He decided to oppose these bills through Satyagraha and for that purpose formed the Satyagraha Sabha. The movement started with a call for a nationwide strike and it met with an astonishing success. But during the strike there were some riots in Delhi and Amritsar. Gandhiji was taken into custody at the Punjab border when he was going there to stop them. The people in Bombay, Ahmedabad and Viramgam got excited when they heard this news and there were large-scale riots at all these three places. There were disturbances in Punjab also. On 13th April General Dyer, a military officer fired on a peaceful assembly of people at Jallianwala Bag in Amritsar killing more than 300 men and women, wounding more than a thousand people. Immediately after the incident, Martial Law was imposed in the Punjab rule and the people were subjected to inhuman torture.

The whole country was agitated. Gandhiji was deeply pained but he did not lose his balance of mind. Following his concept of Ahimsa he withdrew his satyagraha and went to Punjab to console the people there after the restoration of peace in that province. There he had the first experience of the people's love for him which later they were to shower upon him. The Government had appointed a committee to investigate the causes of the disturbances and measures taken by the Government to suppers them. But the Government was not prepared to give enough facilities to the leaders sent to jail in tendering their evidence. So, the Congress appointed its own committee. Gandhiji, as a representative of that committee visited the Punjab villages and took statements of uncounted number of men and women and exposed the unbelieveable tyranny of the Punjab Government in his report. Though Gandhiji thus had an experience of the high-handedn8ss of the Government, he still had faith in the sincerity of the British Government so at the annual session of Amritsar Congress held at the end of the year, he advised cooperation with the Government. In August, 1917, Mr. Montague, Secretary of state for India had announced that the British Government's aim was to take India in the direction of 'Responsible' Government. A new constitution was to be framed in accordance with that policy and with that aim in view Montague visited India in 1918 to consult the Indian leader.

In accordance with the joint recommendations of Montague and Lord Chelmsford, the then Viceroy a law was passed by the British Parliament in December 1919 giving limited self-rule to provincial governments. Signing this law king George had issued a proclamation on 24th December appealing the Indian people and the British officials in India to have mutual trust and cooperation. Gandhiji was impressed by this appeal and so he advised the congress to have trust in the sincerity of the British Government and to accept that law. The Congress accepted this advice and passed a resolution accordingly. But within only five to six months after this Gandhiji's faith in the British Government received shock. Turkey had fought on the side of Germany in the first world War and this gave rise to the possibility of the powers of Sultan of Turkey might be curtailed and the Allies under the peace treaty to be made after the War. So, when the War was in progress, Muslim leaders in India had demanded promise from the British Government that the Sultan of Turkey would not be humiliated. The British Prime Minister had replied to that demand in ambiguous terms. As the time of the peace treaty drew near the Indian Muslims began to press their demand more strongly and sent a deputation to the Viceroy in that connection. Gandhiji felt that Muslim leaders demand to be just. So, he urged the Hindus and the congress to extend their cooperation to the Khilafat committee set up by the Muslim leaders.

The Muslin leaders' demanded was that the authority of the Sultan as the Khailfa over the sacred Muslim place in Arabia should remain in act, and hence their movement was called 'Khailfat' When the terms: of the peace treaty were published in May 1920, it became known that Turkey was deprived of some of its territories and that the Sultan was also deprived of his authority over the holy Muslim places in Arabia. At about this time, the report of the inquiry committee set up by the Government about the disturbances in the Punjab was also published. Gandhiji felt that the report covered up the atrocities committed by the Government and that it did not contain a recommendation for adequate punishment of General Dyer. The General was retired from the Army but his pension granted by the Indian Government was continued. These two measures of the British Government shocked Gandhiji and his faith in the sense of justice of the British Government was shaken. So, he called upon the country to start a nonviolent agitation against the Government and thus started the first country-wide fight of direct action against British rule. In the noncooperation movement, the programme included the four-fold boycott of courts, Government's educational institutions, legislatures and foreign cloth.

Together with these, there was the constructive programme of communal unity, abolition of Untouchability, Swadeshi, Knaaiana National education. Gandhiji toured the whole of India to spread the message of this struggle. In his speeches during this tour, he poured out the pain he had felt in his heart at the country's poverty and holding the British Government responsible for that poverty described as Satanic. To bring about Hindu-Muslim unity he undertook a joint tour of the country with the Khilafat, leaders, Maulana

Mohammed Ali and Shaukat All. The Khilafat movement also brought him into friendly relationships with Hakim Ajmalkhan, Dr. Ansari and Maulana Abul Kalam Azad. While carrying on propaganda for the abolition of untouchability he described the practice as Hindu 'Dyerism', thus inviting the unity of the orthodox Hindus. The noncooperation movement of Hindus produced a country-wide awakening. The boycott of courts was not very successful from the point of numbers, but it got for Gandhiji able leaders like Motilal Nehru, Jawaharlal Nehru, Chittaranjan Das, Vallabhbhai Patel, Vitthalbhai Patel, Sarojini Naidu and Chakravarti Rajagopalacharya as colleagues even the constructive programme did not meet with great success.

But it firmly planted in the minds of the people the idea that Swaraj was not only for political power but also for the amelioration of conditions of the poor in the village, It is possible the it the whole programme would have been successful to a greater extent had not there been violent disturbances in the wake of the movement. But in August 1921, the Arbas in Malabur known as the Moplas indulged in violent riots against the Government and as a result even the local Hindus had to suffer much. The Congress gave a call to boycott the Prince of wales when he visited India in November. In that connection there were disturbances first in Bombay in November 1921 and then in Madras in January 1922. Gandhiji ignored these disturbances and continued the agitation. But finally in February 1922, an excited crowd in place called Chauri Chaura the Gorakhpur district. Uttar Pradesh burnt alive about twenty policemen in their station. Gandhiji, ignoring the opposition of other leaders called off the 'no-tax' movement which was to be started at Bardoli· and stopped aggressive propaganda against the Government though the constructive programme was continued. The Government took advantage of the changed situation. Arrested Gandhiji and had prosecuted him in a court of law.

The judge sentenced him to a six year imprisonment. Till that day the people of India had called him the Mahatma. Now, thanks to this strict adherence of the principle of nonviolence he came to be reputed as the Mahatma even in Western countries. French philosopher, Remain noiana him by writing his biography. Miss Madeleine step daughter of British Admiral on reading that book was fascinated by Gandhiji and in November 1925 she became Gandhiji's disciple and became an inmate of his Satyagraha Ashram. Gandhiji gave her the name Miraben. She continued to take an active part in Gandhiji's missions of service till his death. Because of illness Gandhiji was realised from jail by the Government in February 1924, before he had completed his term but at that time the nationalist forces of the country were in disarray. Some leader like Motilal Nehru, Chitaranjan Das and Vithallbhai Patel had given up the boycott of the legislatures and had formed the Swaraj Party to participate in the elections which were to be held at the end of 1923. On the other hand Rajgopalachary, Vallabhbhai Patel, and Rajendrababu advocated complete adherence to the policy of noncooperation. In Turkey Kemal Ataturk had deposed the Sultan and declared the country a republic. So, the Khilafat movement in India had also collapsed. The bond of cooperation between the Hindus and the Muslims having thus sapped the old animosities between the two communities became intensified and communal riots started at many places. In protest against them Gandhiji undertook a fast for 21 days at the residence.

## GANDHI'S FIGHT FOR INDIA'S INDEPENDENCE

On July 18, 1914, after negotiating a breakthrough settlement with the government, Gandhi left South Africa for good. He embarked on a trip to England, and finally returned to India permanently on January 9, 1915, to a hero's welcome. Under the guidance of G. K. Gokhale, a revered politician, Gandhi spent his first year back rediscovering his homeland by criss-crossing the country, learning its problems and listening to the poor. He reacquainted himself with India's needs and potential and studied how he could apply the lessons of Satyagraha learned in South Africa to India's struggle for independence from Britain.

Gandhi set up another ashram, on the Sabarmati river near Ahmedabad, where he lived for the next sixteen years. Over 250 people eventually joined his community, which practiced the same austerity he originally witnessed at the Trappist monastery in South Africa. Each member professed 14 vows, including truth, nonviolence, celibacy, poverty, fearlessness, physical labour, tolerance of all religions, and making their own clothes. They prayed together, ate together, farmed the land, published newspapers, and prepared themselves to suffer and die in the nonviolent struggle for independence.

In 1917, a determined peasant from the other side of the country begged Gandhi to visit his desperately poor remote region (Champaran) and to help the starving peasants in their struggle against oppressive British landlords. Gandhi agreed, made the long journey by train, and quietly started gathering information about the specific injustices committed against the peasants. He expected to stay a month, but stayed nearly two years. One day, while he was riding along on an elephant, the British arrested him. Overnight, the news spread throughout the region that a holy man had been arrested while seeking their rights. Thousands of peasants gathered outside the courthouse to support Gandhi. He was immediately released, allowed to finish his study of illegal abuses against the farmworkers, and eventually, the Indian government passed a new agrarian reform law to protect disenfranchised farmworkers. Gandhi became the hope of the Indian people.

On March 18, 1919, Britain announce that the repressive measures it set up during World War I against the Indian independence movement, restricting basic civil rights, would continue, even though the war was over. The Rowlatt Acts suppressed freedom of speech, press and assembly, in an effort to crush the ever-growing dissent.

Gandhi announced the next day that he had a dream in which the whole nation had gone on strike against British rule, and he invited the whole nation to consider making his dream a reality.

On April 6th, in response to Gandhi's call for a general hartal, a national day of prayer and fasting, virtually everyone stayed at home to pray and fast and India was shut down for a day. Millions marched in the street to the stunned shock and amazement of the British (and Gandhi). Suddenly, India was waking up. The British government responded by doing what empire's do—repressing the movement, arresting its leaders, killing demonstrators. The following week, British soldiers massacred 379 peaceful protesters and wounded another 1,200 in the city of Amritsar.

In the months that followed, Gandhi prayerfully decided to make a complete break with the British empire and dedicated the rest of his life to achieving India's independence through peaceful nonviolence. He called for massive "nonviolent non-cooperation with the British, until they peacefully realize they are masters in someone else's house and leave."

In 1920, Gandhi persuaded the Indian National Congress to adopt the strategy of Satyagraha to achieve freedom, and the movement officially began. From 1920 to 1921, Gandhi called for widespread civil disobedience against British rule, but after a handful of demonstrators brutally killed 21 police officers in Chauri Chauri, Gandhi suspended the movement, infuriating other protest leaders.

For the rest of his life, Gandhi would wrestle with the movement, calling off every campaign at the slightest outbreak of violence. In the end, he regretted that the Indian people were never as committed to nonviolence as he wanted them to be.

By 1922, over 50,000 Indians were in penitentiary for civil disobedience. When Gandhi called off the campaign, the British released all political prisoners, but then arrested Gandhi. On March 18, 1922, Gandhi was brought before a judge on the charge of sedition and invited to make a statement before he was sentenced. "Noncooperation with evil was as much a duty as cooperation with good," Gandhi said, and since British rule over India was evil, he declared, he was guilty of nonviolent non-cooperation with it. Then he challenged the judge to give him the highest penalty possible or to resign and join the movement. Gandhi was sentenced to six years in prison, the maximum sentence.

For the next two years behind bars, Gandhi meditated, read hundreds of books, wrote countless letters, and worked on his spinning wheel each day. He also began writing his autobiography. Though the British government tried to silence Gandhi, his imprisonment only raised his stature in the hearts of all Indians, who now called him, "Mahatma," meaning "Great Soul."

Gandhi urge all those who risked arrest to embrace suffering with love, as the path to political and spiritual freedom. "We must widen the prison gates," he wrote, "and we must enter them as a bridegroom enters the bride's chamber. Freedom is to be wooed only inside prison walls and sometimes on the gallows, never in the council chambers, courts, or the schoolroom."

On February 5, 1924, Gandhi was released from prison because of poor health. In the following years, while continuing his support for independence, he focused much of his time on reforming Indian life, to prepare India for the coming of independence.

His top priority was Hindu-Muslim unity. At one point, he undertook a grueling 21 day fast for interreligious reconciliation and reformation, which inspired millions of Indians to relinquish past prejudices and pursue reconciliation.

He called for the abolition of Hinduism's lowest caste, the untouchables, the poorest of the poor, who were consigned from birth until death to clean toilets. He advocated daily use of the spinning wheel to make one's own clothing, and a boycott against British clothing. He campaigned for the development of "constructive programs," which would improve village life for ordinary, impoverished Indians. He toured the country, preaching nonviolence and inspiring millions of Indians to change their lives and their nation. Occasionally he met with the current British viceroy and would announce that the time had come from Britain to leave India. Hundreds of thousands of people would turn out to catch a glimpse of the Mahatma wherever he appeared. If the crowd was loud or unruly, he would sit in silence for hours, until everyone became perfectly still. Then, he would quietly depart.

On March 2, 1930, Gandhi wrote to the viceroy and announced that unless Britain lifted the unjust salt tax that deprived millions of salt, he would embark on a campaign of civil disobedience. On March 12, Gandhi set off on a 240 mile march to the sea town of Dandi.Thousands of people turned out to greet the marchers, surprising even Gandhi. Each day, the tension and excitement mounted. On April 6th, after his morning meditation, Gandhi bent down and picked up the illegal salt. The country exulted in jubilation. Hundreds of thousands of people began to pick up, make, sell and distribute salt, thus violating the British salt tax and declaring their independence. Gandhi's simple gesture worked. It woke up the sleeping giant, and the days of British rule were numbered.

Within a month, the British arrested and locked up 60,000 protesters, including all the leaders of the movement. Gandhi himself was arrested on May 4th and imprisoned for eight months. On May 20th, two thousand satyagrahis marched to the Dharsana salt mines and approached the entrance in small groups in order to enter and demand their right to salt. As each group of Gandhian protesters approached, the British soldiers savagely beat them over the head with steel rods, seriously wounding hundreds and killing several of them. The world was horrified by reports of this vicious assault by the so-called "civilized" British empire upon unarmed, peaceful demonstrators who did not to lift a hand in self-defense. Thousands more joined the protest. The British were quickly losing control and becoming ever more repressive. Within the year, the British imprisoned more than 100,000 Indians for nonviolent protest. Millions of people around the world began to call for the British to leave India.

In March 1931, in reaction to mounting pressure, the British released all political prisoners, recognized the right to boycott foreign-made cloth, and lifted the ban on home- made salt. They then invited Gandhi to England for a "Round Table" conference to discuss possible independence for India. Gandhi went to London, where he stayed for four months with Muriel Lester at Kingsley Hall in the poor East End section. Though there was no immediate political outcome from his efforts, Gandhi was able to put the case for independence to millions of British citizens and Europeans. He won them over with his sincerity, charm and truth. Though many of his co-workers concluded that the conference was a failure, Gandhi felt that one should not refuse to meet with one's enemies. One week after he returned to India, on January 4, 1932, the British outlawed the Congress party and imprisoned all its leaders, including Gandhi.

Gandhi continued to speak out for the abolition of the Hindu untouchable caste. On September 20, he began a "fast unto death" in his prison cell "for the removal of untouchability." The country was shocked. His friends, particularly Nehru, said that untouchability had existed for thousands of

years, and such a fast was suicidal. But Indians revered Gandhi and trusted his wisdom. Almost immediately, Hindu leaders around the country welcomed untouchables into their temples for the first time in thousands of years. In just days, Hinduism underwent breath-taking reforms as the faithful feared the death of their mahatma. After five days, Gandhi ended his fast. He would continue to advocate for the untouchables for the rest of his life, and Hinduism would never be the same. Gandhi was released from prison in May, 1933. He and Kasturbai decided to move their home to the poorest region in India, the tiny, inaccessible village of Wardha, located directly in India's centre.

Then, he embarked on a full-time, nationwide tour and campaign to reform Indian village life. For the next six years, Gandhi traveled the country, spoke to millions of people, fought poverty and illiteracy, urged use of the spinning wheel, and raised enormous amounts of money to support the untouchables, whom he now called "Harijans," or "Children of God." At several rallies, over two hundred thousand people turned up to watch Gandhi strike a match and burn huge mounds of British clothing.

Over the years, he built what he called a "model village," or "Sevagram" meaning "Service Village," in Wardha, which became his home for the rest of his life. He chose the location because of its extreme poverty and because this region was inhabited almost entirely by untouchables. He hoped it would be a place of solitude. Instead, it quickly became a pilgrimage site, and tens of thousands of people visited the village over the years. His home was a small, mud and bamboo hut which contained a spinning wheel, a straw mat, a low writing table and two shelves for a few books. He rose for prayer at 4:00 a.m. every morning, and ate only fruit, nuts and vegetables. As before, he and his friends made their own clothes, grew their own food, ran their own school, published their own newspapers, raised funds for the poorest of the poor, and shared everything in common. Once when he was beginning a prison term, he was told to list his occupation and wrote "farmer and weaver." Though a lawyer, politician, and journalist, Gandhi saw himself as a simple, poor man of the people, living in solitude and poverty, devoted to his friends and the struggle for peace and justice. As the world hurried again to war, Gandhi continued to advocate nonviolence and peaceful alternatives to war. When the war began in 1939, Gandhi broke down and wept.

Though he opposed the Nazis, he also opposed warfare and spoke out against it everywhere, pleading for nonviolent resistance to Hitler. His was one of the few voices in the world against World War II. In 1940, Gandhi left the Congress party when they decided to support Britain in the war. He rejoined the following year after Churchill rejected the Congress' party offer to help fight the Nazis. Gandhi announced repeatedly that if the Allies truly stood for the cause of democracy, they must immediately grant independence to India. His public stand against the war threatened Britain even more than his work for independence, and the British government, led by Churchill, hated Gandhi more than ever.

On August 8, 1942, Gandhi called for a new civil disobedience campaign against British rule The next day, the British arrested him and his wife. Riots broke out throughout the country. In early 1943, Gandhi undertook a 21 day fast against both British imperialism and Indian violence. He barely survived.

On February 22, 1944, Gandhi's beloved wife Kasturbai died in his arms in prison, after a long sickness. They had been married for sixty-two years Gandhi buried her ashes on the prison grounds. A few months before, Gandhi's secretary, one of his closest friends, had also died in prison. That spring, after Gandhi contracted malaria and nearly died, the British released him—on May 6, 1944. Altogether, Gandhi was arrested on twelve occasions during his life and spent nearly six years behind bars (2,089 days in Indian prisons and 249 days in South African prisons.)

As the war came to an end and it became increasingly clear that the British would withdraw from India, Muslim politicians demanded that India be divided along religious lines to create East and West Pakistan. Hostility and riots between Hindus and Muslims broke out across the country. Gandhi decided to journey to one of the poorest outskirts of India, where the most brutal riots and massacres were occurring, in a living plea for unity and nonviolence. For nearly six months, Gandhi walked through Noakhali, one of the most inaccessible regions of India, made up of two and half million Muslims living and dying in desperate, absolute poverty Though he was relatively unknown in this remote province, where no one heard any news from the outside world, within weeks, the region celebrated the presence of a mahatma walking barefoot through their villages preaching nonviolence and religious unity. Gandhi would stay overnight with the first peasant who offered to take him in. Altogether, he visited 49 villages. He inspired the Muslims to welcome back the Hindus who had fled the region. Within a few months, the entire region was disarmed and at peace. Later, after his death, Gandhi's associates described the months in Noakhali as the most miraculous period of Gandhi's life. He walked unarmed as a pilgrim of peace into a chaotic warzone, an apostle of nonviolence in a land possessed by violence. Everyone was captivated by Gandhi. He was seventy-eight years old at the time.

As the war broken, the U.S. dropped atomic bombs on Hiroshima and Nagasaki, incinerating over one hundred forty thousand people in two brief flashes. Gandhi condemned the atomic bomb, and pleaded with the world powers not to use these weapons again. He was the most prominent religious voice in the world against the U.S. development of nuclear weapons. He pleaded with his own country never to manufacture or use such weapons. Until the very afternoon of his death, he said repeatedly that the possession of nuclear weapons risks the destruction of the planet. His plea for nuclear disarmament became his central spiritual message until his death.

After Churchill was defeated, the new British government decided to grant independence to India and accepted Muslim demands for the creation of the separate Muslim nations of Pakistan and East Pakistan (now Bangladesh). On August 15, 1947, independence was granted. Gandhi spent the day alone in solitude, prayer and fasting for unity and nonviolence. But as millions of Muslim refugees fled to the two Pakistans and millions of Hindus fled East and West Pakistan for India, the country exploded in violence. Hundreds of thousands of people were massacred within a few short months.

Gandhi search for a way to stop the killing. He decided to move into a poor Muslim home in Calcutta, the scene of the worst violence, and declared a fast unto death until the violence stopped. Within 73 hours, Hindus and Muslims not only stopped the violence, but began to march and pray together by the thousands. As Gandhi approached death, Calcutta came to a standstill and everyone prayed for peace. Gandhi ended his fast. The violence had stopped because no one wanted him to suffer for what they were doing. Gandhi had performed another miracle. Nevertheless, during those terrible years, nearly one million Indians were killed as the country was divided.

Gandhi then moved to Delhi to try to stop the riots there. On January 13, 1948, Gandhi began another fast to the death. This was his eleventh public fast. Huge parades were organized and meetings between local politicians and religious leaders were held, and on the sixth day, fifty leading Muslims, Hindus and Sikhs, signed a peace pledge in Gandhi's presence. But Gandhi said this was not enough, and broke down sobbing. They insisted their commitment to Hindu-Muslim unity was sincere. As he listened to their pleas, he decided to end his fast. The next day, on January 20th, a bomb exploded while he was holding his outdoor evening prayer meeting. While many Muslims hated him as a Hindu leader, many Hindu fanatics hated him for defending and protecting Muslims. On January 29th, he said to a friend, "If someone were to end my life by putting a bullet through me, and I met his bullet without a groan and breathed my last taking God's name, then alone would I have made good my claim." Gandhi expected he would be killed. Gandhi felt that he had failed to convince India that nonviolence was the only way to independence. The partition of the country, the massacres, the riots, the deep hatreds and the world war left him sad and depressed. Still, he continued his public work of disarmament, and planned to travel to Pakistan. On January 30, 1948, at 5:10 p.m., as he walked through the garden to his evening prayer service, Gandhi was shot and killed. He fell to the ground calling out God's name.

"I have not anything new to teach the world," Gandhi wrote shortly before his death. "Truth and nonviolence are as old as the hills. All I have done is to try experiments in both on as vast a scale as I could. In doing so, I have sometimes erred and learned by my errors. Life and its problems have thus become to me so many experiments in the practice of truth and nonviolence."

# Bibliography


Ajeet, Javed: *Secular and Nationalist Jinnah,* JNU Press, Delhi. 1999.

Alam, Kousar J. : *Political Aspects of National Integration,* Meerut: Meenakshi Prakashan, 1981.

Almond, Gabriel A.: *Comparative Politics: A Developmental Approach,* Boston: Little, Brown, 1966.

Alva, Joachim: *Leaders of India,* Bombay, Thacker & Co., Ltd., 1943

Atri, Ajit : *Gandhi's View of Legal Justice,* New Delhi, Deep and Deep Pub., 2007.

Aziz, K. K.: *Complete Works of Patel,* Islamabad, National Commission on Historical and Cultural Research, 1978.

Bapat, S. V.: *Tilak Sukti Sangraha,* A Kesari Prakashan, Pune, 1926.

Bhalla, Alok: *Stories about the Partition of India,* New Delhi, HarperCollins, 1994.

Bhattacharjee, Arun : *Rajiv Gandhi: Life and Message,* New Delhi, Ashish, 1992.

Chatterji, Joya: *Bengal Divided: Hindu Communalism and Partition, 1932-1947,* Cambridge, Cambridge UP, 1994.

Chaudhary, M.: *Partition and the Curse of Rehabilitation,* Calcutta, Bengal Rehabilitation Organization, 1964.

Chaudhuri, Nirad: *Thy Hand, Great Anarch! India: 1921-1952,* London, Chatto & Windus, 1987.

Chopra, P. N.: *Towards Freedom: Documents on the Movement for Independence in India, 1937,* Delhi, Oxford UP, 1986.

Forster, E.M.: *A Passage to India,* New Delhi: Peacock Books, 2005.

Gandhi, Gopalkrishna : *A Frank Friendship : Gandhi and Bengal: A Descriptive Chronology,* Calcutta, Seagull Books, 2007.

Ghoshal, U. N.: A *History of Indian Political Ideas.* London, 1966.

Gurmukh Nihal Singh: *Indian States and British India: Their Future Relations:,* Nand Kishore Brothers, Banaras, 1930.

Haas, Ernst B.: *Beyond the Nation State,* Stanford: Stanford University Press, 1964.

Harrison, John: *The City in South Asia: Pre-Modern and Modern,* London, Curzon Press, 1980.

Hasan, Khalid: *Quaid-i-Azam Mohamed Ali Jinnah: A Centenary Tribute,* London, Information Division, Embassy of Pakistan, 1976.

Hasan, Mushirul: *India's Partition: Process, Strategy and Mobilization,* New Delhi, Oxford UP, 1993.

Jalal, Ayesha: *The Sole Spokesman: Jinnah, the Muslim League and the Demand for Pakistan,* Cambridge, Cambridge UP, 1985.

Joshi, V.C.: *Rammohun Roy and the Process of Modernization in India,* Delhi, 1975.

Kenneth L.: *Ahmedabad: A Study in Indian Urban History,* Berkeley, University of California Press, 1968.

Maheshwari, S.R.: *Public Administration in India.* The Higher Civil Service, Delhi: Oxford University Press, 2005.

Mehta, Vinod :2000) *eforming Administration in India,* Delhi: ICSSR, Har-Anand Publications, 2000.

Menon, Ritu and Bhasin, Kamla: *Borders and Boundaries: Women in India's Partition,* New Delhi, Kali for Women, 1998.

Menon, V. P.: *The Transfer of Power in India,* Bombay, Orient Longman, 1957.

Mir Laik: *In Muhammad Ali Jinnah,* Karachi, Ministry of Information & Broadcasting, 1976.

Moon, Penderel: *India: The Transfer of Power 1942-1947,* London, HMSO, 1970-1983.

Mosher, Frederick C.: *Democracy and the Public Service,* New York: Oxford University Press, 1968.

Nag, Sajal: *Nationalism, Separatism and Secessionism,* New Delhi: Rawat Publications, 1999.

Naik, J. P.: *Political Content of Education,* Socio Research Publications Centre, Calcutta, 1917.

Prasad, Lal Bahadur : *Indian Political System and Law,* New Delhi, Shree, 2005.

Riker, William H. : *Federalism: Origin, Operation, Significance,* Boston: Little, Brown, 1964.

Roy, Ramashray : *Gandhi and Ambedkar : A Study in Contrast,* Delhi, Shipra Pub., 2006.

Singh, Balwant: *An Untouchable in the I.A.S.,* Saharanpur: Prem Printing Press, 1964.

Singh, Kirpal: *Select Documents on Partition of Punjab — 1947, India and Pakistan,* Delhi, National Bookshop, 1991.

Stanley A. Wolpert: *Tilak and Patel: Revolution and Reform in the Making of Modern India,* Berkeley, 1962.

Taneja, Anup : *Gandhi, Women, and the National Movement,* 1920-47, New Delhi, Har-Anand Pub., 2005.

Wolpert, Stanley : *Gandhi's Passion : The Life and Legacy of Mahatma Gandhi,* Delhi, Oxford University Press, 2001.

Yasin, Mohammad : *Indian Politics : Processes, Issues and Trends,* New Delhi, Kanishka, 2004.

Zaidi, A. Moin: *Evolution of Muslim political Thought in India,* New Delhi: S. Chand, 1975-79.

# Index

❑❑❑